MW00447455

COLD WAR ON THE HOME FRONT

COLD WAR
on the HOME FRONT

The Soft Power of Midcentury Design

Greg Castillo

University of Minnesota Press
Minneapolis
London

Copyright 2010 by the Regents of the University of Minnesota

All rights reserved. No part of this publication may be reproduced, stored in
a retrieval system, or transmitted, in any form or by any means, electronic,
mechanical, photocopying, recording, or otherwise, without the prior
written permission of the publisher.

Published by the University of Minnesota Press
111 Third Avenue South, Suite 290
Minneapolis, MN 55401-2520
http://www.upress.umn.edu

Library of Congress Cataloging-in-Publication Data

Castillo, Greg.
    Cold war on the home front : the soft power of midcentury design /
Greg Castillo.
        p. cm.
    Includes bibliographical references and index.
    ISBN 978-0-8166-4691-3 (hc : alk. paper) -- ISBN 978-0-8166-4692-0
(pb : alk. paper)
    1. Consumer goods—United States—History—20th century.
2. Consumer goods—Soviet Union—History—20th century.
3. Capitalism—United States—History—20th century. 4. Socialism—
United States—History—20th century. 5. Cold War. 6. Propaganda,
American. 7. Propaganda, Soviet. I. Title. II. Title: Soft power of
midcentury design.
    HF1040.8.C37 2010
    339.4′709045—dc22

                                                            2009036239

Printed in the United States of America on acid-free paper

The University of Minnesota is an equal-opportunity educator and employer.

17 16 15 14 13   10 9 8 7 6 5 4 3

Contents

TO PROTECT OUR WAY OF LIVING

Domesticity as a Weapon

In 1951, sociologist David Riesman published a fictitious account of an American bombing campaign involving consumer goods rather than explosives. What U.S. officials called "Operation Abundance" was dubbed "The Nylon War" by Riesman's imaginary reporters, following its opening barrage of the USSR with women's stockings. The strategy was inspired and devious:

> Behind the initial raid of June 1 were years of secret and complex preparations, and an idea of disarming simplicity: that if allowed to sample the riches of America, the Russian people would not long tolerate masters who gave them tanks and spies instead of vacuum cleaners and beauty parlors. The Russian rulers would thereupon be forced to turn out consumers' goods, or face mass discontent on an increasing scale.[1]

Operation Abundance "was both violently anti-Soviet and pro-peace," according to Riesman's cold war parody, and entailed "recruitment of top-flight production and merchandising talent from civilian life." Successive waves of air-dropped samples were said to throw socialist society into disarray "as Soviet housewives saw for their own eyes American stoves, refrigerators, clothing and toys." Riesman described the war's outcome as a new Soviet policy that strained state resources in an attempt to enfranchise citizens as consumers. "[T]he Russian people, without saying so in as many words, are now putting a price on their collaboration with the regime. The price—'goods instead of guns.'"[2]

Less than a decade after its publication, Riesman's lampoon came to seem prophetic. In the late summer of 1959, Russians got their first taste of the celebrated American Way of Life at the American National Exhibition in Moscow. Advising on exhibition planning, Llewellyn Thompson, the U.S. ambassador to the USSR, proposed that the displays "endeavor to make the Soviet people dissatisfied with the share of the Russian pie which they now receive, and make them realize that the slight improvements projected in their standard of living are only a drop in the bucket compared to what they could and should have."[3] In the eight years that had transpired since the publication of Riesman's "Nylon War," however, the deployment of U.S. consumer goods behind the iron curtain had become defensive, rather than simply offensive. The successful Soviet test of a ballistic missile, detonation of a hydrogen

(facing page) "To Protect Our Way of Living," a U.S. propaganda poster of the 1940s, presents military and industrial prowess as key ingredients of the American Way of Life. Quality Postcards, Oakland, California, qpfans.com.

bomb, and launch of the first artificial orbital satellite, Sputnik, established the USSR as a leader in cold war technology. At the Soviet Exhibition of Science, Technology and Culture, staged in New York's Coliseum in June 1959, a replica of Sputnik hung like the sword of Damocles above the heads of entering visitors. Installations included a rocket engine, a nuclear particle accelerator, and a scale model of a reactor-powered icebreaking ship.[4] Washington's propagandists took a decidedly different approach for the reciprocal U.S. exhibition in Moscow. They attempted to shift the terms of the debate from military hardware to modern housewares—a domain of uncontested American preeminence. Rather than constituting unilateral assertions of cold war superiority, these two national exhibitions reveal the influence that each superpower wielded over the self-image projected by its rival.[5]

Nestled in the greenery of Moscow's suburban Sokol'niki Park, the American National Exhibition presented Soviet citizens with a

An exterior view of "Splitnik," with its ten-foot-wide central corridor, allowing crowds of visitors to flow easily through the interior. U.S. National Archives, Still Pictures Division, RG306 PS B Subjects "Houses— Model" 59-10679.

smattering of advanced technology and high culture but yielded center stage to a consumer goods extravaganza. It included cosmetics, clothing, televisions, sewing machines, kitchen appliances, packaged convenience foods, soft drinks, sporting goods, mail order catalogs, fiberglass sailboats, and automobiles. Its two furnished model homes bore more propaganda significance as platforms for a consumer life-style than as housing prototypes, bolstering the exhibition's "Trojan house" display strategy. Both residences showcased a kind of commodity production that East bloc economies could not yet emulate, in that consumer durables require a highly developed light-manufacturing sector rather than the heroic heavy industries promoted by Stalin-era socialism.

Covering the Moscow exhibition for U.S. audiences, American reporters ignored the show's model apartment, outfitted with iconic modernist pieces selected by George Nelson, the designer whose firm had coordinated the exhibition. Instead, they wrote into history a prefabricated tract home donated by All-State properties, a New York developer based in Long Island. A bisecting gangway permitted Soviet crowds to flow unimpeded past the home's furnished interiors, inspiring journalists to dub the suburban prefab "Splitnik," an apt nickname, given the U.S. goal of undercutting Sputnik's global publicity coup. *Pravda,* Moscow's Party newspaper, complained: "There is no more truth in showing this as the typical home of an American worker than, say, the Taj Mahal as a typical house of a Bombay textile worker, or Buckingham Palace as the typical home of an English miner." Indeed, there was a grain of truth to the accusation.[6] Splitnik's showroom-new appointments, fresh from Macy's Manhattan department store, were anything but typical for an American working-class household. However, for a skilled worker wielding a federally guaranteed Veterans Administration mortgage (with no down payment required), the 1,144-square-foot home, selling for around $13,000 including its suburban lot, was in fact within reach—if just barely.[7]

Soviet Premier Nikita Khrushchev seemed testy on his opening-day tour of the exhibition, which was hosted by U.S. Vice President Richard Nixon. Their visit to an RCA-sponsored television display began what turned out to be the opening round of an extended sparring match. In front of live video cameras, Khrushchev made a rash wager: "In another seven years we will be on the same level as America. When we catch up with you, while passing by we will wave back to you."[8] U.S.

State Department personnel watched transfixed as the level of tension rose. *New York Times* reporter James Reston wondered, "why [doesn't] somebody pull the plug on the whole thing?"[9] According to Tom Wicker, another *Times* correspondent, Khrushchev was then led to the site of a premeditated ambush. Peter Blake, the curator of an architecture display at the Moscow exhibition, recalls that press photographers had received the tip to stake out Splitnik for a photo opportunity. William Safire, a publicist for All-State properties and a Nixon admirer who would later work on his presidential campaign, steered the two dignitaries toward Splitnik. As the Soviet and American retinues entered the model home, exhibition coordinator Gilbert Robinson deftly removed a crowd control barrier on the opposite side. Spectators and reporters pressed in from the entrance and exit, trapping the two leaders within the suburban home's pastel walls. Seizing an opportunity, the vice president issued the most unusual call to arms in diplomatic history: "I want to show you this kitchen."[10]

Posed beside a GE washer/dryer, Khrushchev and Nixon faced off. The Kitchen Debate pitted Soviet socialism against American capitalism, assessing the two world orders in terms of their ability to "deliver the goods" to citizens. Splitnik's gleaming collection of appliances were revealed not simply to be domestic conveniences. They

The historic Kitchen Debate on July 24, 1959. In central front *(left to right)*: Soviet Premier Nikita Khrushchev, U.S. Vice President Richard Nixon, Communist Party Central Committee Second Secretary Leonid Brezhnev, and a sunshine yellow GE washer–dryer. Associated Press/Wide World Photos.

were also ideological conveyances: the evidence in a dispute over citizen enfranchisement, housework and gender equity, and the economics of mass consumption and planned obsolescence. The arguments continued through a second exhibition tour that evening, prompting a joint statement by the leaders several days later asserting their dialogue had been "frank" rather than "belligerent."[11] From mass-media accounts of the Kitchen Debate, Americans learned that the battle of the superpowers was being waged not only on the front line of military capability but also along a domestic front, a message telegraphed in the *Washington Post* headline: "U.S. Typical Home Enters Cold War."[12] This book tells the story of that campaign from the perspective of both camps. While its mobilization of domestic material culture garnered far less media attention than nuclear weapons tests, diplomatic summits, and the space race, the deployment of America's middle-class home as a yardstick of economic democracy in Marshall Plan Europe changed the strategies and outcome of superpower competition. It encouraged the Soviet bloc to measure its progress through direct comparisons with Western per-capita private consumption, the Achilles heel of economies based on state-owned heavy industries. The Seven-Year Plan for 1959–65 pledged that the Soviet Union would outdistance the United States in productivity, and that by 1980 basic consumer goods would be distributed free of charge. The USSR's Third Party Program, ratified in 1961, established that abundance for all was the precondition for a full transition to communism. A retreat from this untenable position began almost immediately but failed to provide a viable alternate strategy for citizen enfranchisement. The world economy that we are familiar with today, characterized by a single globalization project rather than two, is an outcome of this cold war duel.

THE SOFT POWER OF HOME

Displays of kitchen appliances and stylish living rooms cultivated national prestige through what political scientist Joseph Nye calls "soft power." Hard power, according to Nye, relies upon instruments of compulsion and control: occupying armies, trade embargoes, and payoffs for good behavior among allies are examples. In contrast, soft power wields the force of attraction. Rather than coercing, soft power entices, enlisting support through intangibles like culture, values, belief systems, and perceived moral authority.[13] Soft power has been theorized "to a surprising degree with little reference to empirical studies of the impact of 'soft resources' historically," as Victoria de Grazia notes, or, I would add, to studies of the dynamics of soft-power reception among target audiences.[14] Unlike hard power, which is concentrated in the hands of those at the source, soft power is dispersed and malleable. The allure of effective soft power lies in its capacity for requisition and reuse by foreign recipients to advance their own interests, but in ways that ultimately benefit the donor nation. Riesman's parable, in describing Soviet citizens using U.S. product samples to compel a shift in the Kremlin's economic priorities, illustrates the principle. In practice, however, the targets of U.S. soft-power initiatives were usually elites, the "more politically alert and potentially most influential citizens," as specified in a classified U.S. Information Agency (USIA) report.[15] U.S. cultural policy in postwar Europe "did not reach out to the population at large," according to historian Jessica Gienow-Hecht, "but relied on the multiplier effect: it targeted key individuals who, it was hoped, would absorb the offerings and then pass on to a broader audience what they had learned."[16] Soft power is, of course, a subset of what cold warriors called (somewhat interchangeably) "propaganda," "information," and "psychological warfare."[17] Although propaganda can merely proselytize, it can also supply information with the potential to empower its audience, often in ways difficult to fully predict, at which point it would qualify as an exercise in soft power.

Dwight D. Eisenhower, the former five-star general who, as president, pursued diplomatic agreements paving the way for the American National Exhibition in Moscow, was an ardent advocate of what would today be called soft-power initiatives. In testimony before the U.S. House of Representatives, he defended cultural information programs that represented the nation abroad through "ice boxes, radios, cars, how much . . . [Americans] have to eat, what they wear, when they get to go to sports spectacles, and what they have available in the way of art galleries and things like that."[18] His position put him at odds with his party's House and Senate Republican majority, which put its stock exclusively in the hard power of military forces. Eisenhower rejected as "ignorant and uninformed" the practice of funding rearmament programs without a corresponding budget for foreign aid and cultural diplomacy.[19] In 1953, he established the USIA as a clearinghouse for information intended "to persuade foreign peoples that it lies in their own interest to take actions which are also consistent with the national objectives of the United States"—as concise a manifesto on soft power as any ever issued.[20]

Although journalists and historians credit the Kitchen Debate with turning the American postwar home and its contents into icons of anticommunism, the 1959 Moscow exhibition was the campaign's parting volley rather than its opening shot. Ten years earlier, the U.S. State Department had identified divided Berlin as the ideal proving grounds for cold war consumption propaganda. Just as in Riesman's fictional "Operation Abundance," federal officials recruited "top-flight" civilian consultants, including Edgar Kaufmann Jr., the curator of industrial design at New York's Museum of Modern Art (MoMA). The greatest impresario in the art of transforming domestic comforts into soft-power assets, however, was Peter G. Harnden, a figure missing from most chronicles of postwar cultural diplomacy. Trained at the Yale School of Architecture, Harnden began his federal career as a U.S. Army Intelligence officer but soon changed his institutional affiliation to become the Marshall Plan's chief exhibition organizer in Germany, refining his household propaganda methods during a subsequent posting with the USIA. By the time he struck off on his own in the mid-1950s as a private subcontractor for U.S. overseas exhibitions, Harnden had pioneered most of the cold war techniques used to promote what was called the American Way of Life and its intertwining economic and political ideals. As this book reveals, consumer spectacles staged by Harnden in divided Germany led directly to Khrushchev's fateful encounter with a sunshine-yellow GE kitchen a decade later.

Any chronicle of cold war household exhibitions would be incomplete without an account of Soviet bloc responses to America's calculated provocations. It may seem improbable that the USSR and East Germany (the German Democratic Republic, or GDR) staged model home shows intended to outshine the American competition; after all, the founding axiom of U.S. propaganda about consumer culture was that the capitalist West possessed it and the socialist East did not. As Don Slater, a theorist of consumption, writes:

> Consumer sovereignty was the most popular cold war wedge between East and West, one that . . . struck into the heart of everyday life. The contrast between the bounteous West and the grey, sclerotic Soviet East turned on the notion that stifling the individual's capacity to define and pursue even the most trivial

of their desires resulted both in an entire loss of freedom and in
an inefficient, corrupt and above all materially *unsuccessful* social
system.[21]

Soviet bloc leaders recognized not only the power of Western consumer
propaganda but also the fact that divided Berlin was its ground zero.
"Marxism was born in Germany," the USSR's vice premier Anastas
Mikoyan warned in 1961. "If socialism does not win in the GDR, if
communism does not prove itself as superior and vital here, then we
have not won."[22] As Mikoyan implied, competing postwar soft-power
campaigns were strategically interdependent. Most cold war cultural
scholarship, however, has focused exclusively on the phenomenon of
Americanization, a concept that has been under continuous reconstruction for half a century.[23] From World War II through the 1960s, what
U.S. foreign policy analysts found problematic was not the rapid pace
of worldwide Americanization but the lack thereof. In response, they
called for aggressive overseas propaganda programs. From the 1960s
through the 1990s, scholarly debate shifted to the notion of U.S.
cultural imperialism, defined as the exaltation and propagation of
American values at the expense of native cultures. This concept underwent a rigorous critique in the 1990s. Cultural theorists argued that
far from passively accepting U.S. cultural exports, foreign populations
responded with tactics ranging from outright resistance to subtle
processes of arrogation and reinterpretation. Historians assigned
greater agency to local "culture brokers" and scrutinized their use
of U.S. exports as self-interested actors rather than as proponents—
either conscious or unwitting—of American foreign influence. Recent
scholarship approaches cultural practices and artifacts adopted for local
use from their original U.S. context as indeterminate signifiers rather
than ironclad vehicles of an American Way of Life.[24]

    No matter how it is conceptualized, the phenomenon of "Ameri-
canization" can never be completely understood without taking into
account its cold war competitor. In contrast to the spirited scholarly
debate regarding Americanization, Soviet soft power remains a terra
incognita of contemporary cultural theory.[25] "[C]onsidering the
pretensions of the state socialist system," cultural historian György
Péteri observes, "we can safely claim that the communist project in
Eastern Europe has been the largest deliberately designed experiment

in globalization in modern history."[26] As conceptual frameworks, "Americanization" and "Sovietization" not only "tend to yield reductionist accounts of economic, social and cultural transformations," as Péteri argues, but also fail to fully describe the motives of cold war donor and host cultures alike.[27] In postwar West Germany, the American Way of Life was linked to the notion of Atlanticism: a discursive construct that recast Western Civilization as the collective heritage of nations connected, rather than separated, by the North Atlantic Ocean. "Until 1945 Americans *never* considered themselves fraternally tied to Europe," diplomatic historian Michael Vlahos insists, "nor did they talk about 'The West' as a political and cultural entity. If anything, the smart talk was of American membership in the 'Anglo-Saxon race.'" The Marshall Plan changed that worldview. *Your Eighty Dollars*, a documentary film produced by the U.S. State Department and broadcast nationally on the ABC television network in 1952, informed taxpayers that the 12.5 billion dollars disbursed in Europe over the previous four years had revived the cradle of American civilization rather than two of the nations that had vowed to destroy it.[28] Now dismissed as "a geostrategic slight of hand,"[29] Atlanticism attempted to mediate between New and Old World difference with pragmatic goals in mind: foremost among them, the vision of a pacified Germany embedded safely within an alliance of pro-American nations.[30]

Marshall Plan exhibitions invoked a unified Atlantic community through displays of its imagined household culture. Its aesthetic lingua franca was International Style modernism—a taste in design that was anything but typical for American household consumers. Stalinism's alternative formula for cultural internationalism denounced modernism as a symptom of Western "degeneracy." According to Party doctrine, imperialism, fascism, and monopoly capitalism were America's global afflictions. The antidote was socialist realism, promoted throughout "the communist world system"—a term used by its contemporary proselytizers[31]—as an ingredient in the "Soviet transformation package," as Sheila Fitzpatrick notes.[32] Opponents in this *Kulturkampf* denounced the pernicious effects of an opposing superpower's campaign of either "Americanization" or "Sovietization," a portrayal that purposely ignored the processes of hybridity shaping the postwar era's supranational civilizations, and the impact of local brokers in mediating cold war cultural transfers.[33]

COLD WAR CAPITAL

Until the infamous wall went up in 1961, a socialist capital and a capitalist metropolis met at the permeable border that transected Berlin. West Berliners shopped in their East bloc sister city for cheap goods at favorable exchange rates.[34] East Berliners crossed into their Western border town seeking products and entertainments censured by the Party. Despite disadvantageous currency exchange rates, socialist consumers—particularly the young—frequented cinemas showing Hollywood films, stores selling jazz and swing music, and shops stocked with nylons, jeans, and so-called boogie-woogie shoes.[35] Khrushchev recognized that the "battle between socialism and capitalism" had its front line in Berlin: "There, the borders are simply open, and there is a constant contact with the capitalist world to which the German Federal Republic belongs. . . . There, the comparison is made; which order creates better material conditions: that of West Germany or East Germany."[36] A decade before Berlin became a symbol of geopolitical quarantine, the city served as a populist experiment in how daily life could be transacted across the cold war divide.

Inspired by the ways consumers exploited Berlin's porous boundary for their own ends, propagandists devised new strategies to reach target audiences on either side of the ideological frontier.[37] A two-week Marshall Plan television exhibition at West Berlin's German Industry Exhibition (Deutsche Industrieaustellung) in August 1951 provides a perfect case study. As with other Marshall Plan events, the exhibition intentionally disrupted political life across the border: in this case, the World Festival of Youth and Students for Peace (Weltfestspiele der Jugend und Studenten für den Frieden), attended by tens of thousands of East German youths as well as delegations from a number of East bloc nations. Shipped into East Berlin to attend the mass rally, participants were poached by American and West German exhibition planners. Bargain-rate admissions for citizens holding East German identity cards provided an incentive for a day trip to the capitalist West, and allowed Marshall Plan officials to keep a precise tally of socialist visitors. The commodity spectacle staged in West Berlin was highly politicized, as revealed in opening-day remarks by West Germany's Economic Minister Ludwig Erhard:

> The exhibition has the character of a window display for the East. May our German brothers . . . living in Bolshevist bondage

take from their visit to this exhibition the confidence that a happier fate awaits them if they reunite with us to live in peace and freedom. May the colorfulness and diversity of the products on display dispel the deceptive phrases of Eastern propaganda . . . and demonstrate what a free people are capable of achieving . . . in a free economic order.[38]

With the cooperation of two U.S. corporations, CBS and RCA, Marshall Plan organizers gave postwar Europe its first glimpse of color television transmission technology at the 1951 industrial fair. RCA donated over one hundred black-and-white television sets to be placed in shop windows across the city. Two open-air color TV projection screens—one erected near West Berlin's town hall, the other in Potsdamer Platz, adjacent to the border with East Berlin—were erected for outdoor spectators. By dusk, hundreds of Berliners from both sides of the border were perched on mounds of rubble amid the ruins of Potsdamer Platz to secure clear views of the evening telecast.[39] This continental preview of live television programming, a mediated social communion uniting viewers in locations across West Berlin, was an American analogue of the collectivity expressed under Stalinism by choreographed masses processing along flag-draped boulevards.

The industrial exhibition's allure of free world abundance and entertainment was exploited by U.S. propagandists, who distributed news photos of uniformed members of the FDJ (Frie Deutsche Jugend, the East German Party youth organization) entering Marshall Plan exhibits, faces retouched to protect the identity of these wayward socialists. Another Marshall Plan press release titled "Free Berlin Exhibits Draw Communist Youths" announced that "a steady flow of wide-eyed visitors, some who had come to Berlin from many parts of the world, 'played hooky' from the phoney-peace propaganda of the East and saw for themselves the exhibits put on by the Columbia Broadcasting Company in color, and the Radio Corporation of America in black and white."[40] In June 1952, Walter Ulbricht laid down the law: "Every young person at a university or any other kind of school will be immediately expelled if he has any connections with West Berlin. Whoever is a member of the state youth organization will be kicked out of the FDJ. . . . There is no other way."[41] Given the threat of ideological contamination West Berlin posed for socialism, it should come as little surprise that it would be described bitterly by Khrushchev as "a bone in my throat."[42]

On West Berlin's fashionable Kürfurstendamm, a shop window containing RCA television sets and a female model provides onlookers with their first experience of live telecasting during the Marshall Plan–sponsored Berlin Television Exhibition, August 1951. U.S. National Archives, Still Pictures Division, RG286 MP GER 1148.

In Berlin, constant exposure to an antithetical other subjected both East and West to a process of ongoing redefinition.[43] Domestic design spectacles functioned within their resultant cold war image economy, or "iconomy," as the international traffic in media symbols is conceived in the work of art historian Terry Smith. West Berlin's model home exhibitions conjured overworked and unrewarded East German workers, underscoring the Marshall Plan's promise of abundance. In response, East Berlin's home exhibits derided the promised American Way of Life as an embalmed bourgeois fantasy premised on proletarian exploitation. Competing household spectacles functioned both as propaganda and a channel of communication, provoking retaliatory position statements on reconstruction of both the economic and social varieties, the appropriate relation of a satellite nation to its superpower patron, and the relationship of all of these postwar issues to Germany's convulsive past. Postwar "dream homes" were an ideal medium for such complex messages. Idealized domestic settings lent physical and emotional immediacy to abstract ideological concepts. The cozy intimacy of the staged household obscured its mechanics of pedagogy. Model homes invited viewers to imagine the texture of a daily life in a capitalist or socialist future and to project themselves into economic and political systems still "under construction." As ultimately realized, both postwar regimes of private consumption and their infrastructure of domestic

Members of the Free German Youth organization (FDJ), marching with a banner reading "Defend our national cultural heritage from American cultural barbarity!" and a placard bearing a portrait of Goethe, parade through East Berlin during the World Festival of Youth and Students for Peace in August 1951. U.S. National Archives, Still Pictures Division, RG286 MP GER 1912.

space were not simply outcomes of a given approach to reconstruction but also the products of carefully wrought indoctrination campaigns.[44]

OVERVIEW

The cultural cold war was characterized not only by "fierce competition between the superpowers for possession of the future," as David Crowley and Susan Reid have noted, but also by their struggle for authority over the past.[45] Chapter 1, "Household Affluence and Its Discontents," examines how notions of a modernist *Wohnkultur,* or "residential culture," devised in Germany's Weimar Republic after World War I informed initial conceptions of household reform in the wake of World War II. Interwar visionaries affiliated with the Bauhaus design academy and the Werkbund, a voluntary association of manufacturers, architects, and government officials, championed the *Existenzminimum* (subsistence minimum) home, an approach revived in the late 1940s by designers in both East and West Germany. By the early 1950s, however, domestic minimalism came to seem more like a throwback to the past than a blueprint for the future. In the socialist East, the Party advanced a Stalinist cultural revolution that expropriated neoclassicism as the cultural patrimony of an enlightened working class and demonized modernism as a capitalist deviation. In West Germany, it was not

interwar modernism per se but only its celebration of asceticism that
fell afoul of the postwar future envisioned by the U.S. Marshall Plan,
which prescribed productivity and barrier-free trade as the underpinnings of a peaceful consumer society. Model home exhibitions in
divided Germany's two new nations nurtured two opposing postwar
subjectivities: the East's aesthetically cultivated proletarian, and the
West's cosmopolitan consumer-citizen.

Cold war Germany's two politicized styles of consumer culture—
socialist realism and International Style modernism—are examined in
chapter 2, "Cultural Revolutions in Tandem."[46] Both were institutionalized as vehicles of reform but under very different circumstances.
Most U.S. State Department officials, focused on the goal of Western
European economic recovery, were proponents of modern consumer
practices that enfranchised citizens and yet were relatively uninterested
in the modernist design of products. Many of the public servants and
private consultants engaged as propagandists by the Marshall Plan's
"state and private network," however, saw modernist design and
democracy as complementary ideologies.[47] The resultant fusion of art
and politics was reflected in U.S.-supported initiatives ranging from
domestic consumer goods exhibitions to the pedagogy of a new design
academy, Ulm's Hochschule für Gestaltung (HfG), understood to be a
postwar successor to the Bauhaus. Stalinist aesthetic theory, by contrast, was an explicit domain of Party functionaries rather than their
design consultants and thus inherently political in nature. Years of
wartime exile in Moscow had served as a finishing school in Soviet
cultural politics for East Germany's Party leaders, who regarded aesthetic modernism as symptomatic of capitalist degeneracy. Its remedy
was socialist realism, a Soviet creative method that infused a shared
neoclassical patrimony with locally specific national and folk art
influences—or so the theory went. Few East German domestic designers dared openly resist the Party's cultural revolution, and modernists
who did not flee to the West "disappeared" into internal exile, a refuge
that preserved their talents for a time when they might be appreciated.

Chapter 3, "Better Living through Modernism," examines the
promotion of modernism in West Germany as a state-sponsored
aesthetic and "free world" analogue of socialist realism. Modernist
home furnishings became an object lesson in transnational economic
citizenship at We're Building a Better Life (Wir bauen ein besseres
Leben), a 1952 exhibition mounted by the Mutual Security Agency

(MSA), a Marshall Plan successor organization. In accord with economist James S. Duesenberry's recently theorized "demonstration effect," the Better Life exhibition home employed a model family to enact the rituals of daily life in a consumer wonderland. In concert with another traveling exhibit, a model supermarket in which visitors could grab a shopping cart to discover the pleasures and convenience of American self-service retailing, the MSA's model home inculcated the cultural and economic cosmopolitanism associated with a new postwar citizen of Western Europe: the modern mass consumer.

Domestic design was one of the pet projects of Walter Ulbricht, the general secretary of the Central Committee of the SED (Sozialistische Einheitspartei Deutschland, or German Socialist Unity Party), whose personal interventions at East Berlin's home exhibitions support assertions that German communists, rather than their Soviet patrons, impelled the nation's Stalinist hard line.[48] Live Better—More Beautifully! (Besser leben—schöner wohnen!), a 1953 conference and exhibition that transplanted Soviet aesthetic theory into the East German home—and unwittingly revived a Third Reich discourse about modern art's degeneracy—is examined in chapter 4, "Stalinism by Design." The Party's program of cultural reorientation ultimately alienated consumers and design professionals alike. In the wake of Stalin's demise and Khrushchev's reforms, unrepentant East German devotees of Bauhaus design founded a new postwar avant-garde: that of socialist modernism.

Chapter 5, "People's Capitalism and Capitalism's People," assesses the impact of an electrifying "Red Scare" on U.S. propaganda campaigns. Anticommunism was a multipurpose tool, empowering individuals and institutions through its rhetoric of vilification. Attacks on the State Department and its foreign initiatives led President Dwight D. Eisenhower to use private enterprise as a cover for federal propaganda at international trade fairs. The Ad Council, an advertising industry group, took the privatization of U.S. cultural diplomacy a step further, voluntarily creating a new exhibition to promote the American economic system abroad. People's Capitalism used the suburban home as an icon of grassroots capital accumulation. A second stratagem in Eisenhower's anticommunist campaign was to invite Soviet delegations to the United States under the presumption that they would return to their homeland transformed by their experience of the American Way of Life. In fall 1955, Soviet housing officials touring construction sites across the United States purchased a complete prefabricated suburban house, including its furnishings, and shipped it back to the USSR—ironically, just as Eisenhower's "psych warriors" were planning cultural infiltration missions aimed at striking "as close to Moscow as possible."[49]

The 1959 American National Exhibition in Moscow was the culmination of the U.S. home propaganda offensive. It bombarded Soviet visitors with multimedia images of American daily life and then deposited them in a multistory warehouse overflowing with retail goods. American journalists relayed accounts of an American triumph in Moscow, depicting the Kitchen Debate as a bitter Soviet admission of defeat on the consumption front. Soviet news sources told a very different story, dismissing the exhibition's more improbable home amenities as products of an economy based on invented desires rather than needs. Chapter 6, "The Trojan House Goes East," reveals how Party criticism of American household excess bolstered a Promethean Khrushchev-era initiative: the retooling of mass consumption to support rather than erode the ideological underpinnings of Soviet socialism.

The East bloc program to reinvent consumer modernity did indeed yield a new socialist subject, but it was not the ideologically motivated citizen envisioned by Khrushchev. At the front line of the cold war's battle for economic credibility, the East German Party in 1958 unveiled a new initiative calling on the nation to "catch up and overtake" West Germany in per-capita consumption by 1961. Stalinist notions of cultural and economic autarky collapsed as delegations from East Berlin toured Western Europe to keep abreast of "world class" design in order to improve life for socialist consumers while making East bloc products viable in the capitalist marketplace. Rather than leaping ahead, however, the East German economy foundered. In 1962, to stem the tide of fleeing citizens, Ulbricht cast Berlin's partition in concrete with an "anti-Fascist protection wall." Insulated from the West's siren song, East Berliners witnessed the socialist rehabilitation of modernism at the new life—new dwelling (neues leben—neues wohnen) exhibition. As explored in chapter 7, "Consuming Socialism," the new supply of housing allowed socialist citizens to withdraw from the public sphere into capsules of domestic privacy. Consumer modernity turned out to be communism's poison pill, unwittingly ingested by the Party to counter the pathologies of Stalin-era privation.

Having mapped in the preceding pages what this book is about, I should close with an accounting of what it is not. This study examines

Household Affluence and Its Discontents

After spending the war in American self-exile, in 1945 Heinrich Hauser published *The German Talks Back,* a defense of cultural autonomy so inflammatory that it was never distributed or even reviewed in his homeland. Hauser seized upon the kitchen as a metaphor for what he described as the "spiritual chasm" separating America from Germany. A pair of sixteenth-century works, *The Fat Kitchen* and *The Lean Kitchen,* by the Flemish master Pieter Brueghel provided symbols for this cultural clash. Hauser characterized the United States as a "fat kitchen" stocked with physical comforts reflecting a "corresponding philosophy of [a] more abundant life." The "lean kitchen" represented the flinty asceticism he associated with "Prussianism," a trait that Hauser felt had spread beyond Germany to all of war-ravaged Europe as "a new Spartan philosophy, which prides itself . . . on how many things it can do without." America's prosperity made it alien and alienating to the inhabitants of a continent in ruin, Hauser insisted. "Everything American—every broadcast, every piece of merchandise, even the food shipped as relief from the U.S.A.—speaks to the European mind as if in so many words: 'This is the way *they* live over there; their circumstances are very different from ours.'" As in Brueghel's paired interiors, in which the estrangement of obese burghers and starving peasants is "mutual, and the indignation of the lean is even greater than of the fat," Hauser predicted that American materialism and wealth would only further alienate Europeans in the new postwar era.[1]

Attitudes in Germany substantiated Hauser's claims. Following Hitler's defeat, faith in an ennobling asceticism purged of class gradations was shared by social elites in all four zones of Allied occupation. Through 1946 and 1947, Germans struggled with consumption in its most elemental sense. Food supplies were desperately short. Widespread starvation seemed entirely possible. Rationing schemes instituted by the Allied occupation, given their inherent "bias against inherited wealth and meritocracy and . . . favor of the working man," helped create postwar expectations distant from bourgeois norms, as Konrad Jarausch and Michael Geyer observe.[2] Intellectuals, ranging from writers and architects to social reformers and politicians, envisioned themselves at the threshold of a new era that would muzzle glorifications of material excess. By common consensus, a post-Nazi society would be egalitarian and socialist—but not Bolshevist.

(*facing page*) Two generations of German women cook on an outdoor stove built of scavenged debris as barefoot children watch and wait in the ruins of Nuremburg, June 1945. Photograph by Tony Vaccaro from akg-images, London.

1

The Fat Kitchen and its companion piece, *The Lean Kitchen,* were engraved by Pieter van de Heyden in 1563 after paintings by Pieter Brueghel the Elder. In *The Lean Kitchen (above right),* emaciated peasants crowd around a bowl of mussels while a well-fed burgher flees. Although the table overflows in *The Fat Kitchen (above left),* a starving peasant is ejected from the room. From *Honderd teekeningen van oude meesters in het Prentenkabinet der Rijksuniversiteit* (Rotterdam: W. L. & J. Brusse, 1920).

Two journals, *Der Ruf* (The Call) and *Ende und Anfang* (End and Beginning), were dedicated to the search for a "third way," navigating between *Kasernensozialismus* (barracks socialism) and unbridled monopoly capitalism—the latter widely seen as having aided and abetted the rise of fascist warlords. "Private ownership of the means of production seems just as absurd [today] as slavery 2000 years ago," declared Alfred Andersch, the coeditor of *Der Ruf.*[3] Statesmen across the spectrum of postwar German politics vied to define European socialism's middle ground. In 1945, Kurt Schumacher, the fiercely anti-communist leader of the SPD (Social Democratic Party) in the British sector, advocated a path between the economic models of the United States and USSR, asserting that neither could simply be transferred to Germany. At its 1946 convention, the SPD championed central planning mixed with elements of market capitalism as the recipe for a postwar order characterized by freedom and diversity. Members of the SPD's more conservative rival, the CDU (Christian Democratic Union), voiced their commitment to the establishment of a "truly Christian socialism."[4] These visions of a variant of socialism unique to its time and place radically redefined the notion of a *Sonderweg,* the belief that Germany's path through history was utterly exceptional. Even German communists concurred on the necessity of a socialist *Sonderweg.* In its manifesto of 11 June 1945, the KPD (German Communist Party) rejected the Soviet model as "inappropriate" and proclaimed that "an entirely new way must be blazed!"[5] In the absence of a normative conception of postwar socialism—or at least one that German citizens were privy to—politically galvanized architects joined the fray, proposing domestic environments for the vague but enticing "new democracy" that would mark the nation's special path into the postwar era.[6]

Given an economy in ruin, a spartan lifestyle seemed to complement the quest for an indigenous socialism. As envisioned by scores of German modernists in the mid- to late 1940s, the postwar home would be characterized by radically limited consumption. Minimalist design provided an opportunity to aestheticize poverty as a form of redemption and forged a historical link to the legacy of Weimar-era modernism. A manifesto submitted by the author Alix Rohde-Liebenau to a 1947 competition for new concepts in residential design sponsored by Berlin's Soviet-licensed Insitut für Bauwesen (IfB) recast the nation's tragedy as the catalyst for a cultural revolution. Recalling the spectacle of six million refugees displaced by bombardment and advancing armies, she launched her tract with the declaration: "We have become urban nomads! Just as we ourselves have become mobile, we must have movable possessions." Her prescription for domestic reform banished sofas, club chairs, feather beds, and decorative odds and ends as artifacts of a vanished past. Even bathtubs were slated for extinction, to be replaced by the compact shower stall. Postwar furnishings would conform to a binary taxonomy. Storage pieces like chests and drawers would persist only as "built-in" furnishings, a category that included wall-mounted shelving and fold-down tables and desks. "Nomadic" objects, the alternate category, would comprise simple chairs and stools and the wheeled "camp kitchen"—a "lean kitchen" in spatial terms—as the antidote for what Rohde-Liebenau condemned as the bourgeois practice of cooking as "a hobby, a pastime like playing the flute." This stringent reconfiguration of domestic environments, it was claimed, would expand the function of living space by a factor of two.[7]

Germany's first postwar years were a time of patching up and making do, rather than of ambitious construction programs. Rohde-Liebenau's prescriptions for household reform found expression in an unbuilt, state-sponsored commission for worker apartments designed in 1948 by Hermann Henselmann, an up-and-coming talent in the IfB, the organization that had solicited her minimalist manifesto. Henselmann's project was for the Thuringian textile-mill town Niederschmalkalden. Of the twelve hundred workers employed by the

Hermann Henselmann's design for a communal residence for East German textile workers, 1948. At top, two sleeping "cabins" open onto a mezzanine walkway lined with built-in cabinets; below, the communal living room is furnished with lightweight chairs and tables and a tea cart. *Neue Bauwelt* 7 (1949): 29.

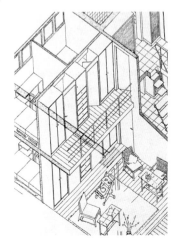

mill in the late-1940s, two-thirds were women, most of them single: either young and unmarried, or war widows. Henselmann resolved the dialectic of residential companionship and privacy by appending a communal living room to individual "cabins," as he labeled the scheme's tiny single bedrooms. His cutaway drawing shows two floors of stacked cabins opening onto a double-height common room and its outdoor deck. The shared living space is appointed with a few lightweight chairs and side tables, and—just as proposed by Rohde-Liebenau—a wheeled trolley with cook plate for preparing snacks and tea. Full meals were to be taken at an adjoining residential cafeteria, eliminating any possibility of cooking as a "hobby" or gender-specific chore. Another renunciation of bourgeois convention is evident outside the sleeping cabins, where the most personal of possessions, clothing, was to be stored in built-in cabinets arrayed along a shared corridor.[8] Throughout Henselmann's design, the two-part typology of "nomadic" and "built-in" furnishings proposed by Rohde-Liebenau supported socialist collectivity and suppressed private consumption.

Henselmann's design recruited women as the avant-garde of postwar collective housing and Stalinist labor relations, an amalgam of idealism and repression that heralded the arrival of East Germany's new order. Between March and September of 1947, as a series of crises strained American and Soviet diplomacy to the breaking point, divergent plans for German economic reconstruction emerged. The U.S. policy of Soviet containment, announced by President Harry Truman in March, was followed in June by the unveiling of the U.S. Marshall Plan, administered by the European Recovery Program (ERP). In September, the Kremlin issued its response at a pan-European communist party conference held in the Polish town of Szklarska Poręba. The "two camps" thesis issued by Andrei Zhdanov, head of the USSR's new Department of Foreign Affairs, called the Marshall Plan a program of colonial subjugation and vowed Soviet resistance. At this first conference of the postwar Cominform (Communist Information Bureau), participants denounced the ideal of a socialist *Sonderweg* as "the illusion that there is some third possibility between freedom and imperialism." During the course of the meetings, Eastern Europe's postwar nations underwent a titular transformation from "states of new democracy" to "people's republics," signaling their induction into a consolidated Soviet bloc.[9] Soon after, Germany's Soviet Military Administration (SMAD) instituted the fundamentals of Stalinist economic planning in the eastern zone of occupation. Labor unions were stripped of political autonomy and integrated into a top-down command structure. Party-affiliated industrial management trumpeted piecework—wages based not on the number of hours worked but production quotas—as a breakthrough in socialist productivity. Rather than introducing Soviet remuneration systems at German industrial sites with established working-class communities, which had long embraced the union motto "Akkord ist Mord," or "piecework is murder," SMAD planners launched their campaign at textile enterprises "manned" primarily by women, who were relative latecomers to labor politics. "Not surprisingly," economic historian Jeffrey Kopstein notes, "by the end of 1947, twice as many female workers received piecework wages as male workers."[10] Henselmann's textile mill collective, like similarly "utopian" plans by Russian Constructivist architects a generation earlier, envisioned environments for proletarians motivated by ideological passion rather than material acquisition.[11] Melding beneficence with subjugation, Henselmann's plan for a socialist company town presaged the "welfare dictatorship" that came to define East German society.

Minimalist housing design developed under a different set of political and economic circumstances in the western sector, with one notable parallel: the occupying power's intention to staunch the quest for an indigenous German socialism. Local advocates of a "third way" quickly discovered the limits of America's democratization campaign. In 1948, the U.S. military government revoked publishing licenses for Der Ruf and Ende und Anfang.[12] That June, the British and American zones introduced a new currency, the Deutschmark (DM), as monetary reforms devised by Ludwig Erhard, the manager of the bi-zonal economy, went into effect. Erhard dismantled the Nazi-era price controls Allied administrators had left intact to control the distribution of goods in a postwar economy of shortages. With prices suddenly deregulated and paid in a new currency, businesses released their hoarded stock. Shop windows that had long been empty were suddenly crowded with goods—including furnishings that appalled German design reformers. "A veritable flood of old remainders and new kitsch inundated household consumers, who purchased—out of necessity or ignorance, naively and at fantastic cost—the abominations offered by unscrupulous manufacturers and merchants," lamented Bauhaus alumna Vera Meyer-Waldeck. Shoppers recovering from shortages, she insisted, were in no condition to resist the "orgy of ever-wilder products."[13] According to Meyer-Waldeck and fellow members of the German Werkbund, a voluntary organization calling itself "the design conscience of the nation," the situation demanded immediate action.

Founded in 1907, the Werkbund united industrialists, designers, social reformers, and government representatives in their advocacy of German goods that met the needs of modern life and the demands of export markets.[14] During the 1920s, the Werkbund abandoned its arts-and-crafts orientation to champion modernist functionalism as industrial design's cutting edge. With the rise of the Third Reich a

The Day/Night Dwelling by Jupp Ernst and Josef Lucas, displayed at the German Werkbund's 1949 New Dwelling exhibition in Cologne. Rheinisches Bildarchiv.

decade later, the organization underwent another transformation. Confronted with the prospect of dissolution, the Werkbund ceded control to the Kampfbund, a rival association affiliated with the Nazi Party.[15] Postwar Werkbund members buried all memory of Third Reich collaboration to revive their organization, pledging to advance "the values of economy, honesty, and good form, which are the very witnesses of spiritual order."[16]

A battle-patched exhibition hall in a Cologne suburb was the setting for New Dwelling (Neues Wohnen), the first major exhibition staged by the postwar Werkbund. Hanging from bare steel roof trusses, a placard announced "Werkbund is no Luxury" (*Werkbund ist kein Luxus*), a slogan implying that good design was a necessity rather than a privilege.[17] A literal reading would have been just as accurate. The 1949 exhibit showcased simple, modest objects as an antidote to the "false abundance" conveyed by stylistically overwrought furnishings.[18] Exemplary in this regard was the "Day/Night dwelling," a minimalist manifesto in habitable form by Jupp Ernst and Josef Lucas. Their one-room residential mock-up, designed to be a living/dining room by day and a bedroom by night, consisted of a flush-mounted storage wall, simple wooden chairs and tables, and a fold-down cot, with only an oriental carpet and single flower vase as decoration. The exhibition's opening-day speeches equated asceticism with social and spiritual redemption, foreshadowing the thesis of "Building Dwelling Thinking," Martin Heidegger's 1951 address at the Werkbund's Darmstadt conference.[19] "Privation purifies and tests every object, narrowing it down to just what it should be: a bed, a table, a kettle," argued architect Rudolf Schwarz. "All of these simple things . . . arrive at pure design in the home of the poor, and are no more embellished than their use."[20] Comparing the new postwar era with its Weimar predecessor, Erik Nölting, the economic minister of Nordrhein-Westfälen, remarked, "hard times in the past also forced downsizing and thrift upon us, but it was a healing force that led to new form and a modest yet refined domestic culture."[21] Other speakers defended asceticism against profligate consumption. "Our men and women . . . should learn to distinguish for themselves which perceived needs are real and which are false," warned architect Hans Schmidt. "False needs can be awakened by appearances, by envy, by advertising. It is essential to induce wariness and introspection in people."[22] Werkbund minimalism envisioned consumer practices shaped by moral choice and collective commitment as the remedy for a corrupt (and corrupting) materialism stoked by advertising's "dream merchants."[23] However, the hodgepodge of New Dwelling offerings, which ranged from product designs that were decades old to new furniture prototypes so provisionally constructed that they lay in pieces by closing day, only served to underscore the backward state of German household manufactures.[24] For a nation that had set the global standard for modernist home design a generation earlier, the 1949 Werkbund exhibition was the demoralizing reminder of a former avant-garde's fall from grace.

POSTWAR FUTURES PAST

The New Dwelling show prompted reactions "oscillating between the highest praise and the most bitter reproach," according to Alfons Leitl, the editor of the architecture journal *Baukunst und Werkform*.[25] The exhibit showcased the gap separating reformist design intentions from marketplace realities, a disjuncture rich in historical precedent. Werkbund associates had experimented with household minimalism once before to address a postwar housing crisis—that following Germany's World War I defeat. Interwar modernists commended downsized apartments for their efficient floor plans and reduced construction costs. The former, they claimed, would eradicate a bourgeois domestic culture more concerned with conveying status than satisfying needs; the latter would ensure that decent housing was made available to the masses.

Postwar minimalists were heirs to not only the legacy of Weimar modernism but also its discourses on American modernity. As Heinrich Hauser reflected, "For ten years after the First World War, Germany's most popular slogan was '*Wir Amerikanisieren uns!*' (We Americanize ourselves!). Rarely, perhaps never in history, has there been a defeated nation so completely enamored of the victor's efficiency as were the Germans after 1919."[26] Time-and-motion studies developed in the United States by industrial efficiency expert Frederick Winslow Taylor, subsequently applied to the scientific analysis of household tasks by the home economist Christine Frederick, inspired Europeans to rethink residential design and its orthodoxies. Weimar-era social housing became the preeminent laboratory for modernist experiments in the functionalist ethos of spatial compression. The *Existenzminimum* (subsistence minimum) dwelling was also, at least nominally, the product of breakthroughs in nutritional science made during World War I. By determining the subsistence minimum diet needed to prevent starvation, German nutritionists helped their nation survive the famine created by an Allied shipping blockade. Their methods of calculating minimum human caloric requirements provided a paradigm for calculating residential spatial requirements at war's end, a transfer of empirical methods that should have raised questions.[27] Domestic space needs are culturally rather than physiologically determined, usually through comparisons with the living conditions of others. As cultural theorist Don Slater points out, "people do not take such a zero degree of existence as the baseline for assessing *their own* needs."[28] Intoxicated by the aesthetics of architecture's "*Neue Sachlichkeit*" (new objectivity), avant-garde designers reinvented domestic environments and practices for the new machine age. The subjective preferences of working-class clients were to be replaced by the empirically derived solutions proposed by upper-middle-class housing professionals.

From America's Taylorist techniques of measuring human movement, analyzing performance, and increasing assembly line efficiencies, the German ideal of a radically modern *Wohnkultur* (dwelling culture) was born. After reading Frederick's manifesto on rational housekeeping—"something of a 'bible' to young architects" in Weimar Germany[29]—Grete Schütte-Lihotzky conducted her own time-and-motion studies to create the "Frankfurt kitchen" for that city's pioneering social housing program. Her design squeezed all food storage, preparation, and clean-up functions into a 6.2-by-11.3 foot (1.9-by-3.44 meter) room reminiscent of the galley in a train's restaurant car.[30] Every detail reflected efficiency analysis and planning, from the linear arrangement of counters, appliances, and storage cabinets to the integration of linoleum floor and baseboard for easy cleaning.[31] The compressed floor plan eliminated not only unnecessary steps but also the traditional heart of working-class home life, namely, the ample table found in the conventional *Wohnküche,* or "live-in kitchen." Schütte-Lihotzky's kitchen displaced family activity into an adjacent living/dining room, a move said to be consistent with modern hygienic principles but that also precluded any temptation to emulate bourgeois domesticity by keeping a parlor reserved for formal use. The Frankfurt kitchen was part of a broader program of reforms intended to modernize residents along with their residences. As proclaimed in *Das Neue*

The Frankfurt Kitchen by Grete Schütte-Lihotzky, 1926. The functionalist layout places the primary work surface below the window; to the right is the sink, a rack for drying dishes hanging above the drain board, wall-mounted cabinets, and a grid of undercounter containers for flour and other cooking ingredients. Victoria and Albert Museum, London.

Frankfurt, the city's home journal, "The new person demands new housing, but new housing also demands new people."[32] *Wohnkultur* enthusiasts exploited the *Existenzminimum* apartment as an "island of opportunity" for the rationalization of private lives through functionalist design.[33]

Unlike the single-purpose Frankfurt kitchen, the primary living area of an *Existenzminimum* residence was planned to accommodate multiple uses, including relaxing, entertaining, dining, studying, and in some units even sleeping. Programmatic flexibility was made possible by a new generation of lightweight furnishings that could be rearranged or folded away to reconfigure the space for changing activities. Traditional dining suites, sideboards, and upholstered seating, intended to be moored in static arrangements, looked clumsy and bloated in such small confines. The chairs and tables designed for a modernist *Wohnkultur* were skeletal in form, their visual transparency creating the illusion of spaciousness even in cramped quarters. In an effort to influence furniture purchases, the municipal housing authority compiled a catalog of approved designs, published as the *Frankfurt Register.* A full complement of such domestic appointments outstripped most household budgets, resulting in *Existenzminimum* units clogged with archaic furnishings from the tenant's previous home.

Frankfurt's campaign to reform living habits also collided with ingrained categories of social "distinction," a term often associated with the theoretical work of Pierre Bourdieu but originally developed in a 1925 study by Edmond Goblot, a French professor of logic.[34] Goblot coined the concept of distinction while analyzing behavior and possessions as semaphores of class membership. Frankfurt's modernist social housing, interpreted in Goblot's terms, reflected a reformist attempt to displace bourgeois domestic culture (and its emulation by working-class aspirants) with an invented realm of distinction that was iconoclastic in design and egalitarian in character. *Existenzminimum* housing, however, proved ill-suited to the task. Amenities like central heating and electric kitchens pushed rents in Frankfurt's social housing so high that most working-class families were excluded. Only a household headed by a salaried white-collar worker or skilled laborer could afford to live in Frankfurt's sleek new apartment blocks.[35] With the proletariat priced out of the new *Wohnkultur,* cosmopolitan trendsetters soon claimed its modernist furnishings as the lifestyle icons of their own realm of social distinction.

The Dwelling (Die Wohnung), a building exhibition staged in 1927 by the Werkbund, showcased the contradictions of the new *Wohnkultur*. Ludwig Mies van der Rohe, who would soon assume directorship of the Bauhaus, designed the site plan for a model home development in Stuttgart's Weißenhof district. It surveyed housing advances across Europe, featuring Mies's four-story apartment block as the development's dominant structure. According to a Werkbund policy statement, Weißenhof model homes were to be "built with an eye to the city of Stuttgart's most urgent housing needs, which is to say for families of low and middle income."[36] Mies solicited advice on kitchen design from Dr. Erna Meyer, a disciple of Christine Frederick and the author of a popular bestseller, *Der neue Haushalt* (*The New Household*), who distributed suggested guidelines to all participating architects. For interiors within his own housing block, Mies developed a system of movable partition walls with matching floor-to-ceiling doors, all of which could be rearranged at the tenant's discretion. Specifying mass-produced rather than custom-designed furnishings to appoint apartment interiors, Mies, along with Bauhaus associates Marcel Breuer and Mart Stam, unveiled a new breed of modernist "sitting machines" at the exhibition. These distilled the chair's form down to a diagram of function, with bent metal tubing as a structural framework supporting leather, canvas, or rattan seating surfaces.[37] Weißenhof interiors established a signature look for "Bauhaus design":

(*above*) A bedroom interior designed by Lily Reich for the Mies van der Rohe apartment block at the Weißenhof housing development. Vitra Design Museum.

(*above left*) The apartment block designed by Ludwig Mies van der Rohe for the German Werkbund's exhibition The Dwelling (Die Wohnung) in Stuttgart's Weißenhof district in 1927. In this photograph, the building is a backdrop used to advertise a Daimler-Benz motorcar. Daimler-Benz Archiv, Stuttgart.

ascetic astringency enriched with the glint of chrome, polished leather, and black varnish. Was this modernist *Wohnkultur,* with its brittle elegance and unmistakable air of luxury, really intended for "families of low and middle income," as stipulated by the housing exhibition's organizers?

Mies had openly abandoned the design brief, advising another participant, the French architect Le Corbusier, that Weißenhof would feature "houses for the educated middle-class."[38] Aesthetic license ultimately compromised function as well as social policy. Erna Meyer found only one kitchen design worthy of praise among the exhibition's hundred-plus housing units. The cell-like maid's quarters found in many of the model homes provided a concise assessment of the attitude toward housework that prevailed among the exhibition's fifteen architects.[39] Kurt Schwitters, a Bauhaus art instructor, dissected the conflict between stylistic and social reform after a visit to Mies's model apartment:

> Mies combines the spirit of the times with class. What is class? A new catchword for architects . . . Class means quality in contemplation. A tiny object can therefore have class. But Mies' [apartment] house is large . . . and the interiors appear huge as well, with doors that are as high as the ceiling. I don't think that one is simply to walk through these doors, one is to stride through them. Tall and noble people will stride through these "doors of the new spirit" . . . Of course, it could turn out to be like the Frankfurt estates, where occupants arrive with their green plush sofas. It is possible that the future residents of the Weißenhof housing estate will not turn out to be as mature and free-spirited as their own doors. But let us hope that the apartment house ennobles them.[40]

In both an opening-day address and exhibition catalog essay, Mies shunned any mention of the economic context of "the great struggle for new forms of living," which he framed as a crusade for cultural modernity. "The issue of rationalization and standardization is only part of the real issue," he announced. "The problem of the New Home is ultimately a problem of the mind."[41] At the Werkbund's Stuttgart housing exhibition, modernist furnishings were transformed from the tools of a reformist *Wohnkultur* to symbolic "stand-ins for its intents."[42]

The "tall and noble people" whom Schwitters described as the ideal Weißenhof residents found their ultimate lifestyle expression at a subsequent Werkbund installation in Paris. Germany's contribution to the 1930 Spring Exhibition of the Société des Artistes Décorateurs, designed by Bauhaus founder Walter Gropius in collaboration with faculty colleagues Herbert Bayer, László Moholy-Nagy, and Breuer, was the full-scale interior of a visionary housing collective. A spacious

The café-bar and communal gymnasium *(top left)* of a model housing collective created by Bauhaus design talents for the German Werkbund exhibit at the Exposition de la Société des Artistes Décorateurs, Paris, 1930. Foto Marburg/Art Resource, NY.

lounge invited the building's imaginary residents to sit at a café bar, read, listen to radio, dance, or exercise together. This invocation of a communal future, while analogous in program to the socialist utopias proposed by Soviet modernists in the 1920s, was created as a showcase for German export luxuries. Suspended above the common room on a metal mezzanine bridge, visitors gazed down at a glittering collection of tableware, office equipment, and chromium-steel furniture that combined functionalism with hard-edged opulence. The congregate lifestyle depicted in Gropius's installation, while plausible for a luxury ocean liner, was patently absurd when linked to the rhetoric of social housing. Each resident of the futuristic commune, whether single or married, inhabited an individual *Existenzminimum* apartment. The male version took the form of a study, sober yet handsome; the female version was a chic boudoir stocked with modernist *objets de toilette*. Absent was any indication of a communal kitchen, a facility celebrated in Soviet modernist utopias as an incubator of social collectivity but elided from the Werkbund's Paris fantasy in the manner expected of a five-star hotel. Weimar-era critics of the Bauhaus often scorned its designers as "salon Marxists."[43] Anyone curious to discover what physical form a Marxist salon might take could examine the furnished, full-scale prototype assembled by the Werkbund in Paris. It was also the last opportunity to witness the short-lived conflation of Weimar municipal socialism and export modernism, a design legacy described in jaundiced terms after the war by Bauhaus alumnus Hubert Hoffmann as one "which (with exceptions) consisted of the creation of a few pieces of furniture, houses and appliances for snobs."[44]

As design historian Paul Overy observes, the 1930 Werkbund exhibition represented, in fact, "a 'Bauhaus idea' that no longer existed at the Bauhaus."[45] The school's pedagogy had taken a hard left turn in 1928 under a new director, Hannes Meyer. An impassioned communist, Meyer called for a return to *Existenzminimum* fundamentalism as a springboard for social revolution. His design for a worker's dormitory cell, the Co-op Interieur, depicts a *Wohnkultur* stripped to bare necessities: a pair of folding camp chairs, a metal-spring mattress (oddly supported by truncated cones), a shelf stocked with preserves, and— the one concession to leisure—a gramophone.[46] If proletarians were, by Marx's definition, the proprietors of nothing other than their own commodified labor, Meyer's model home was their proper domain: a temporary encampment for the foot soldiers of a class war. More an

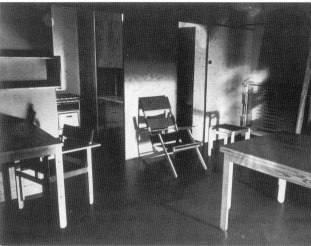

exercise in housing theory than praxis, the Co-op Interieur surely would have alienated workers of the flesh-and-blood variety, but as an experiment in domesticity it proved revelatory, bringing together the axioms of Bauhaus design—functionalism, mass production, standardized furnishings—to create a radical (and radicalizing) environment for "the semi-nomads of today's economic life," as Meyer described his imagined clientele.[47]

The prototype for a standardized Volkswohnung (People's Apartment) produced by Bauhaus students and exhibited in Leipzig in 1929 reveals Meyer's influence. Like the cheap, mass-produced camp chair he chose for his Co-op Interieur, Volkswohnung prototypes of canvas-and-wood chairs, designed and built by Gustav Hassenpflug and Vera Meyer-Waldeck at the Bauhaus furniture workshop, incorporated the skeletal framing of tubular steel chairs while scrupulously avoiding their voluptuous forms and finishes. With the dissolution of the Bauhaus and the Nazi appropriation of the Werkbund in 1933, the radical minimalism of Meyer's "Red Bauhaus" seemed destined for extinction in that it advanced neither German luxury export sales nor the interests of Third Reich nationalism. Under new ideological parameters, however, militant asceticism enjoyed a brief revival in the wake of Hitler's annexation of Poland. In conjunction with the Third Reich's plans to create large-scale agricultural enterprises in the newly conquered East, Hans Schwippert—who would later become the first

(*above*) The Bauhaus "Volkswohnung," produced in 1929 by the school's wood workshop under the direction of Josef Albers and displayed in November of that year at the Grassi Museum in Leipzig. Bauhaus-Archiv, Berlin.

(*above left*)A mock-up of the "Zimmer Co-op," Hannes Meyer's proposal for a radically minimal home, 1926. Deutsches Architektur-Museum, Frankfurt.

postwar president of Werkbund—drafted self-build patterns for austere wooden furnishings to be assembled by the "Germanized" Poles conscripted as an agrarian labor force.[48] A more humane revival of Meyer's modernist fundamentalism surfaced in initiatives mounted by postwar Werkbund associates like Hassenpflug and Meyer-Waldeck, and in the work of Bauhaus alumni like Franz Ehrlich, Selman Selmanagič, and Mart Stam. A luxurious version of Weimar-era *Wohnkultur* analogous to that of the 1930 Werkbund exhibition in Paris would also find its place in the new postwar order. Having disappeared from production due to Third Reich restrictions on the use of steel for nonmilitary manufacturing, tubular steel chairs by Breuer and Mies were relicensed for production in the 1950s by Knoll International and became the gold standard in decor for corporate offices and U.S. Department of State diplomatic facilities, as discussed in the next chapter.

SELLING THE AMERICAN WAY OF LIFE

The future of West German consumption catapulted into political debate in 1949, the year of the Werkbund's New Living exhibition and a federal election. What seemed to be at stake was West German economic reconstruction as a "Prussian lean kitchen" or an "American fat kitchen," as Hauser would have it. SPD policies favored egalitarian consumption integrated within the structures of a centrally planned economy. The Party's position was consonant with that of the Werkbund and echoed in a New Living show opening-day address by Erik Nölting, the SPD economic spokesman. Nölting's political opponent, CDU economic strategist Ludwig Erhard, instead stressed competition and private investment within a "social market economy" (*Marktwirtschaft*). Erhard's objective was to secure social welfare planning and its sources of funding through increased productivity and private consumption, a position consistent with that of the U.S. Marshall Plan. CDU candidates won a bare majority in West Germany's first national election. For West Germans, the 1950s turned out to be not the era of aestheticized austerity proposed by the SPD and Werkbund but the dawning of a legendary Economic Miracle (*Wunderwirtschaft*). CDU leaders and U.S. advisors promoted changes in consumer behavior that, in aggregate, were intended to facilitate the miracle. Consumption emerged as a target of propaganda campaigns and state interventions as West Germans, bent on putting the war behind them, proceeded to construct new lives rooted in material aspirations.

Marshall Plan administrators faced a two-front battle in Western Europe. On one hand, intellectuals and public opinion leaders often regarded America as the purveyor of "a primitive, vulgar, trashy *Massenkultur* (mass culture), which was in effect an *Unkultur* (non-culture), whose importation into postwar Europe had to be resisted," as historian Volker Berghahn notes.[49] On the other, local communist labor unions and party propagandists leveraged these stereotypes to portray the United States as a military empire ruled by parvenus. Dispelling "the old stereotype of the Yank as a cross between a cinematic gangster and an uncultivated bumpkin" was crucial to America's postwar "fight to wage the peace," according to Paul G. Hoffman, the former corporate executive who administered Marshall Plan initiatives through the Economic Cooperation Administration (ECA).[50] Fulmination against U.S. "cultural barbarism" became a staple of Germany's Soviet-sector media in 1947, when Alexander Dymschitz, the SMAD officer in charge of cultural affairs in the eastern sector, denounced America's purported contamination of German arts and letters.[51] These allegations of a U.S. consumer "non-culture" were more than just insulting. By denigrating American materialism, they also subverted the Marshall Plan blueprint for postwar recovery. European reconstruction would be built upon a New Deal variant of "Fordism," the linkage of mass production to mass consumption used by Henry Ford to mollify workers as his efficiency engineers raised productivity by rationalizing assembly-line tasks.[52] In Marshall Plan Europe, low-cost mass-produced consumer goods would reward organized labor and its compliance with U.S.-sponsored productivity campaigns, while restoring market principles to an economy long dominated by industrial cartels serving a military state. "Today's contest between freedom and despotism is a contest between the American assembly line and the Communist Party line," Hoffman declared.[53] The Marshall Plan's subsequent efforts to unleash European consumer desire redefined Franklin D. Roosevelt's "Four Freedoms," transforming "freedom from want" into the freedom *to* want.

As depicted in U.S. State Department propaganda regarding European consumption, the postwar home and its commodity culture were inherently political. A 1952 Marshall Plan publicity photo shows a man standing in front of a wooden trailer with a bowl of food in his hand; a woman peers from a curtained window behind him. Titled "A Potential Danger," the accompanying press release states:

> Proudly standing behind his rickety old car in front of the caravan which is his home, this German is one of the millions who today—seven years after the end of the war—still live in discomfort and insecurity. . . . But this man, taken as a type, is more than just a name on a waiting list. He represents a potential danger to Germany, for in the years of this type of existence he has developed a taste for insecure living and has acquired a mentality which is an easy prey for communist propaganda.[54]

The Marshall Plan's portrait of a latent communist drew upon prejudices and fears directed at millions of displaced "expellees" who had arrived in western Germany from the East disoriented and destitute. Unwelcome newcomers, they were forced to compete with established

"A Potential Danger," part of a photojournalistic essay distributed to European newspapers by the U.S. Marshall Plan, 1952. U.S. National Archives, Still Pictures Division, RG286 MP Ger 1695.

locals for scarce postwar resources and were quickly stereotyped as shiftless and untrustworthy.[55] American propagandists added political volatility to this list of imagined shortcomings. If nomadic living invited Marxist subversion, rooted, middle-class domesticity was the logical antidote.

Although the Marshall Plan policy of encouraging private owner-ship shared the consumer ideology of America's postwar boom, both traced their origins to the Great Depression and federal attempts to end it. Franklin D. Roosevelt's ill-fated National Recovery Administration (NRA) tried to interrupt a self-perpetuating cycle of underconsump-tion through collective wage agreements intended to increase incomes, thus stoking consumer demand. Wary of government regulation, business interests fought back with a public relations campaign cele-brating private enterprise as the guardian of an American Way of Life characterized by abundance.[56] In effect, NRA administrators and their private-sector detractors, while operating at cross-purposes, simultane-ously endorsed guaranteed consumption as a prerogative of American citizenship.[57] Another New Deal initiative, the National Housing Act of 1934, and its offshoot, the Federal Housing Administration (FHA), used the single-family suburban house as a instrument of macro-economic intervention. New federally guaranteed loans persuaded lenders to reformulate their three- or five-year mortgages as fifteen- or twenty-year repayment plans with far lower down payments. Reduced mortgage payments permitted more Americans to invest in a home and its furnishings, interrupting the cycle of underconsumption. Meanwhile, federally funded public works programs improved roads, created reservoirs, and constructed hydroelectric stations, creating the water, power, and traffic infrastructure required by an anticipated boom in suburban development. The high wages and low unemployment needed to realize a New Deal consumer republic remained its missing ingredients, however, throughout the 1930s.

The breakthrough came with World War II. Industrial mobiliza-tion and soaring federal spending created full employment in well-paid defense industry jobs.[58] In the early 1940s, as weapons manufacturing boomed, millions of Americans pursued employment opportunities in areas of fresh suburban growth.[59] New industrial facilities, decentralized to limit their vulnerability in the event of enemy bombing, spawned instant communities in places like Westchester, California; Midwest City, Oklahoma; and McLoughlin Heights, Washington. As innovative

Westchester, California, a suburban community of 3,230 new homes within proximity to three major aircraft manufacturing facilities, in 1942. The automobile, commuter, and partially prefabricated homes foreshadow a postwar American Way of Life. Courtesy of Huntington Library.

builders rethought the conventions of residential construction, FHA building standards formulated during the Depression were put to the test. Developers applied mass-production techniques to suburban construction, assigning specialized work teams to precut and preassemble portions of homes before trucking them to the building site. As urban historian Greg Hise has observed, these wartime experiments predate the famed assembly-line building methods of postwar suburbs like Levittown, New York, by a decade.[60] By war's end, all the elements later celebrated as the American Way of Life were in place: the New Deal conflation of democracy with mass prosperity, a generous system of

federally subsidized private home mortgages, and demand for a grow-
ing assortment of household durables. America's first generation of fully
enfranchised "citizen-consumers" was created "from the top down as
well from the bottom up," as social historian Lizabeth Cohen points
out.[61] In its attempt to guide the postwar reconstruction of Western
Europe, the Marshall Plan would attempt to orchestrate a similar chain
reaction of public-sector economic policy with private-sector production and consumption.

The United States launched its campaign to promote the American Way of Life on the continent under the problematic rubric of
"propaganda." For most Americans, the word was synonymous with
"deceit and trickery, with totalitarian rather than democratic methods,"
as ECA director Hoffman was painfully aware. He defended Marshall
Plan propaganda by referring back to the term's original meaning: the
propagation of a belief system. Hoffman defined information as a
form of communication intended merely to enlighten. In contrast,
propaganda connoted "the communication of facts (or non-facts) and
opinions in an effort to *influence*." Hoffman had initially believed that
his mission in Europe could be accomplished through information:
"a man or two in each of the ECA missions overseas to get out press
releases, contact local editors, and report back home." He soon was
persuaded otherwise and warned that in Italy, France, and Western
Germany, with the help of lavish Soviet funding, "sleight-of-hand
practitioners of Communist propaganda" created campaigns that were
"incredibly adroit, incessant, and tailored to the prejudices and emo-
tions of people in all walks of life." Combating anti-Americanism
required "a creative approach to the propaganda task" and "a continuing
program of research and testing, just as [in] our military forces." It
would be led by "men who can use all the tools of propaganda with
imagination, boldness and skill, tempered by . . . a sensitive awareness
of the forces of world ferment." They would advance a "free world
doctrine" based upon religious freedom, political civil liberties, and
a "socially conscious capitalism" that would maximize economic
opportunity while insuring citizens against "life's common hazards."[62]
Hoffman's "propaganda task" promoting the Marshall Plan's New Deal
synthesis provides an inventory of America's soft-power assets as the
nation entered the cold war.[63]

A classified U.S. intelligence report of 1947 examined Soviet
propaganda ridiculing the American Way of Life, and recommended a

counter-propaganda offensive based on the themes "American living standards" and "try it our way."[64] In the spring of 1948, U.S. military administrators in Frankfurt launched their first attempt to link American consumption with anticommunism. They contracted Frederick Gutheim, an expatriate German architect with a host of Weimar-era social housing projects to his credit, as an advisor for an exhibition on U.S. housing. Patricia van Delden, the chief officer of the OMGUS Information Centers and Exhibitions Branch, questioned the wisdom of the plan:

> In the years since the war, the Congress has failed to pass an adequate housing bill, and our own publications, easily available to the Germans in [U.S.] Information Centers, draw constant attention to that fact. . . . European countries, notably Switzerland, Denmark, Holland and the Scandinavian countries, are leading the world in their . . . low cost housing programs. It is therefore questionable about drawing the attention of the Germans at this point to American low price housing systems. Unless we are in the position to explain to the German people how they can acquire these houses . . . we could be criticized for raising false hopes.[65]

Van Delden's alternative plan, to "confine ourselves to material showing American concepts of architecture," was disregarded by her superiors.

Peter Harnden, the director of Exhibitions Programs at OMGUS, was charged with producing postwar Germany's first official display of American housing. It initiated a steep learning curve that culminated in his transformation into what Hoffman would describe as "the born propagandist":

> He is most likely a man who knows something of all the methods and means of mass communication and how to orchestrate them. But he must also think in terms of the deed which generates its own propaganda and how to bring it about, and he knows the power of word-of-mouth communication to support more formalized techniques. The propagandist is not satisfied to inform— he seeks to persuade.[66]

Trained in architecture at Yale, Harnden shifted to a career in army intelligence during the war. Stationed in Germany after the Nazi defeat, he met and married Marie Vassiltchikov, a Byelorussian noble whose family had fled the Bolshevik revolution for Weimar Germany. A peripheral figure in the failed plot to assassinate Hitler, Vassiltchikov was an ideal informant in the anthropological sense: culturally informed, educationally accomplished, admired by local elites, and capable of sharing a hard-earned "awareness of the forces of world ferment" with her propagandist husband.[67] Despite Harnden's burgeoning career as an emissary of the American Way of Life, he would end his career by "going native," refusing to relocate to Washington for a promotion and opting instead to remain in Europe with his aristocratic wife and children.

Hampered by limited resources, Harnden's first attempt to promote American housing in Europe relied on photographs solicited from architecture schools at Harvard, Columbia, and MIT to illustrate prefabricated construction, advanced household technology, and new trends in suburban planning. He contracted the OMGUS Exhibitions Workshop, led by Joost Schmidt, the former master instructor of graphic design at the Bauhaus, to produce eight scale models and 150 display panels depicting residences ranging from single-family houses and apartments to "homes of the American wealthy." How America Lives (So wohnt Amerika) opened in Frankfurt in August 1949. Visitor attendance was modest, to put it nicely. Despite stellar production talent, the show was a critical flop. The paean to U.S. household affluence was largely ignored by journalists but managed to incur the wrath of a proponent of domestic austerity. "We know with what pleasure and childish enthusiasm the American plays with the idol of technology, and how much money this toy consumes," wrote Rudolf Pfister in the architectural journal *Der Baumeister*. "We have no time for robots, and . . . it should go without saying—we want to remain sentient human beings."[68] Photographs and scale models of houses neither captivated the general public nor dissuaded elites of the idea that cultural barbarism had made itself at home in America. The head of Frankfurt's U.S. Information Center, Donald W. Muntz, recognized the error and prescribed a solution:

> If real honest-to-god electric stoves, refrigerators and deep-freeze units had been on hand, the general attendance figures would have been astronomic. I can well imagine that the problems in bringing these gadgets together would be manifold, but an effort here would have paid off.[69]

West Germans examine a wall panel titled "Homes of the Well-to-do" at the How America Lives exhibition in Frankfurt, 1949. U.S. National Archives, Text Division, RG260 390/42/21/3 Box 323.

The "particular failure" of How America Lives would not be repeated in subsequent American household exhibitions.

In the battle to win European hearts and minds, the notion of conscripting America's household "gadgets" (and the housewives who used them) found academic support in 1949. An enthusiastic reviewer deemed the "demonstration effect" theorized by James S. Duesenberry "one of the most significant contributions of the postwar period to our understanding of economic behavior."[70] Duesenberry broke from economic orthodoxy, which conceptualized consumption as a set of individual choices based on relative price and real income. According to Duesenberry, rational decision-making was less important than acquired and learned habit in consumer preference. Consumers informed their choices by observing and assessing other people's consumption, not just in terms of social status, as proposed by Thorstein Veblen's notion of "conspicuous consumption," but on the basis of perceived need. Utility, in other words, was subjective, and purchasing habits based on need changed with exposure to more affluent versions of need. Duesenberry's theory of a "demonstration effect" posited that individuals became dissatisfied with their consumption standards after seeing superior products in use by others. "Mere knowledge of the existence of superior goods is not a very effective habit breaker," he wrote. "Frequent contact with them may be."[71] While State Department documents make no mention of Duesenberry, given his theory's broad reception, it seems likely to have influenced U.S. propaganda intended to expose Europeans to "real honest-to-god electric stoves, refrigerators and deep-freeze units"—the gleaming essentials of an "American fat kitchen."

Within five years of Nazi Germany's unconditional surrender, America unleashed the largest international propaganda effort ever mounted in a time of peace. Marshall Plan administrators orchestrated a forceful response to European fears that mass consumption threatened the integrity of home and family. *Konsumterror*, or "consumption terror," as sociologists Theodor Adorno and Helmut Schelsky dubbed it, had run rampant at the Werkbund's 1949 exhibition and in its aesthetic of modernist household austerity. American propaganda, by contrast, attempted to induce "a radical shift in the priorities of individuals, towards new ideals of personal progress which could be defined in the language of income and consumption," as historian David Ellwood observes.[72] *Productivity, Key to Plenty,* a Marshall Plan film dubbed into a number of languages, took audiences through an American suburban home to examine its amenities and appliances as the narrator asked, "What housewife has not dreamed of a kitchen like this? . . . One can remain attached to moral values which give a precise meaning to existence without neglecting the material factors which contribute to the good things in life."[73] Model homes exhibitions sponsored by the Marshall Plan were not intended to sell a specific type of housing or its

Germans waiting to tour the America at Home exhibit. U.S. National Archives, Text Division, RG59 862A.191, Box 5225.

showcased product lines but the idea that escalating private affluence was a crucial outcome of good postwar governance.

America at Home (Amerika zu Hause) debuted at West Berlin's first annual German Industrial Exhibition (Deutsche Industrie-Ausstellung) in October 1950 as a national election was in progress across the border in East Germany. Within the new George Marshall-Haus, a permanent trade fair pavilion built with U.S. funds, an installation produced by Harnden extolled collaborative efforts by American labor unions and industrial managers to increase productivity. The culminating display sat outside the Marshall-Haus against a lush backdrop of poplars. It was a single-family suburban home shipped from Minneapolis to Berlin as a kit of prefabricated components. German carpenters working in round-the-clock shifts had assembled the home from crates in just five days, a feat said to demonstrate how American productivity advances and harmonious labor relations could benefit Europeans. The six-room home plus carport lent substance to the American promise that workers would be better off supporting innovations in production rather than conspiring against them.[74] An internal memorandum was more bombastic, calling America at Home a "patriotic reaffirmation of our way of life" and the icon of "a struggle as vital to the peace and prosperity of the world as any military campaign in history."[75] John McCloy, the U.S. High Commissioner for Germany, saw the exhibit as "the chance to put [a] living monument to American life in Berlin."[76] And as monuments go, this one was a bargain: $24,000 exclusive of assembly labor but including shipping costs for the prefabricated components and a full complement of furnishings.[77]

Earlier predictions of astronomical attendance for an exhibition featuring "real honest-to-god" appliances proved right on the mark. From the moment America at Home swung open its front door, it was mobbed. The surfeit of visitors prompted exhibition sponsors to post police at the front and back doors, and to limit foot traffic to groups of ten in order to avoid damage to the home's timber floor joists. Interiors were coordinated by Bernard Wagner, a German-speaking architect on loan from the U.S. Home and Housing Finance Agency, whose father, Harvard professor Martin Wagner, was the famed urban planner of Weimar-era Berlin.[78] Young female American studies majors from West Berlin's new Free University worked the floor as tour guides, answering questions about "such household miracles as the . . . electric washing machine, illuminated electric range, vacuum cleaner, mix

Merchandise Mart brought the museum's patronage of International Style modernism to the world's largest home furnishings show, attended biannually by twenty to thirty thousand buyers. A trek through its showrooms had been cause for despair, as related by an impresario of postwar modernism, George Nelson:

> Ninety-eight percent of the merchandise on display is appalling in its colorless mediocrity. . . . One goes from floor to floor in a daze, seeing the same imitation period pieces repeated without end, radios artfully hidden in sewing tables, bars tucked away in hassocks, and beds that try to look as if George Washington had slept in them. A substantial proportion of the furniture labeled "modern" is no better, frequently suggesting a point of origin near a jukebox factory.[31]

Kaufmann made no secret of his agenda, which was nothing less than transforming "the buying habits of American consumers and the selling practices of retailers," a curatorial initiative "without precedent in the United States," as Terence Riley and Edward Eigen have observed.[32] In the same way the Good Design project blurred distinctions between the museum and department store, Kaufmann's Marshall Plan collaboration eroded another set of institutional boundaries: those separating U.S. cultural diplomacy from MoMA's mission to establish the aesthetic hegemony of modernism in America.

MoMA's Good Design shows struck Kaufmann as tailor-made for foreign export:

> In Europe, as well as America, we have found a wonderful response in the press to our *Good Design* exhibitions. . . . This encourages the belief that a discriminating show of American home furnishing design can present the best and most progressive side of our life to the European public in terms which are intentionally understandable and sympathetic.[33]

Others were not as sanguine. Harold Van Doren condemned the "air of Lady Bountiful going democratic" conveyed by "$60 dollar salad bowls" and "pretty ash trays," a collection of objects betraying a mindset "incapable of coming to grips with the realities of design in everyday life."[34] Undaunted, Kaufmann oversaw the installation of the New Home Furnishings exhibit at its Stuttgart debut.[35] It juxtaposed upscale furniture by American design luminaries like George Nelson, Saarinen,

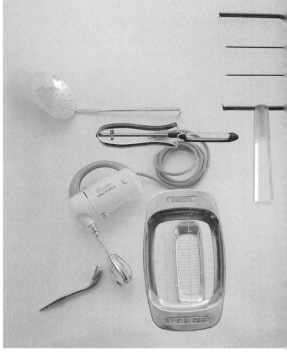

At Stuttgart's American Home Furnishings exhibit in 1951, modular storage units by Charles Eames form a backdrop for an Eames molded fiberglass rocking chair, both for the Herman Miller collection; and a Hamilton Beach electric mixer with an assortment of kitchen utensils demonstrates the innovation in product design promoted by the Marshall Plan. U.S. National Archives, Still Pictures Division, RG286 MP GEN 1001 and GEN 925.

Ray and Charles Eames, and Isamu Noguchi with prosaic items, including a Chemex coffee carafe, Pyrex measuring cups, and Tupperware containers, a combination said to demonstrate that "a contemporary lifestyle" involved a mix of "many low-cost items and a few luxury items."[36] Kaufmann displayed these consumer goods in art-gallery isolation, rather than domestic contexts, granting aesthetic redemption to household consumption. Cameo appearances by an Eva Zeisel casserole, a Select-a-Range modular stove, and an Elco potato peeler may have revealed the secret lives of domestic products as aesthetic objects but not their relationship to the activities of a postwar kitchen. Still-life tableaux featuring a Nelson sectional sofa and side table, a Saarinen "Womb" chair, or an Eames modular storage unit conveyed tasteful consumption without any "orchestrating concept" indicating how such commodities support a lifestyle.[37] Kaufmann, however, ascribed enormous political significance to modernist household objects. His 1950 manifesto *What Is Modern Design?* declared it indispensable to democracy, asserting: *"Modern design is intended to implement the lives of free individuals*" (emphasis in original).[38] Werkbund activist Heinrich König was correct in more ways than one when he noted that the products shown at the New Home Furnishings exhibition were not "representational" in style.[39] Rather than merely representing an American Way of Life, modernist consumer goods were its physical embodiment, according to Kaufmann.

The New Home Furnishings exhibition catalog interpreted MoMA's International Style as the apotheosis of German design culture. Kaufmann's essay explained that the Werkbund and Bauhaus had provided the foundation for their heir apparent, American midcentury modernism.[40] The assertion was echoed in a review of the exhibition by Bauhaus alumnus Wilhelm Wagenfeld, who declared that American product design, with its "carefree, ingenious lightness and an obvious joy taken in empirical experiment," proved New World modernism "more perfectly resolved and less problematic than [its German precursor] the first time around. . . ."[41] Discourses establishing a continental provenance for postwar American design congealed into dogma over the course of the 1950s. "In this period," as the historian Paul Betts observes, "the Bauhaus assumed a privileged position within West German culture in part because it played a crucial role in the larger Cold War project to draw the Weimar Republic and the [postwar] Federal Republic into the same elective lineage, while at the same time conjoining West German and American cultural modernism."[42] The message that modernist design bridged transatlantic difference was broadcast across Western Europe as the New Home Furnishings show took to the road. The exhibition traveled to venues in Stuttgart, West Berlin, Munich, Milan, Paris, London, Amsterdam, and Trieste, and as featured in the newsreel *Welt im Film* (World on Film), was seen by movie theater audiences in cities and towns across West Germany.[43]

Despite its claim of displaying "American design and craftsmanship as adapted to American home living," New Home Furnishings was "in no way typical of the contemporary American household," as a German reviewer recognized.[44] The nostalgic and regional furniture styles that dominated the U.S. market were nowhere to be found in Kaufmann's exhibition. American freedom of choice for consumers, no matter what their taste (or lack thereof), was an aspect of economic democracy that seemed to embarrass Marshall Plan officials. William C. Foster, a former steel industry executive acting as the ECA deputy administrator for Europe, claimed that the "especially progressive" consumer designs showcased by Kaufmann were displacing more "conservative and conventional" products in the United States. This dissimulation of populist taste became a recurring motif in American cultural diplomacy and its national self-portrait concocted for foreign consumption. By the mid-1950s, State Department exports included avant-garde sculpture, abstract expressionist painting, modernist product design, and International Style architecture, all offered as evidence of American freedom of expression.[45] In this dubious marriage of art and politics, abstract works that were by common definition "nonrepresentational" were used to represent the nation's core values—a propaganda tactic so improbable that it was nothing short of sublime.

MODERNIST PEDAGOGY AND ITS PRODUCTS

Postwar American advisors pronounced the New Home Furnishings show a public relations breakthrough. "Interest is enormous," reported the U.S. Foreign Service Office of Public Affairs.[46] Design education provided another opportunity to mobilize modernist design in support of economic reconstruction. The U.S. State Department became the majority stakeholder in financing the start-up of Ulm's Hochschule für Gestaltung (Academy of Design, or HfG), often regarded as the postwar German successor to the Bauhaus. West Germans successfully co-opted the project, meeting some of the goals set by its superpower patron but shifting others in conformance with the wishes of the school's founders.[47] Far from demonstrating the imposition of American will upon a client state, the HfG's creation is a study in soft-power renegotiation.

The HfG was the brainchild of Inge Scholl and Otl Aicher, who as children were linked to the underground circle of "White Rose" insurgents executed by the Gestapo. As a postwar memorial to her martyred siblings, Scholl wanted to found an institute of higher learning that would bolster a postwar democracy distinctly socialist in inclination. "The world of bourgeois imagination is no longer sufficient," she wrote in 1946. "[Socialism] should no longer be merely the cry of the dispossessed, but must become the obligation of a new culture."[48] Scholl and Aicher shared a common interest in Bauhaus pedagogy as a vehicle for social reform. While teaching design at Ulm's municipal community college, they met Bauhaus alumnus and Swiss Werkbund affiliate

Max Bill, who had been employed by the U.S. occupation government as an educational consultant.[49] Bill's faculty position in Zurich's Kunstgewerbeschule (Arts Trade School) provided important credentials for the proposed design academy, and Scholl and Aicher enrolled him in their project. Scholl presented her ideas to U.S. High Commissioner John McCloy at his headquarters in 1949. A "quiet arrangement" emerged from their meeting. The United States would contribute half the cost of establishing a new school if Scholl could locate donors for the other half. She was given six months to produce a document specifying educational goals, curriculum, and construction plans.[50] John P. Steiner, a U.S. educational advisor, added another criterion: "I put forth the question: how will your planned institute help in the reconstitution of a free and democratic nation?"[51] As occupation authorities made clear, funding would be contingent as much upon political ideology as design education.

Scholl's proposal aimed to put all questions to rest. The curriculum would offer training in politics, press, broadcasting, film, photography, advertising, industrial design, and urbanism: disciplines supporting a liberal capitalist democracy across its spectrum of practices, ranging from the technologies of shaping public opinion to the design and promotion of mass-produced consumer goods. Consistent with the school's patronage, Scholl excluded socialism from the pedagogical agenda.[52] The curriculum plan was submitted to U.S. authorities in June 1950.[53] It satisfied McCloy, who praised Scholl's "crusade to enlighten the German people" on their "democratic road" to forging "a close association with the peoples of Western Europe."[54] However, the political commitment that McCloy praised set off alarms for another authority figure. Seeking support for the Ulm project, Bill appealed to Bauhaus founder Walter Gropius, a State Department consultant on German reconstruction with a faculty post at Harvard.[55] Before agreeing to join the school's board of advisors, Gropius wanted to see the curricular emphasis placed "clearly and unambiguously" on design rather than politics. He insisted that architecture, urban planning, and product design be moved to the top of the inventory of course offerings, with political studies given the lowest priority. "However, I believe it quite possible that the inculcation of democratic attitudes could be included as a peripheral pursuit of the institute," Gropius wrote, adding, "if you want me to help with the American officers who are in charge of cultural issues under McCloy, please let me know."[56]

In 1951, one of Scholl's detractors—a former Gestapo officer, as it turned out—denounced her as a communist sympathizer. It took nearly a year to convince her American patrons that the charge was a fabrication.[57] Bill's damage-control efforts painstakingly extricated the Ulm project from the legacy of Hannes Meyer's "Red Bauhaus":

> The object of the school in Ulm is not simply to educate new people, but to stiffen the spine of a larger cohort already active [in society] so that they do not fall into the communist camp. It is a known fact that the "Bauhaus" was politically neutral, yet in practice took on German leftist tendencies. At that time, the "light from the east" appeared to many as the only possible solution to social problems . . . for the most part they have changed their minds. Others, however, are still working in East Germany, albeit under increasing difficulties, since the agenda of a progressive contemporary culture is incompatible with the conditions that they strive for there.[58]

In resuming support for the project, McCloy may also have been influenced by a letter from Gropius pledging that modernist design would produce democratic citizens. "Every successful student leaving the school to enter as a designer into the field of industry or teaching will represent a broad method of approach based on a consistent democratic conception which then will make him a potential cultural factor in his environment." Ulm's higher education program would enhance the prospects for a West German democracy, or so he argued.[59]

When McCloy presented Scholl with a check for one million DM on 23 June 1952, he was funding a school in which a curriculum in politics had been replaced with a minor course of study under the anodyne title of "Cultural Information." Bill, taking Gropius's comments to heart, had established architecture and city planning as the school's focus of instruction. Why would McCoy fund a design institute in which political education had been all but eliminated? Apart from the claim that modernist pedagogy yielded democratic subjects, McCoy's rationale paralleled the motives of the West German industrialists who co-funded the school. In his previous post as director of what would become the World Bank, McCloy was an outspoken advocate of economic and political stability through free trade, going so far as to contemplate "complete economic union" as the ultimate answer to Europe's problems.[60] Given the crucial role of export manufactures in

Hans Gugelot (*seated*) and other faculty members of the Ulm HfG pose with various consumer products developed at the school, including hi-fi equipment designed for Max Braun GmBH. Ulmer Stadtmuseum/ HfG Archive.

his vision of postwar geopolitics, McCloy's continued support for the HfG was a calculated gamble in which the potential gain from subsidizing West German design innovation far exceeded the risks.

Ulm's new design academy ultimately represented a strategic investment in economic reconstruction. The HfG, inaugurated in 1953, reinvigorated Bauhaus functionalism, making its postwar variant the hallmark of high-quality West German consumer goods. HfG instructor Hans Gugelot, a former associate at Bill's Zurich design office, pioneered minimalist design in home electronics, beginning with high-fidelity audio equipment designed in collaboration with Dieter Rams for the Max Braun company. Gugelot's M125 modular storage system for home and office made all-purpose functionalism chic among West German elites. Working in concert, Gugelot and Aicher refined modernist graphic conventions for corporate branding, with Braun and Lufthansa among their early clients. Rather than designing single objects, Gugelot and Aicher specialized in creating market identities for families of goods and services, now the standard method of establishing global brands. McCloy's support for a school specializing in cutting-edge industrial design may have shortchanged American political goals, but it yielded high dividends in advancing Marshall Plan strategies for European economic reconstruction.

SOCIALIST MODERN

Inge Scholl's dream of reviving Bauhaus pedagogy as a springboard for postwar social reform was by no means unique. For a cohort of politically galvanized modernists, East Germany's socialist future inspired hope for a worthy successor to Hannes Meyer's "Red" Bauhaus. All such educational initiatives ultimately failed, including one by Hubert Hoffmann at the famed Dessau Bauhaus, and another by the architect Hermann Henselmann in Weimar, the site of the original Bauhaus academy.[61] Only Mart Stam, who had taught architectural design at the Bauhaus under Meyer, could claim any measure of success in this regard. By the early 1950s, however, every attempt to apply modernist design to the task of East German reconstruction had collided with the Party's project to import socialist realism from its Soviet homeland. In terms of aesthetics and power dynamics, socialist realism was the antithesis of West German modernism. American support for modernist design gave West German elites like Scholl and Aicher the latitude to shape cultural initiatives in ways that met the needs of both locals and a superpower patron. This soft-power approach was anathema to the bureaucratic avant-garde of a Stalinist cultural revolution.[62] In comparison with Marshall Plan modernism, socialist realism was cultural hard power.

In 1948 Stam introduced himself to Gerhard Strauss, a top official in the East German Ministry of Education, announcing: "The [Party] Central Committee sent me. I want to help build socialism. What can I do, where can you use me?"[63] His arrival was perfectly timed. Currency reform had just coupled West Germany to the capitalist economies of Marshall Plan Europe. Soviet administrators launched the East German alternative: an initial Two-Year Plan of centralized economic management modeled upon Soviet precedent. Strauss was looking for pragmatic educational reforms that could be harnessed to the project of socialist reconstruction.[64] He engaged Stam to merge Dresden's two art academies into a single institute charged with training a fresh cadre of industrial designers. Stam proposed the name "bauschule" (building school) for the new institute, echoing Bauhaus tradition. In keeping with its namesake, Stam's bauschule would expunge all remnants of academic atelier culture. To cultivate a proletarian intelligentsia, student recruitment would favor candidates from agrarian and working-class backgrounds.[65] Rather than teaching fine arts, bauschule instruction would emphasize the design of "progressive household goods" for working-class consumers.[66] At Stam's new academy, Bauhaus pedagogy would be exercised by and for the proletariat.

Strauss was delighted by the replacement of fine-arts instruction with an industrial design curriculum, but the same could not be said for faculty displaced by the change. Stam's dictatorial manner and contempt for atelier tradition provoked a mutiny among the teaching staff. Believing that Stam's talents might be better used elsewhere, Strauss and the SED approved his transfer to another institution in need of an

Students in Mart Stam's Institute for Industrial Design at the Berlin-Weißensee Art Academy work on prototypes for mass-produced consumer ceramic goods, 1951. Bundesarchiv, photograph 183-12940-4. Photograph by Kemlein.

overhaul. In 1948, Strauss had censured the Berlin-Weißensee Academy, founded as a private initiative at war's end, for "muddling along in the characteristic academic art orthodoxy."[67] As the school's new director, as of May 1950, Stam again advanced the goal of socialist reconstruction through educational reform.[68] Aided by new faculty members, including Bauhaus alumnus and fellow Party comrade Selman Selmanagič, Stam applied his formula for turning a fine-arts academy into an industrial design laboratory. Finding the school hobbled by mediocre students, Stam cracked down on the lax work ethos—a disciplinary effort that would come back to haunt him.[69] Rather than using classroom time for hypothetical assignments, he collected the school's best talent in a research group charged with real-world tasks. The resulting Institute of Industrial Design was a cooperative initiative involving the East German Bureau of Standardization and Product Testing and the Ministries of Heavy Industry and Popular Education. Stam envisioned the joint venture as the catalyst for a breakthrough in socialist material culture. "There are hundreds of superfluous and tasteless petit-bourgeois products to be scrutinized and discontinued," he insisted. Improving the design of household goods would take East German workers to "a higher plane of taste and culture."[70]

Would-be socialist consumers agreed. Despite a goods famine gripping East Germany, traditionally crafted furnishings remained in production and on the market at exorbitant prices. These wares were presented to foreign wholesalers at the Leipzig trade fair, used by locals as a source of vicarious thrills. Its visions of household abundance had little to do with public need, as a newspaper critic noted:

> In the Fair pavilions it was like a bath for the eyes to find so many beautiful things brought together at one time. Glass, porcelain, ceramics; color and form equally complete and balanced. . . . How did the new furniture look? There all expectations were disappointed. Amazed, one asked oneself: don't the interior designers, woodworkers and furniture producers have any insight—or are they still of the opinion that each family lives in a multiple-room apartment? Nowhere does one see a truly fitting solution to the one-room apartment in which so many [of us] today reside.[71]

Stam was not the only Bauhaus associate to address the dearth of consumer durables suitable for mass production. At the Deutsche

Werkstätte (German Crafts Studio) in Dresden-Hellerau, founded in conjunction with the Werkbund in 1909, Franz Ehrlich, a Bauhaus alumnus under Meyer and collaborator in the school's 1929 *Volkswohnung* project, worked with engineer Erich Menzel to create molded plywood furniture using half the raw material needed for a conventional wooden chair.[72] Gustav Hassenpflug, another Bauhaus protégé, focused his efforts on modern storage and shelving units, a vector of research motivated by social concerns. "Modular furnishings," he wrote, "will fulfill their purpose when they can be purchased and put to good use, above all else, by the truly needy: that is, the bombed-out, the relocated, the immigrants who are living in twos and threes in single-room apartments, or in fours and fives in two-room dwellings."[73] East German designers bearing Bauhaus pedigrees were poised to realize Hannes Meyer's call for "people's necessities instead of luxury goods" (*Volksbedarf statt Luxusbedarf*) just as the Party issued a new round of directives aimed at stopping them in their tracks.

HARD-POWER CULTURE

The fortunes of East German modernism foundered in 1951. With policies in place calling for the emulation of Soviet precedents in economic planning, labor organization, and class structure, East Berlin's politburo, led by Walter Ulbricht, mandated the import of Stalinism's signature aesthetic. Described as "socialist in content and national in form," socialist realism proclaimed that art's true purpose was to celebrate the triumph of communism and reveal its historical foreshadowing. Its doctrinal adoption in 1932 by the USSR's Communist Party Central Committee ended political infighting by competing avant-garde factions and consolidated Party control over cultural production. Socialist realism expropriated bourgeois taste and aesthetic achievements in the name of the proletariat, supporting Lenin's vision of proletarian culture, which he decreed "simply has to be the systematic further development of the sum of knowledge that mankind has accrued under the yoke of capitalist, feudal, and bureaucratic social orders."[74] The official Soviet aesthetic disappointed modernists farther West, who had seen Stalin's USSR as the last best hope for an empowered avant-garde patronage. It confronted Soviet designers of the 1930s with an even more disconcerting prospect: charting the unknown waters of an aesthetic based on ideological proclamations, rather than any proven system of creative practice. To facilitate the developmental process, the Soviet Party Central Committee reorganized all fields of artistic endeavor into centrally managed unions and academies charged with turning doctrine into art. Writers, painters, musicians, sculptors, and architects examined neoclassicism for its latent socialist content, scrutinized folk art for its lessons on national character, and combined these divergent elements in a new cultural admixture. Failure to combine these ingredients in a way that satisfied colleagues and Party authorities was admonished in terms bearing a confusing similarity to the lexicon of Western art criticism. In Stalinist discourse, "eclecticism" meant slavish imitation of historical styles without the compulsory process of socialist realist synthesis. "Kitsch," said to be an exclusively capitalist phenomenon, was the exploitation of vulgarity for its market value. What was called modernism in the West was dubbed "formalism" in Soviet parlance, denoting the manipulation of form as an end in itself rather than to convey socialist ideology: an absence that implied the presence of antisocial content. All of these shortcomings were, by default, politically suspect in that they mangled the message of communist progress.[75]

During the war, the battle for national survival had trumped Soviet campaigns against internal subversion. When it was over, Andrei Zhdanov, a high-ranking politburo member and the future founder of Cominform, renewed the Party's crusade against aesthetic deviance. The so-called *Zhdanovshchina* of 1946 expanded outward to encompass Soviet client states.[76] East German design professionals received their call to arms in 1950, after Ulbricht authorized the retraining of highly placed reconstruction bureaucrats in Moscow. Upon return to East Berlin, they became the deskbound firebrands of a Stalinist cultural revolution.[77] The SED Central Committee dissolved the IfB, the state-supported design bureau that had sponsored Henselmann's investigation of *Existenzminimum* housing for millworkers a few years earlier. The organization's employees were reorganized as the Deutsche Bauakademie (German Building Academy), a new state institute named after a nineteenth-century Prussian precursor, but modeled on the Soviet Academy of Architects. Former IfB member Kurt Liebknecht, the nephew of the German communist martyr Karl Liebknecht, was appointed to head the state's new clearinghouse for design commissions. Bauakademie management was linked to the Party by a web of cross-memberships, allowing the SED Central Committee to intervene in anything from urban planning and architectural design to the development of new furniture prototypes.[78]

The "Formalism Discussion" at the SED Third Party Congress in July 1950 called upon the nation's cultural intelligentsia to abandon modernism. Its imported Soviet replacement proved a hard sell, however. Many East German designers still equated socialism with the Bauhaus, not neoclassicism. One possible resistance tactic consisted of superficial acquiescence combined with a cautious attempt to reformulate socialist realist practice to include modernism. For example, in a public lecture on postwar architecture's rediscovery of national tradition, a leitmotif of socialist realism, Henselmann suggested the Bauhaus as an appropriate starting point.[79] This attempt to reform socialist realism's "Nati-Tradi" orthodoxy, as it was later lampooned, was a high-risk strategy, as Henselmann quickly learned. An article in *Neues Deutschland*, the national Party newspaper, enumerating his ideological and aesthetic infractions brought the architect back into the fold.[80]

Intimations of the coming cultural revolution were felt at Berlin-Weißensee prior to Stam's arrival as the school's new director. A controversy erupted in 1950 over the use of "hostile" avant-garde imagery in posters for school events. Six instructors, denounced as "bourgeois" and "reactionary," were forced to resign.[81] As the head of the school's SED committee, Stam was expected to spearhead efforts to root out formalists. He evaded this responsibility, as indeed he had to: by Party criteria he also was guilty of the charge. The rhetorical trail left behind at Berlin-Weißensee suggests that Stam sought a discursive accommodation with socialist realism. While demanding postwar consumer objects that were "honest, good and true"—adjectives redolent of the Werkbund's "design conscience"—he proclaimed the need for a new style expressing socialism's "comradely and life-affirming" qualities, terms saturated with Stalinist pathos.[82] In attempting to attune modernism to his party's ideology, Stam worked toward an unlikely (and largely unwanted) resolution of the dialectical clash between Bauhaus design and its socialist realist antithesis. Other modernist partisans forged their own rapprochement with the Stalinist paradigm shift. At the Department of Industrial Design in Weimar, up-and-coming faculty member Horst Michel declared war on kitsch, a pathology reviled by modernists and socialist realists alike. Railing against "pointless design buffoonery, dishonest splendor and feigned quality," Michel warned, "If people are surrounded by furnishings that are superficially grand, untruthful, hollow and senseless, they will be influenced likewise."[83] His alarmist rhetoric found favor with SED ideologues, just as it would have among cultural critics representing the Werkbund, Bauhaus, or, for that matter, the Third Reich. An unwavering stand against kitsch proved to be the perfect statement of political commitment in the uncharted waters of East Germany's cultural revolution. Modernists like Hubert Hoffmann and Gustav Hassenpflug opted for the less ambiguous response of voting with their feet, immigrating to West Berlin.

The Party proclaimed a national "Battle against Formalism in Art and Literature" at the Fifth Congress of the SED Central Committee in March 1951. Press coverage informed East Germans of the threat posed by modernism. "In architecture, which faces great tasks in the context of the Five-Year Plan, what hinders us the most is the so-called 'Bauhaus style.' That is also the case with designs for mass-produced furniture and household utensils."[84] The politics of Bauhaus design could be discerned from the behavior of its adherents, insisted Bauakademie director Liebknecht. "Today, where are the architects who represented the Bauhaus, such as Gropius, Mies van der Rohe, Martin Wagner and others? They are in America; they seem to like it there, and from this we can infer that they have decided in favor of American imperialism."[85] In fact, the Party's quarrel was not with these émigré celebrities, who nicely illustrated the proclaimed connection between modernist design and monopoly capitalism, but with Bauhaus recidivists in East Germany. As Hans Hopp, a well-placed Bauakademie leader and former Weimar-era modernist, remarked, "the accusations made against the Bauhaus then must be made against all architects [who are products] of this time."[86] As Hopp understood, enthusiasts of modernist design had become, by definition, enemies of the socialist state.

East Germany's newly minted socialist realists struggled to master an unfamiliar ideology of Soviet provenance. For example, four months after the Party declared war on formalism, the director of the Bauakademie Institute for Interior Design, Peter Bergner, issued an inadvertent defense of household functionalism:

> Furniture is produced in runs of up to 5000 pieces, making it simply an article of mass production. That is a fact that can be praised or deplored, but not ignored. This explains why, in building construction and architectural representation, the retention of forms

from our classical heritage presents far fewer difficulties than in the industrial manufacture of furnishings.[87]

Within a fortnight Bergner had revised his position. Some socialist commodities still were exempted from the neoclassical imperatives: "No one would consider asking more of a washbasin or frying pan than to fulfill its purpose perfectly." Bergner's evaluation of these objects echoed the Marxist notion of "use value." However, armoires, china

Captioned "What should our furniture look like?" the cover of an East German news journal shows a Deutsche Bauakademie functionary pointing out neoclassical cabinetry details to three would-be modernists: *left to right,* Friedrich Engemann, Horst Michel, and Mart Stam. *Bild-BZ* 7, no. 23 (June 8, 1952).

cabinets, and chairs reflected "the intellectual, economic and cultural disposition of the inhabitant"; they had qualities inextricably linked to cultural heritage. "Kitchen appliances are tools," Bergner explained; "furnishings should be housemates."[88] A century earlier, Marx had drawn a mental map locating bourgeois commodity fetishism within "the mist-enveloped regions of the religious world," a realm in which man-made objects were regarded "as independent beings, endowed with life, . . . entering into relation both with each other and with the human race."[89] Although Marx predicted that socialism would eradicate commodity fetishism, socialist realism had spawned its own unique variant: a domestic culture in which chairs and tables were housemates rather than tools.

THE INTERIOR WORLD OF STALINISM

The Bauakademie unveiled East Germany's new native style at a two-day conference, "Issues of German Interior Design and the Design of Furniture," held in March 1952 at East Berlin's House of Soviet Culture. Participants included architects, interior designers, furniture manufacturers, representatives of state retailing organizations, and Party officials.[90] The keynote address was delivered by the general secretary of the SED Central Committee, Walter Ulbricht, who emphasized the role played by beauty in nurturing socialism. "Furniture manufactured in the Bauhaus style," he explained, "does not correspond to the sensitivity to beauty possessed by the new Germany's progressive human beings." Under the pretense of economical mass production, "designs were developed that had nothing to do with beauty." According to Ulbricht, "crate-like furniture"—meaning modular storage units—of "primitive design" served "neither the needs nor the demands of the working population." Designers who failed to grasp that fact demonstrated their alienation from the working class. "Is it not time, after all, to establish a closer connection between craftsmen and architects and the working people?"[91] Ulbricht's rhetorical question underscored the gravity of socialist realist "beauty," a construct charged with the portent that another superficially neutral term, "function," bore for modernism. Subsequent conference presentations revealed beauty's foundation in national tradition. Beauty was the antithesis of formalism: that vehicle of "the so-called American lifestyle, which claims global validity, is nothing other than a direct continuation of [bourgeois] decadence, and serves to uproot human beings, making them suitable as objects of exploitation in all forms, straightforward and veiled." The fact that German designers could no longer create "beautiful details that come together harmonically in a beautiful whole" revealed the pernicious influence of modernism's "colorless international language."[92] Beauty also had the power to rehabilitate the ideologically misguided. "We know that political consciousness, for many, is not sufficiently developed to enable citizens to distinguish the beautiful and good from the ugly and bad. Only when such material education penetrates one's most inner being, including the world of his dreams and fantasies . . . will such changes bear fruit."[93] Rather than being defined by the eye of the beholder, socialist realist beauty defined the beholder. It was the nexus linking socialist subjectivity, resistance to capitalist imperialism, a revival of national cultural tradition, and—crucially for conferees—the reconciliation of former modernists with Ulbricht and the proletariat he spoke for.

East German newspapers avoided any mention of the differences of opinion at the Bauakademie conference. At a session on "Working Women and the Issues of Interior Design," Alice Lingner, an advocate of domestic reform, insisted that housing was experienced differently by men and women, and that the repose men found at home would not be shared by women until apartments were "more functionally built, furnished and serviced."[94] Bauakademie associate Madeleine Grotewohl argued for the "extreme rationalization and mechanization of housework" to facilitate the entry of women into the workforce.[95] Another Bauakademie member, Liv Falkenberg, reported on new Czechoslovakian housing, noting its inclusion of built-in kitchen cabinets and thus implicitly challenging the argument that East Germany could not afford to provide such amenities.[96] These presentations, out of sync with the conference's overarching theme of beauty and national tradition, went unreported. Ulbricht had the last word. He rejected the "formalist" proposition that "the kitchen should be merely a workshop for women." "Women want a beautiful room," he declared. "In the home, every surface should not be blank (*glatt*). That is a piece of Weimar-era propaganda that interprets the primitive as beautiful."[97] Ulbricht's grasp of the psychology of East German homemakers was literally unquestionable. To dispute his judgment challenged the axiom that he represented the citizens of socialism, an apostasy that no conference participant was foolhardy enough to commit. With feminist

A model housewife with her home's "beautiful" kitchen cabinets in an apartment on East Berlin's Stalinallee. From Gerhard Puhlman, *Die Stalinallee: nationales Aufbauprogramm 1952* (East Berlin: Verlag der Nation, 1953).

concerns dismissed, discourse shifted back to a predetermined message: that modernism was atavistic, and that socialist realist beauty embodied social progress.

A session on "Criticism and Self-Criticism" showcased another Soviet cultural import: the political ritual called *kritika/samokritika* in Russian. A staple of Stalinist daily life, it demanded that individuals publicly admit their failings and those of their coworkers as a Party functionary recorded the proceedings. As a tool of administrative control, the ceremony created tension among colleagues, preventing their mutual enrollment as coconspirators. Having spent the war years in Soviet exile, Bauakademie director Liebknecht was well versed in the method. He introduced the session by noting "talented architects such as professor Selmanagič, professor Stam [and] the architect Ehrlich have not as of yet taken a self-critical position regarding their work."[98] Instead of confessing, however, one of beauty's discontents seized the opportunity to criticize. Franz Ehrlich opened his litany of dissent by thanking female conferees for their "reprimand." Since no women served on the Bauakademie presidium, he observed, it was no wonder that those in attendance had to instruct their male colleagues in the realities of domestic labor. Relieving the burden of housework called for a fundamental reform in household design, Ehrlich insisted. By combining the expertise of housewives and industrial engineers, a kit of parts for furniture could be devised consisting of cabinet doors, side panels, shelves, and legs, from which citizens could assemble objects according to need—from a chest of drawers to a storage wall. The socialist home's distinctive character, he maintained, should come not from ornament-laden furniture but from family possessions and craft objects displayed against a neutral background of modular storage. Ehrlich also dared to disagree with the knee-jerk criticism of modernism dispensed at the conference: "Because it is not historically accurate, I must protest this cheap way of describing anything one doesn't like as Bauhaus." He closed the abortive criticism and self-criticism session with a parting shot at the dogma of national tradition. The work of a self-critical designer was based on an exacting study of history, Ehrlich insisted, rather than "words with nothing behind them."[99] Why the insult did not cost him his career is difficult to fathom. At a time when skilled East German technicians were fleeing westward in ever-greater numbers, perhaps his production experience was too valuable to be discarded. In any case, for the time being Ehrlich failed to trigger the Party's purge reflex. But the issues he raised regarding feminism, functionalism, and socialist domesticity would remain suppressed from East German design discourse for years to come.[100]

The Bauakademie conference closed with a volley of paper resolutions that had little discernable impact on East German manufacturing. Meanwhile, the Party's cultural revolution swept academia, leaving few aspects of design education untouched. The Ministry of Popular Education reorganized Weimar's design academy, making its first class graduating with a degree in industrial design also its last.[101] Although ministry officials considered reassigning Horst Michel, the head of the defunct department, to a post in a ceramics factory, he managed to remain at Weimar as a lecturer in interior design.[102] At about the same time, ministry officials arrived at Berlin-Weißensee demanding to know what Stam had done to eliminate formalism at the school. Faculty members bristled at the combative tone. Stam urged the warring parties to show a measure of mutual tolerance. A transcript of his comments went directly to the SED Central Committee.[103] Denunciations were solicited from disgruntled students whom Stam had considered mediocrities but whom Party authorities declared "politically and ideologically farther advanced than their professors."[104] Stam was dismissed from his post, and a restraining order was issued to prohibit him from setting foot on school grounds. Having abandoned his native Holland five years earlier "to help build socialism" in East Germany, Stam again became an immigrant, fleeing his adopted nation for a new life in the West. Purged by the political system he had devoted his life to serving, he spent much of its remainder as a recluse, in his wife's words, "sick in heart and soul."[105]

Better Living through Modernism

A profound loss accompanied the rising postwar fortunes of the International Style, according to architectural historian Colin Rowe. As the "vision of . . . [a] unitary future world" receded after the war, modernism suffered a "rapid devaluation of its ideal content."[1] The same could be said for the promise of modernist product design as a vehicle for social reform. In his *Enquiry into Industrial Art in England* of 1937, Nikolaus Pevsner maintained that modernism demanded "a certain leveling of social differences." He wondered whether "a sweeping change in social conditions, such as the establishment of some kind of State Socialism, might lead to a sweeping change in the appearance of industrial products."[2] A world war later, as modernism went mainstream, such speculation all but vanished. Asked about the American market's lack of high-quality modern furniture at affordable prices, George Nelson shocked a Chicago lecture audience in 1948 by confessing, "I think I ought to tell you that, as a designer, I don't give a damn about the people." His catchphrases—"There is a market for good design" and "Nothing is less consequential in the creation of a work of art than good intentions"—epitomized a postwar modernism stripped of social idealism.[3]

In Europe, an unexpected patron reasserted modernism's potential as the springboard to a "unitary future world." In its efforts to anchor Marshall Plan member nations within a West of its own making, the U.S. State Department discovered the visionary appeal and propagandistic potential of International Style modernism. We're Building a Better Life, a domestic spectacle mounted in 1952 by the Mutual Security Agency (MSA), a Marshall Plan successor agency, hypothesized the transatlantic *Wohnkultur* of a modernist middle class. Its new postwar people, exhibited along with the exhibition's model home, would be affluent, cosmopolitan in taste, politically democratic, and culturally hegemonic. Their domestic environment—the native habitat of either a "John Smith or Hans Schmidt," as stated by Michael Harris, the German division chief of the MSA—embodied the principles of global mass consumption and barrier-free trade.[4] At We're Building a Better Life, modernism escaped its postwar sentence as "the acceptable decoration of a certainly non-Utopian present," in Rowe's words.[5] Under the aegis of the State Department, the International Style returned to its continent of origin as a triumphant expression of Atlanticism: the

(*facing page*) A young, affluent, two-parent–two-child model family enjoys a modernist home environment at the Marshall Plan's We're Building a Better Life exhibit as a crowd of spectators peers in through a living room window. U.S. National Archives, Still Pictures Division, RG286 MP GEN 1903.

cultural unification of the United States and Western Europe as conceived by the former and revealed to the latter.

ATLANTICISM BY DESIGN

Divided Berlin's competitive market in ideologies shaped what was, to date, America's most ambitious household exhibition. Three weeks following the close of East Berlin's conference on "Issues of German Interior Design," U.S. exhibit planners, having traded their Marshall Plan letterhead for that of the MSA, proposed a shift in strategy for their nation's contribution to West Berlin's 1952 German Industrial Exhibition. Rather than creating separate installations related to industry and consumer goods, as had been done in 1950—with America at Home representing the latter—they would dedicate the entire U.S. display to private consumption. The potential impact on East Germans was a primary consideration, as a State Department memorandum makes clear:

> The Berlin Industrial Fair in 1950 was most impressive because it showed large machines being produced by the West at a time when Eastern factories were suffering from dismantling by the Soviets and when raw materials in the East were in extreme shortage. Since that time, however, the Eastern emphasis on heavy machinery and production goods has brought about a changed situation. It is particularly appropriate at this time, therefore, to show West Berliners, and more especially East Zone and [Soviet] Sector visitors, the progress made in the West in developing consumer goods designed to raise the standard of living of the average family.[6]

The name chosen for the MSA exhibition, We're Building a Better Life (Wir bauen ein besseres Leben) reflected cold war rivalry as well. It echoed the East German mantra "Produce More—Live Better" (*Höhere Arbeitsproduktivität—Besser Leben*), a slogan used to motivate "worker activists" to boost productivity through labor techniques imported from Stalinist Russia. Party officials in East Berlin asserted that a socialist labor policy based on voluntary overproduction and piecework wages would yield collective abundance. At the 1952 Berlin Industrial Fair, MSA officials would strive to refute that economic formula and provide a glimpse of the capitalist path to postwar prosperity.

Exhibition plans were finalized in May at a moment of heightened border tensions. To exert a measure of control over its porous boundary with the West, East Berlin blocked some two hundred streets linking the city's two halves.[7] Nevertheless, officers of the MSA presentations branch were confident that they could draw crowds of East German visitors to their exhibit. It would feature a house within a house—a full-scale "ideal dwelling" built within West Berlin's Marshall-Haus pavilion. With respect to previous U.S. exhibits, We're Building a Better Life was a breakthrough in what Barbara Kirshenblatt-Gimblett has called the "political economy of showing."[8] Just as in a nineteenth-century ethnographic display stocked with exotic subjects, the MSA model home would be populated by model inhabitants: a "man-wife-child family team actually going through [the] physical actions of living in [the] dwelling, making proper use of [the] objects in it," as outlined in a State Department telegraph.[9] Unlike the unambiguous sense of superiority conveyed by colonialist displays featuring "primitive" peoples, popular responses to the MSA display were bound to be fraught with contradictions. Germans, encouraged to identify with the showcased residents, would inevitably be reminded of their relative penury. The exhibition's gamble was that observation of a fictive German family living in a postwar dream home would trigger Duesenberry's "demonstration effect," inducing desire for a higher standard of living rather than the alienation pervading Hauser's notion of an "American fat kitchen." To enhance audience identification, the MSA show would assemble its visionary home from local materials: "wherever possible, equipment [is] to be European rather than American."[10] The result was to be an American Way of Life formulated for export and "developed in terms of arguments for a high-production, high-wage, low-unit-cost, low-profit-margin, high consumption system. . . . Emphasis [is] to be placed upon [the] fortunate outcome of American economic philosophy when combined with European skills and resources." The Better Life narrative asserted that prosperity, rather than cultural difference, was what distinguished New World domesticity from its Old World counterpart, and that this disparity could be eradicated through hard work and sound economic policy.

Many of the interior appointments showcased in the Better Life home were manufactured in Europe under license by Knoll International—an inspired choice, given that Knoll's midcentury modernism not only symbolized Atlanticism but was also the product of its economic policies. As a corporate entity, Knoll International was born from a proposition made by U.S. State Department officials to the German expatriate Hans Knoll, a charismatic entrepreneur known in Washington through his firm's refurbishing of federal office buildings.[11] His Manhattan-based company, Knoll Associates, provided interior design services for business and government clients, and imported modern Scandinavian furnishings. With his file of European contacts, Knoll was the perfect partner for a strategic investment scheme initiated by the State Department to create a prototype for the private enterprises needed to plug what U.S. economic planners called the European "dollar gap."

Marshall Plan financial support for Europe was based not on cash grants but on dollar-denominated loans to be repaid in local currencies into continental bank accounts controlled by the State Department, creating stockpiles of so-called counterpart funds. U.S. officials intended to leverage their counterpart funds to influence continental monetary policy. The ultimate goal, according to the ECA's chief administrator, would be "a single large market within which quantitative restrictions on the movements of goods, monetary barriers to the flow of payments, and eventually all tariff barriers are eventually swept away."[12] Putting this plan into practice proved anything but simple. The crawling pace of market integration among Marshall Plan member nations frustrated American advisors.[13] Exports to the United States declined, threatening to increase the "dollar gap"—that is, the deficit created when imports of the dollar-denominated goods vital to postwar

Florence Knoll's interior design for the Knoll International Showroom in Munich. *Design* (London), no. 49 (January 1953).

reconstruction outstripped Western European export income. According to a Marshall Plan midterm review, the level of monetary imbalance would hit a disastrous three-billion-dollar mark by 1952.[14]

In response, Marshall Plan economists examined European export opportunities, surveyed American market preferences, and devised a number of intervention strategies.[15] A large order for furnishings to be used in a State Department expansion program for postwar diplomatic facilities provided the start-up capital, paid in Marshall Plan counterpart funds, that transformed Knoll Associates into Knoll International.[16] Hans and Florence Knoll scoured the continent for suitable subcontractors for their new manufacturing venture. "We drove from Stuttgart to Paris, from Paris to Milan, from Milan to Stuttgart," Florence Knoll recalled. "We started producing our designs for Europe, and once this job was done, the companies were there."[17] Wooden furniture was fabricated in Germany and France, textiles in France, and metalwork in Italy, where, after a decade-long disappearance from the market, the chromed steel furnishings designed by Bauhaus masters Marcel Breuer and Mies van der Rohe went back into production under an exclusive Knoll contract.[18] The result was a model enterprise demonstrating the potential of "American economic philosophy when combined with European skills and resources," as extolled at the Better Life exhibition. Knoll International embodied the transnational flows of goods and capital promoted by the State Department as postwar Europe's path to economic recovery.

Knoll International's modernism, according to sociologist Herbert Gans, epitomized the "progressive upper-middle culture" of a "new class," which saw itself as "forward-looking, enlightened and enlightening, contemporary and reformist, out to vanquish the obsolescent, the unnecessarily complicated, and the dishonest in American culture and everyday life."[19] In summer 1952, Knoll unveiled its new showroom in Stuttgart, the capital of the West German furniture industry. Local manufacturers had much to learn from its bold, fresh interiors, according to a British design journal:

> When one sees the pieces that the postwar Deutscher Werkbund selects as examples of good current design . . . one sense[s] the loss over the years since 1932. The forms are pure, the lines straight, the angles right and the colors pale. The impression . . . is of a somewhat outmoded puritanism.[20]

Knoll's Stuttgart showroom contrasted signature furnishings against the glossy surface of black rubber flooring and swatches of color-coordinated fabric draped floor to ceiling. Abandoning traditionally matched suites of furniture, Florence Knoll's subdued tables and sofas provided a visual foil for bravura modernist chairs by the firm's stable of international talents, whose designs were manufactured under exclusive license. Examining this "laboratory" of export-ready European products, a West German design critic put his finger on what distinguished Knoll modernism:

> In all objects on display, despite the correctness of form, one always has the impression that there are no dogmas here, but instead that the free development of a [design] direction is left open. That, beyond the perfection of execution and color choice, is what strikes us as so extraordinarily congenial.[21]

Knoll's "new look" graced the interiors of new U.S. diplomatic facilities throughout Europe and was commended for private use by the MSA Better Life dream home. Given these ties to the U.S. State Department and its propaganda initiatives, it is not surprising that International Style modernism was a high-profile target for East bloc detractors. Socialist realists called it part of the capitalist conspiracy to "disassociate the people from their native land, from their language and their culture, so that they adopt the 'American lifestyle' and join in the slavery of the American imperialists."[22] Party ideologues portrayed modernism as the handmaid of Marshall Plan economics, which they condemned as an assault on European sovereignty. While alarmist, their assessment was not baseless. As demonstrated at We're Building a Better Life, MSA officials were indeed grooming modernism as the stylistic lingua franca of transnational consumer capitalism and its globalized American Way of Life.

"The American bludgeon as the solution for the market problem." A Soviet cartoon, from the November 3, 1949, issue of *Izvestia*, portrays Marshall Plan administrator Paul Hoffman wielding a dollar sign as a club and smashing a signpost that reads "sovereignty of Western European countries." Underfoot, two fences, labeled "tariff barriers," lie in pieces. Averell Harriman Papers, Manuscript Division, Library of Congress.

WEAPONS-GRADE FURNISHINGS

The Better Life show reunited a tried-and-true cast. The MSA's initial choice for curator was Edgar Kaufmann Jr., whose work at MoMA manifested an increasingly transnational approach to home design.[23] Good Design II, which opened in Chicago in January 1951, featured products from Denmark, Finland, France, England, Italy, Germany, and the United States.[24] Although Kaufmann apparently turned down the MSA commission, the roster of American designers featured in Good Design I and its Marshall Plan spin-off—including Knoll, Saarinen, Eames, and Nelson, among others—was put to good use at the subsequent West German show. Curatorial responsibilities for We're Building a Better Life fell to Peter Harnden. In his new position as chief of the MSA presentations branch, he assembled an international team to mount the exhibition. Harnden contracted a German architect, Fritz Bornemann, to draft plans for the Better Life model home. In Bonn, U.S. public affairs officer Herwin Schaefer was enlisted to secure the show's West German household durables, many available through the Stuttgart office of Knoll International. Freelance consultants were hired to track down additional domestic goods in France and Italy. To deliver the required objects to the exhibition site on short notice, Department of Commerce officials considered asking the air force to mount a new Berlin airlift—one dedicated to the emergency transport of chic furnishings rather than food and coal.[25]

A publicity photograph of a fully clothed model housewife in the home's bathtub at We're Building a Better Life. U.S. National Archives, Still Pictures Division, RG286 MP GEN 1888.

The production team's most harrowing moment occurred just days before the grand opening. Describing the show, Harnden had stated at a press conference that the model housewife "would demonstrate household appliances and equipment," including a bathroom shower. The next day, United Press correspondent Joseph Fleming broke the news that the U.S. State Department would be staging a "striptease" at West Berlin's upcoming German Industrial Exhibition. A flurry of confidential telegrams between administrators in Washington and their West German envoys ensued. MSA officers denied responsibility for the public relations disaster, insisting that Harnden

> did not (rpt not) say or allude to: (A) any sort of "strip tease" (B) "luscious young Germ[an] girl" hired for "leading role" (C) "modeling nylons, panties and brassieres." . . . In view of widespread play given this misleading, erroneous account, plans for shower routine cancelled.[26]

Days later, following a preview of the exhibition for invited guests, a jubilant MSA officer telegraphed news of visitor responses to the secretary of state. Local journalists, business leaders, and state officials, including West German Economic Minister Ludwig Erhard, had found the show delightful. "Contrary to UP story implications, there is nothing vulgar or cheap about [the] role of actors demonstrating household equipment," he reasserted.[27]

The main attraction at We're Building a Better Life, which opened
in September 1952, was a single-family dwelling—two bedrooms, a
living-dining room, bath, kitchen, laundry/home workshop, nursery,
and garden—realized down to its kitchen gadgets and garden tools but
built without a roof. All six thousand products in and around the house
were modern in design and manufactured in a Marshall Plan member
nation. A billboard beside the home's front door announced: "The
objects in this house are industrial products from many countries in
the Atlantic community. Thanks to technology, rising productivity,
economic cooperation and free enterprise, these objects are available
to our Western civilization." A model family—alternately portrayed
by two couples and eight pairs of children, all professional actors or
models—worked the floor in shifts, demonstrating the tasks and leisure
rituals of "an average skilled worker and his family" living in a consumer
wonderland. Perched overhead in a crow's nest, a narrator dressed in
white coveralls explained the features of this exotic household environment. Visitors became voyeurs, staring through windows or crowding
overhead catwalks to observe the ways in which modernist domestic
objects constructed new postwar subjects.

A visitor's journey through the exhibition concluded at a gallery
introduced with a nearly life-size photograph of a blue-collar male
laborer, captioned: "This man is a worker and at the same time a
consumer." Given the era's gender conventions, which regarded home
interiors as a female preoccupation, the panel alerted visitors to an
exhibition discourse of importance to men as well as women. For the
East Germans in the audience, it was also a reminder of the lack of
material rewards for workers under a Stalinist labor economy. In this
final display area, all furnishings seen within the model home could be
examined as closely as a shopper might. A tag attached to each item
indicated country of origin, retail price, and the number of hours of
labor—as measured by a skilled worker's wage—needed to purchase
the object. This seemingly guileless calculation of purchasing power
challenged a tenet of communist faith. Marx had used "labor value" to
define capitalist manufacturing and distribution as exploitive. Profit, he
had claimed, was the unpaid labor value that industrialists appropriated
from workers when products were sold at retail prices. A century later,
MSA exhibit planners radically redefined labor value as the amount of
work needed to *purchase* an item rather than produce it. This changed
emphasis turned the concept devised by Marx to reveal the abuses of
capitalism into a means of measuring its rewards.

(*facing page*) Hovering
above the roofless model
home at the We're Build-
ing a Better Life exhibit,
a narrator dressed in
white coveralls explains
the lifestyle rituals of the
installation's resident
model family. U.S.
National Archives, Still
Pictures Division, RG286
MP GEN 1841.

The second gallery at We're Building a Better Life displayed modular Eames storage units, a pair of Butterfly chairs by Jorge Ferrari-Hardoy arranged around a Florence Knoll table, a set of chairs by Hans Wegner, and a birch bedroom chest by Florence Knoll. Referring to the Marshall Plan community, a panel announces, "We possess the world's highest standard of living." U.S. National Archives, Still Pictures Division, RG286 MP GEN 1974.

As a primer in "the modern approach to interior decoration," the Better Life exhibition taught that "rationally designed products from different countries in the Atlantic community can be combined harmoniously," according to MSA publicity materials.[28] Another press release explained that "just as these items from the various countries combine to form a homogenous whole, so the nations themselves can combine to form a homogenous community."[29] The underlying message was summarized in the West German daily *Der Tag*:

> The new style, realism plus simplicity, finds its strongest expression in the U.S. Marshall-Haus. . . . There are different versions of one style and one way of life typical for a "Western bourgeois" household. Nothing is foreign to us, whether it comes from Berlin or Los Angeles, from Stockholm, Sicily or New York.[30]

"To some visitors, this home of a future 'average consumer' would appear perhaps to be 'American,' but that is incorrect," a design journal reported, reiterating the talking points of an opening-day address by Michael Harris, chief of the German branch of the MSA. "John Smith

or Hans Schmidt would be perfectly capable of affording such a house when certain conditions were met: we must make the Atlantic community of nations a reality, eliminate tariff barriers, and raise productivity, thereby allowing us to lower prices and raise wages."[31] The Better Life's International Style was not simply an aesthetic but also a mode of production and consumption intended to cultivate a transnational middle class.

We're Building a Better Life was a hit among German audiences. Over a half million spectators, over 40 percent of them from the East, waited in line to view the MSA's topless house. Newspaper reports were positive, "with no (rpt no) reference whatsoever" to the striptease scandal, a State Department telegram reported.[32] Word of the exhibition spread through promotional tie-ins, including a newsreel seen in movie theaters across West Germany, and a brochure, *Wir alle können besser leben* (We can all live better), published and distributed free of charge by West Germany's Regional Federation of Employer Associations. By the decade's end, as historian S. Jonathan Wiesen notes, the term "better life" would become an informal trademark of West Germany's economic miracle.[33] *Der Tag* told its readers: "Take your time to inspect this exhibit. With respect to the arts, handicrafts and technics, it reveals that America is the grown-up daughter of Europe. . . . You will see there what it means to live a decent life."[34] The adjective "decent" (rather than "pampered," for example) described a lifestyle that most postwar Americans would have found enviable. In this textbook example of the "demonstration effect," witnessing a model family's casual use of imported luxury goods had, at least for one local journalist, turned them into objects of necessity.

West German architects also expressed enthusiasm for We're Building a Better Life, reading into it the promise of a superpower patron with a taste for modernism. As noted in a State Department memorandum, "Many visitors expressed surprise that [the] modern design of furniture and household appliances originated in Europe, since many said that they thought such [a] modern touch to household equipment was available only in the U.S."[35] In a review of the Better Life show titled "The Domestic Culture of the Western People," architect and editor Alfons Leitl asserted that "whoever might not have known it learns emphatically through this exhibition [that] in all countries of the Western world one deals with the same questions, with the same design themes."[36] The fact that the exhibition was a form of propaganda was common knowledge, Leitl claimed, judging from a comment he had overheard at the exhibition, which he shared with readers: "You have to understand that this whole thing isn't put together just from a professional point of view . . . but with political intent." "A political exhibition, then?" Leitl mused. "Domestic reform with 'industrial design' as a responsibility of the Foreign Minister? Not bad. After the Werkbund, we'll give it a try with [West German Chancellor Konrad] Adenauer and [French Foreign Minister Robert] Schumann!"[37] Werkbund advocate Heinrich König perceived the show as a call for state-sponsored cultural reform, exhorting, "This exhibition is also an appeal to ministries, especially the one administering public education, finally to introduce 'The Study of Living' as a course of instruction. . . . It goes without saying that this class is only to be entrusted to teachers who are truly receptive to the New [style of] Living."[38] König's call for a modernist cultural revolution echoed tactics used by East Germany's Party to institutionalize socialist realism. His enthusiasm for a government-mandated program of aesthetic reorientation shows how little was sometimes learned from firsthand experience of totalitarian cultural politics.

Werkbund activists were not the only ones to approach the Better Life exhibition with a hidden agenda. For the United States, more was at stake than a change in consumer habits. The Mutual Security Act of 1951 had linked American aid and technical assistance for foreign nations to their participation in U.S. military alliances. This broadened definition of Atlanticism prompted the Office of the U.S. High Commander in Bonn to reject an initial proposal to develop the 1952 MSA exhibition around the theme "A Day in the Life of an American Worker," and to issue a statement clarifying the sponsor's goals:

> [The] MSA information program [is] designed to . . . further the defense contribution of West European nations, bring about [a] greater degree of economic integration in [the] Atlantic community, and raise [the] standard of shared agricultural and industrial productivity. These aims will not best be served by presenting [an] exhibition based on [the] theme of how an American worker lives or how U.S. trade unions operate.[39]

Atlanticism, as defined by the MSA, was an economic and military alignment that required West German rearmament—an idea unpopular among the nation's citizens and neighbor states. The Better Life

construct of the postwar housewife was limiting but also liberating. She was situated "in discourses of reconstruction as the bearer of the values of a specific form of postwar modernity, one dominated by scientific and technological rationality."[73] National chauvinism was another Third Reich legacy undermined by the Better Life housewife. She was a cultural cosmopolitan, judging by her home's interior, which mixed modernist decor from across the entire "Atlantic community." As envisioned by the MSA, the feminine roles of kitchen technician and consumer connoisseur came with heightened social status, at any rate for those affluent enough to buy their way in.

No appliance within the Better Life kitchen played a more celebrated role in West Germany's economic miracle than the refrigerator. It topped the list of household items desired by women *and* men throughout the 1950s (with washing machines and vacuum cleaners coming in at second and third place, respectively). Half of all households polled in 1955 dreamed of buying a refrigerator, but only one in ten owned one. In West Germany of the early 1950s, as recalled by a family that had pooled its resources to acquire a gleaming white Bosch, refrigerators were status symbols: "We were terribly proud. Everyone who visited us was led into the kitchen and shown the refrigerator.[74]" This chilly luxury sparked a heated controversy involving the standard-bearers of West Germany's main political parties. In 1953, when Alfred Müller-Armack of the CDU proposed federal financing for installment purchases of refrigerators in order to expand their market, *Welt der Arbeit*, a labor union journal, decried the initiative for its exclusion of citizens of limited means—retirees, for example—who would not qualify for the credit. CDU Finance Minister Ludwig Erhard stepped in, defending his party's platform with an article titled "A Refrigerator in Every Household." Erhard insisted that "luxuries of today" could only become "the general consumer goods of tomorrow . . . if we accept that in an initial phase, they will only be available to a small group with elevated incomes who will have the purchasing power to obtain these goods."[75] If the refrigerator came to define a gap between the haves and have-nots, it would have to be tolerated in the interest of egalitarianism.[76] Erhard's paradoxical contention proved correct. By the decade's end, the cost of a Bosch refrigerator had decreased to 40 percent of its 1951 price.[77] West Germany was poised to emulate America, where between 1940 and 1950 home ownership of refrigerators had nearly doubled.[78]

Far from reflecting an unambiguous process of Americanization, however, West Germany's state-sponsored love affair with the refrigerator came with its own troubled history. Promises of a refrigerator in every kitchen dated back to a Third Reich pledge to provide *Volksprodukte* (people's products) as harbingers of Nazi industrial modernity. These included the *Volksempfänger* (people's radio), *Volkswagen* (people's car), and *Volkskühlschrank* (people's refrigerator)—the latter complementing a campaign to "Fight Food Spoilage!" as Germany headed for war. By 1937, less than one hundred thousand "people's refrigerators," selling at luxury-market prices, had been manufactured. Weapons production pushed refrigerators off the list of Third Reich priorities in 1939, at which time less than 1 percent of German households owned one.[79] Although Hitler's promise to build an Aryan consumer society proved hollow, it had long-term repercussions, as S. Jonathan Wiesen has observed. Postwar consumer rhetoric echoed "language about economic renewal—indeed language about 'miracles'—that had been presented fifteen years earlier."[80] The appliance-laden Better Life kitchen may have sparkled with postwar novelty, but it was a repository of faded memories associated with an older and far less palatable recipe for modern living.

Refrigerators changed far more than West German cooking. They were a stepping-stone between the *Fresswelle*, or "feeding-wave," as historian Michael Wildt has dubbed the economic miracle's opening act, and its subsequent incursion into durable goods. In 1953, 58 percent of West German wages were spent on food, more than twice the average U.S. amount.[81] Tight budgets and careful food management, rather than the effortless entertaining portrayed in the Better Life home, characterized the kitchen of the early 1950s.[82] Daily rounds to the butcher, baker, and greengrocer were standard household chores, absorbing seventy hours of the West German housewife's typical week. Household thrift and the fight against food spoilage remained a selling point for refrigerators. "If you don't have a cool basement, see that you get a refrigerator," a household hints column advised. "You need it for your leftover sausage and your milk more than the rich man does for his fancy pickled herring and champagne." While the logic was dubious— "for the price of a refrigerator, one could replace a great deal of sour milk," as Jennifer Loehlin notes—the notion of pinching pennies through an extravagant purchase speaks volumes about the West German consumer mind-set of the 1950s.[83]

(facing page) A West German supermarket stages a "USA Week" promotion. The original caption of this Marshall Plan press release reads, "Supermarket chains in Europe and the Far East promote American foods, helping consumers become aware of the wide range of American foods available." U.S. National Archives, Still Pictures Division, RG306 PS-D Subjects Germany (W) 67-4001.

A refrigerator promised not just fewer trips to specialized shops but the ability to avoid them altogether. Newly introduced American-style self-service markets meant reduced prices for those who could buy larger quantities, refrigerating purchases and using them gradually, instead of buying small amounts that without refrigeration had to be used in a day. Beyond this quantitative change in retailing, supermarkets offered a qualitatively different consumer experience. "Shopping is one of those disciplines of the body by which we find our place in society," writes Sharon Zukin, a historian and theorist of consumption.[84] Shopkeepers traditionally served as intermediaries between products and people, dispensing consumer advice as well as neighborhood gossip, and sometimes using both to influence buying behavior.[85] Self-service purchases, made without having to call the order out to a shopkeeper, denied fellow shoppers a glimpse, in the words of a West German contemporary, "into my cooking pot, and thus into my purse."[86] Eliminating the shopkeeper as arbiter and overseer of consumer choice lent packaging new prominence as the product's "second skin," conveying contents, value, and social cachet.[87] The postwar era's supermarket novitiate learned the skills of commodity *flânerie,* negotiating a dense semiotic environment in which products communicated directly through slogans and graphics designed to compete with similar goods sharing the same shelf.[88] "Now everything was within reach," writes Wildt, "ready to grasp at the level of eyes and hands; the arrangement of goods, lighting, decor—everything was organized around the presentation of commodities."[89] For the West German shopper, the promenade down bright fluorescent aisles lined with eye-catching labels marked the culmination of a *Bildungsreise,* a journey of self-discovery, into the promised land of postwar consumption.

Self-service food markets increased exponentially in West Germany over the course of the decade, from 39 in 1951 to 17,132 by 1960, by which time they accounted for one-third of all grocery sales.[90] In keeping with America's self-appointed role as Europe's economic tutor, the MSA's Caravan of Modern Food Service introduced retailers and shoppers to supermarket basics across Western Europe. Produced by Peter Harnden, the exhibit was contained inside a collection of expandable cargo trailers. Trucked from city to city, it brought the gospel of self-service retailing to an ever-widening circle of disciples. Mounted outside the installation, placards in seven languages explained supermarket theory and practice. Inside, visitors found a complete library of reference materials, a small theater for screening technical films, and a mocked-up supermarket display, complete with shelves of products, refrigerator cases, and a check-out stand. By grabbing a shopping cart, rolling it down the aisles, selecting packaged foods, and proceeding to the register, visitors discovered for themselves the pleasures of modern shopping. Panels informed local entrepreneurs that "all materials used in the construction of the exhibit are available in Europe."[91] As with its promotion of household mass consumption, the U.S. State Department had a vested interest in publicizing self-service retailing in Western Europe, just as it had in South America a few years earlier. At the 1949 inauguration of Venezuelan supermarket operations by the International Basic Economy Corporation, its director, Nelson Rockefeller, had announced, "lower food prices represent the same thing as an increase in wages."[92] The increased purchasing power resulting from more efficient retailing, State Department officials believed, would enfranchise workers within capitalism's reward system, eroding the appeal of communist trade unions and the tactics of labor confrontation used to disrupt economic reconstruction.

After its Paris debut in May 1953, the Caravan of Modern Food Service toured Belgium, Holland, Denmark, Germany, and Italy. Its itinerary overlapped that of another traveling exhibition produced by Harnden for the MSA: We're Building a Better Life, which hit the road following its 1952 West Berlin opening. The Better Life model home proceeded to two more West German venues, Stuttgart and Hannover, before heading to France and Italy, countries in which disruptive communist labor unions had greatly alarmed Marshall Plan officials. The exhibition continued to pitch its vision of "what the ideal modern home could look like if customs barriers were abolished" under a new name: Home Without Borders (Maison Sans Frontièrs for its Paris opening in February 1954, and Casa Senza Frontiere for an April

The interior of the Caravan of Modern Food Service exhibit, transported through Western Europe in the interest of enhancing economic productivity through streamlined food retailing. U.S. National Archives, Still Pictures Division, RG286 MP GEN 1990.

showing at Milan's International Samples Fair).[93] Although conceived in—and for—divided Germany, We're Building a Better Life remained true to its Atlanticist creed, addressing citizens across Marshall Plan Europe with a universal message: that transnational consumer practices fostered economic recovery and integration. The Better Life and Modern Food Service exhibits conveyed interlocking facets of the State Department's message about American-style affluence and its modes of perception, apprehension, and behavior—the cluster of dispositions that structure everyday life practices according to Pierre Bourdieu's concept of "habitus."[94] European aspirants to the good life depicted at Harnden's exhibitions learned that it could not be acquired piecemeal, bit by glittering bit. The American Way of Life demanded collective commitment to a total package of economic, cultural, and political transformations no less comprehensive than that of any other revolution.

Stalinism by Design

Across Germany's internal border, the West's model housewife encountered resistance from another mythologized female: the East's worker-activist. One of her more vivid manifestations was Marianne Brose, a character created by proletarian author Theo Harych for his novel *Stalinallee,* commissioned by the National Building Program for Germany's Capital (Nationales Aufbauprogramm der Haupstadt Deutschlands). Like the Better Life housewife, the worker-activist was a social narrative incarnate. Fresh-faced and fervent, striving selflessly to construct socialism, she was the antithesis of the stay-at-home *Hausfrau* promoted by the U.S. State Department. These two feminine ideals embodied Germany's divided economic paths. The Better Life housewife epitomized a postwar consumer lifestyle and challenged its threadbare East bloc alternative. The worker-activist, rejecting Western promises of mass affluence, dedicated life and labor to creating a socialist future.

Harych plotted Marianne's socialist coming-of-age within the story of a single evening of misadventure in West Berlin. Unlike the border crossings made by real-life East Berliners—which, in the years before the construction of the wall, typically involved commuting to work, taking in a Hollywood film, or going shopping—Marianne heads West to undertake a daring mission. Armed with a roll of posters and a pot of glue, she proceeds to plaster Party propaganda across shop windows, obscuring capitalist advertising with its communist equivalent. As she observes her surroundings, the West's consumer wonderland quickly dissolves and is revealed to be a shimmering *Scheinwelt,* a "world of illusion":

> Delicious American jams, coffee, citrus, [along with] furs and shoes, filled shops and storefronts. But the bags carried by window shoppers were empty. Perhaps hunger drew them to these display windows, or they were drawn to the streets out of boredom. Their own apartments were cold; light was expensive. Their cupboards were bare. Out here, however, light, life, warm clothes, and groceries were found in abundance. "For whom?" Marianne wondered.

Marianne's amazement turns to terror as Fritz, an unemployed bricklayer (and future refugee *to* East Berlin) pulls her off the sidewalk and

(facing page) Frau Hacke, helped by her son Rainer, puts up curtains in a new apartment on East Berlin's Stalinallee in 1955. Bundesarchiv Koblenz, 183/12940/4/Kemlein.

pushes her into a darkened building. His motives, like the shop windows, are not what they seem: he is keeping her from falling into a trap set by the novel's brutal West German police. Hiding in his dingy tenement apartment, Marianne gets her first shocking view of the interior world of capitalism. "Two moth-eaten bedsteads and an old overstuffed sofa stood beside a table and three chairs. The room also had a chest and shelves curtained off with a worn blanket."[1] Under the blanket are goods waiting to be sold on the black market, a system of commodity distribution that sums up the West's fantasy of affluence. The rescue propels Fritz eastward into a melodrama populated by socialist workers, cement mixers, and saboteurs: in this boy-meets-girl story the love interest is driven not by sexual chemistry but by the magnetic attraction exerted between Stalinist programs for human and urban reconstruction. Although Harych's novel was never published, his depiction of West Berlin tenement life is historically significant—not as a document of life in the capitalist West but of the pledge that working-class life in the socialist East would boast a higher standard of living. By that narrative thread, the fate of a nation—and indeed an empire—would dangle.

THE BATTLE FOR A NEW INTERIOR DESIGN

Marianne Brose and her activist-to-be boyfriend, Fritz, were promotional by-products of East Berlin's flagship reconstruction project. The Stalinallee, a new Soviet-style boulevard, marked East Berlin's triumphal entry along the land route from Moscow. The street's kilometer-long run of neoclassical facades bracketed tree-lined sidewalks and six lanes of traffic.[2] Ground-floor shops and restaurants, ennobled by travertine sheathing and Doric columns, consciously recalled the architecture of imperial Prussia.[3] Stacked above commercial amenities were apartments sheathed in lustrous tiles from the Meissen porcelain works— once famed for the fine china adorning aristocratic tables, subsequently a supplier of building materials for proletarian palaces. For the boulevard's Karl Marx Bookstore, Bauakademie interior design specialists reprised the building's monumental facade in hardwood paneling and casework. Inside the Haus Budapest Restaurant, they explored socialist realism's Hungarian mood with Magyar-inspired embroidery and folk-art scraffito. Down the street at the Café-Restaurant Warschau, customers savored a corresponding recipe for Polish decor. These linked expressions of national character traced their origins to a cultural

strategy that attempted to neutralize the centrifugal effects of nationalist sentiment. Stalin's 1913 treatise *Marxism and the National Question*
proposed a middle course between nationalist factionalism and Party-
imposed internationalism. He proposed a new category of nationalism,
the "oppressed-nation" variety, characterized by a struggle for independence and compatible with the goal of dismantling capitalism. In
Stalin's first administrative position at the helm of Narkomnats—the
People's Commissariat of National Affairs—this nationalities policy
nurtured native Party elites loyal to Kremlin leaders. Similarly, the call
to create an architecture "socialist in content and national in form" in
the early 1930s gave socialist realist representatives of the USSR's
national minorities an ideological advantage over the modernist establishment, which was predominantly Russian in nationality.[4] The result
was an institutionalized collection of styles expressing the individuated,
yet unified, identity politics of "socialism in one country," and the
socialist realist depiction of the USSR as a world unto itself, complete
with its own colorful assortment of regional cultures.

The Soviet occupation of Eastern Europe brought with it the
apotheosis of socialist realist internationalism. Its reflections could be
found throughout the Stalinallee, from restaurant interiors to state retail

(below) The stolid
neoclassical aesthetic
imported from Moscow
and favored by East Ger-
man Party leaders is dis-
played in the Karl Marx
Bookstore, designed by
the Deutsche Bauaka-
demie. Bundesarchiv,
DM2 VI .06.3, volume 3,
figure 8.

(below left) Hungarian-
inspired curtain embroi-
dery and a scraffito panel
in the Stalinallee's Haus
Budapest restaurant
exemplify the aesthetics
of socialist realist identity
politics. Bundesarchiv,
DM2 VI .06.3, Volume 5,
Figure 18.

outlets stocked with socialist indulgences like Bulgarian cigarettes and feta cheese, Romanian Riesling and Hungarian Bikavér wines, Polish eggs, and canned pineapple from China.[5] The Stalinallee's material culture evoked a wider world spreading outward from the boulevard in a single direction—east. From a vantage point framed by the continuous frontage of new seven-story facades, East Germany's reconstructed capital could be perceived in its imaginary totality. "Multiply this image by one thousand: the generous appointments of the street, the mechanical comforts of the housing, the attractive shops, social amenities and restaurants," exhorted an East German tract, "and you will get a general idea of the good life in the socialist residential district of the future."[6] Walking the broad sidewalks, gazing into well-stocked shop windows, touring the street's spacious apartments, residents of both Berlins would undergo a conversion experience—or so it was hoped. The Stalinallee was East Germany's ultimate marketing tool: a model of the socialist future built at one-to-one scale.

With the completion of the first Stalinallee apartment units in December 1952, model residences outfitted by the Bauakademie Institute for Interior Design opened for public inspection as "an example of how the working population should live."[7] The results, which fell short of the boulevard's neoclassical grandeur, disappointed Party leader Walter Ulbricht. Advances in socialist realist architecture had outpaced those of furniture design. In the United States, savvy entrepreneurs like Hans Knoll and George Nelson had made it their business to close the gap between modernist architecture and the market's tired selection of mainstream furnishings.[8] In East Germany, with market responses dismantled and the profit motive demonized, out-of-sync interiors created an ideological crisis rather than a commercial opportunity. A Bauakademie memorandum reported that socialist realism's cultural revolution had faltered. Formalism was rampant among East German designers and—far worse—their proletarian clients:

> Popular opinions expressed at the [Stalinallee open house] exhibit again have provided striking evidence that the consequences of the capitalist brutalization of taste are more deeply spread and rooted than the feeble initial development of the new [aesthetic]. It should also be taken into account that if the populace were allowed to choose between furniture of the familiar formalist-modernist sort which the majority still like, and the new

[furnishings] linked to the [nation's] cultural heritage, which the
majority do not yet like, the latter would be left on the showroom
floor while the former would be sold by the thousands, even if
both were of the same quality.[9]

With the quest to create a "realist" home culture stalling, a follow-up to
the 1952 conference on "Issues of German Interior Design" seemed
imperative.

The initial Bauakademie colloquium on household design had
resounded with defamations of Western modernism but had been
notably short on positive exemplars suitable for emulation. Advice to
would-be socialist realists had emphasized hindsight. Conferees had
learned that "all that is truly new is developed out of the old" and that
"the last great unified epoch of German furniture and domestic design
was the beginning of the nineteenth century."[10] While anachronistic
from a modernist perspective, the postwar revival of neoclassicism con-
formed to Stalinist notions of a contemporary socialist heritage. East
German arts rediscovered the late-eighteenth and early-nineteenth cen-
turies in the 1950s. At the DEFA motion picture studios in Babelsberg,
"heritage films" revealed Beethoven, Goethe, and Hölderlin to have
been "fervent supporters of the French Revolution, and thus harbingers
of socialism."[11] Promoting neoclassicism as a paradigm for contemporary design was part of this broader trend. The furniture of imperial
Prussia, with its "comforting cosiness and human warmth, [and] beauty
in its overall features," belonged among "the cultural goods of our
people," according to Bauakademie design theorists.[12] Their "Battle for
a New Interior Design" reached back in history to appropriate the cultural capital of a vanquished bourgeoisie in the name of Germany's
postwar proletariat.

Neoclassical reclamation in the decorative arts generated its own
state-sponsored research programs. In summer 1952, photographers
under contract to the Bauakademie traversed East Germany document-
ing late-eighteenth and early-nineteenth century furnishings, lighting
fixtures, textiles, and even tiled stoves. Sites included national museums,
stately homes in public ownership, and the dwindling number of
antique collections that remained in private hands.[13] The final product
was a catalog intended as a source of information and inspiration for
postwar designers. Of course, the notion of sorting through the past in
search of a twentieth-century patrimony was by no means unique to

socialist realism. Two generations earlier, in a project analogous to Bauakademie efforts, and which may well have been their model, Paul Mebes published *Um 1800* (Circa 1800), an evaluation of German neoclassical works suitable for contemporary emulation.[14] Published just as a youthful Walter Ulbricht was beginning his apprenticeship as a furniture craftsman in the Leipzig workshop of Ernst Werner, *Um 1800* was a foundational text of its era—and thirty years later, a reference text in the Bauakademie library.[15]

For aspiring socialist realists, *Um 1800* advanced several appealing arguments. Mebes advocated German neoclassicism as a "modest, truly economical" alternative to Jugendstil excess: "After the long, fruitless wandering, truly it is not a step backwards but an advance when we reconnect with the architecture of the eighteenth century."[16] His neoclassical canon, like that of the Bauakademie, excised the mannered Biedermeyer style. Comparing Germany after the Napoleonic wars—Mebes's golden age of neoclassicism—with circumstances after World War I, the 1920 edition of *Um 1800* prescribed neoclassicism for postwar reconstruction, insisting "beauty is also possible with the greatest simplicity and the most modest of means." The only requirement was a "vital transmission of tradition" and a rejection of "formalism," described as "the new aesthetic ideal, which . . . seeks in all its expressive endeavors to overturn the classical tradition."[17] *Um 1800,* however, also contained Stalin-era profanities, including the notion of neoclassicism as "cosmopolitan," which in Soviet parlance denoted capitalist cultural degeneracy, and the assertion that "local and folk traditions slowly are dying."[18] This admixture of orthodoxy and heresy made *Um 1800* unsuitable for citation by socialist realists, and indeed Mebes is nowhere mentioned in Bauakademie documents. But parallels ranging from rhetorical tropes to aesthetic prescriptions suggest that East Berlin's postwar style was as dependent on interwar precedent as was its modernist West German adversary.

At Ulbricht's direct behest, the Bauakademie launched another research venture in 1953. The organization's director, Liebknecht, and two colleagues toured venerable furniture manufacturers in Leipzig, Zeulenroda, and Waldheim. An archive at Zeulenroda contained an exhaustive collection of patterns and decorative details that had survived two world wars intact. The researchers pulled samples for immediate transfer to East Berlin and made plans to ship the rest of the archive to the capital. Unlike the Bauakademie's survey of German antiques, analysis of the Zeulenroda material would not attempt to identify exemplars for contemporary emulation, but exactly the opposite. "We are unanimous in our conviction that one must study this material, in that it is especially important to find the initial configurations, that is, the original configurations, (*Ausgangs- bzw. Ursprungsformen*) of bad design." The researchers believed that the trove of furniture patterns documented the nineteenth century's trajectory of aesthetic decay and that buried within the archive they would find evidence of a formalist "*Ursprungsmodell*": the ancestor of all subsequent generations of ugly furniture. This empirical breakthrough would reveal the historical circumstances of beauty's decline under capitalism.[19] Bauakademie investigators were poised to create a definitive history of household formalism, mapping its evolutionary origins with absolute precision. Like the archaeology of modernity undertaken by Walter Benjamin a generation earlier, the Bauakademie initiative traced its own origins to the *Kulturwissenschaft* ("cultural science") tradition that had flourished during the Weimar era.[20] While sharing some aspects of Benjamin's investigative method, which also sifted through seemingly trivial artifacts to discover unexpected orders of meaning, the Bauakademie project was pessimistic, teleological, and reductive. In any case, as their ambitious research plan makes clear, Bauakademie officials were not content merely to reproduce epistemological structures of Soviet provenance. They aspired to become the pioneers of a Marxist-Leninist discipline of aesthetic archaeology, a breakthrough capable of propelling East Germany to the forefront of socialist realist theory and practice.[21]

As the Bauakademie pondered the origins of cultural decadence, the Party was engaged in a life-or-death struggle with its proletarian constituency. In July 1952, the Socialist Unity Party (SED) announced its accelerated program for the national Construction of Socialism (Aufbau des Sozializmus). It called for forced agrarian collectivization, massive industrial investment, and the suppression of private entrepreneurship, organized religion, and all ties to the West among socialist citizens.[22] Unexpectedly, the Kremlin also mandated that East Germany create a national army to counter West Germany's rearmament under mutual security agreements with the United States. To preserve capital for industrial investment, Ulbricht's Politburo deducted the cost of East German remilitarization from state funds earmarked for the production of consumer goods. Public provision

"An example of unartistic redevelopment" of national design heritage, as depicted in the catalog of Live Better—More Beautifully! an exhibition staged in East Berlin's Alexanderplatz in 1953. Deutsche Bauakademie, *Besser leben—schöner wohnen!* (Leipzig: VEB Graphische Werkstätten, 1954).

„Zürich"

faltered, morale plummeted, and the gap between socialism as lived and as publicized grew ever wider. By winter 1952, butter and sugar had all but disappeared from shops.[23] In the first quarter of the new year, nearly eight thousand East Germans were arrested for black market transactions or for speaking critically of the regime. Every month, between fifteen and twenty-five thousand East German citizens fled westward.[24] The most remarkable socialist tempo turned out to be not the speed of economic reconstruction but the rate at which the proletariat was abandoning the nation established in its name.[25]

Stalin's death in March 1953 stoked hopes for change. The SED promptly dashed them. In mid-May, the Party announced a 10 percent escalation of labor norms—which in effect decreased wages by the same amount, reduced state subventions for public transport and basic foods, and called for a lavish public celebration of Ulbricht's sixtieth birthday at the end of June. Aware that the situation was spinning out of control, the Kremlin's new leadership convened an emergency meeting in Moscow with Ulbricht and his top colleagues. On 2 June, the Soviets presented their German colleagues with a policy program called the New Course. It abandoned the accelerated Construction of Socialism and proposed improvements in living conditions in order to stem the westward exodus. The rise in labor norms was revoked, but its alienating effects could not be retracted. A group of construction workers at the Stalinallee put down their tools to march on the politburo's House of Ministries headquarters in protest on 16 June 1953. The next day, thirty thousand citizens—15 percent of East Berlin's labor force—took to the streets. Demonstrators trampled national flags, defaced portraits of Stalin, and torched the socialist state's flagship retail outlet in Potsdamer Platz in a visceral expression of consumer dissatisfaction.[26] Protests quickly spread to other cities. In Leipzig, crowds jammed downtown streets chanting demands for "butter, no cannons, freedom and higher wages."[27] The Party ultimately remained in power only through the intervention of Soviet army tanks followed by arrests, prison sentences, and executions.

In the wake of the uprising, Ulbricht purged the SED of any potential opponents while trumpeting the New Course reforms he had attempted to resist.[28] The Party announced increased state investment in food and household goods "to bring about a real improvement in economic and political conditions . . . in the immediate future and, based on this step, to raise the living standard of the working class and white collar workers significantly."[29] The promise was hollow. East Germany's agenda for post-Stalinist reform proved so amorphous that when asked what the New Course was, Ulbricht answered "Marxism-Leninism."[30] As far as domestic design was concerned, "Stalinism" would have been an accurate response. Ulbricht enlisted New Course mandates to propel socialist realist furnishings off the drawing board and onto showroom and living room floors.

LIVING SOCIALIST REALISM

On 17 November 1953, five months to the day after the East German uprising, Ulbricht and the Bauakademie turned their attention back to the crisis in household design. The House of Ministries, where angry crowds had gathered to mock Party leaders and demand their resignation, was the venue for a second national conference on East German interiors. The conference and its concurrent exhibition bore a shared title: Live Better—More Beautifully! (Besser leben—schöner wohnen!), establishing beauty as the missing ingredient from West Germany's Better Life ideal. The intended message for East German citizens was that "Bauhaus machine-furniture is Enemy Number One," according to internal Bauakademie documents, with "eclecticism" and "kitsch" the runners-up for "Enemy Number Two."[31] Presentations would trace socialist realism's provenance back to the Renaissance.[32] The target audience consisted of designers, manufacturers, retailers, and—recognizing the crisis in proletarian taste and behavior—the East German public. Flyers, cinema advertisements, and sidewalk placards announced, "In conjunction with the New Course that our government has embarked upon, this exhibition represents a breakthrough in . . . the furnishings industry, and benefits consumers."[33] Far from departing from the policies that had incited riots, however, Live Better—More Beautifully! offered yet another dose of Stalinist culture as a cure for the nation's malaise.

A temporary pavilion erected on East Berlin's Alexanderplatz housed the Live Better—More Beautifully! exhibition. To convey socialist realism's native patrimony, a "Cultural Heritage" display included rare Gothic, Renaissance, baroque, and neoclassical antiques. Museum curators were persuaded to loan their treasures for a show staged on a downtown pavement after receiving a letter from the Bauakademie stating, "The conference and its corresponding exhibition

is of entirely exceptional significance, in that Minister President Walter
Ulbricht is intensely interested in this event, and will be participating
personally."[34] A second installation forecast a socialist realist future
for East German households with thirty new suites of neotraditional
furnishings. A third display, introduced by the broadside "Formalism
and kitsch serve only the misanthropic interests of imperialism and
its politics of warmongering," was called the "Chamber of Horrors"
(*Schreckenskammer*) by the exhibition's planners.[35] Inside, a collection
of "reactionary" modernist objects provided evidence of capitalist cultural decay. By highlighting the "emphatic primitiveness" of modernist
armchairs and "complete decadence" of minimalist light fixtures, the
Bauakademie hoped to reeducate citizens duped by modernism and
Bauhaus design.[36] Four photographs in the Live Better—More Beautifully! catalog illustrated the Chamber of Horrors concept: a 1927
Weißenhof housing exhibition interior designed by Mart Stam, a room
outfitted with modular storage units designed by Bruno Paul in the
1930s and still in production at the Hellerau workshops, the Manhattan
showroom of Knoll International (incorrectly identified as a "New
York living room"), and a contemporary West German home furnished
with pieces from Knoll and its competitor Herman Miller.[37] The last of
these illustrations was cribbed from the West German design journal
Architektur und Wohnform—the same issue featuring the dream home
interiors showcased by the Better Life show.[38] Bauakademie propagandists clearly were aware of the work of their MSA competitors, and Live
Better—More Beautifully! resumed a cross-border dialogue transacted
in the language of exhibitions.

The Live Better—More Beautifully! catalog contained a statement acknowledging "the generous support of the government of the
USSR" in helping stage the exhibition. However, its Chamber of Horrors strayed far from contemporary practices of Soviet art exhibition.
The first Chamber of Horrors was a gallery antechamber at London's
Victorian-era Museum of Ornamental Art (the precursor of the Victoria and Albert) that showcased objects selected explicitly for their taste-
lessness, setting the stage for the "proper" displays that followed.[39]
Early Soviet exhibitions employed similar installation techniques,
shifting their didactic content from art education to political denunciation.[40] Art from the Age of Imperialism and Art of the Great Industrial
Bourgeoisie on the Eve of the Proletarian Revolution, mounted in 1931
and 1932, respectively, accompanied their negative exemplars with a

Three "chambers of horror," as defined by the Deutsche Bauakademie, arranged chronologically: (a) an office, interior design and furnishings attributed to Mart Stam, 1927; (b) Knoll International showroom, New York, featuring Barcelona chairs, ottoman, and table by Mies van der Rohe, designed in 1929 and reissued by Knoll in 1948; (c) a guest room in a private West German residence of the early 1950s. Deutsche Bauakademie, *Besser leben—schöner wohnen!*

narrative accusing the avant-garde of leading Soviet culture down a "blind alley of formalism."[41] The Chamber of Horrors strategy fell out of favor in the mid-1930s as Soviet curators strove to express the aesthetic hegemony of socialist realism as an aesthetic totality. Displays of "bad art" had become obsolete as well as potentially dangerous, in that they placed ideologically discredited artifacts on view. The "Stalinist museum" relegated to storage all objects deemed illegitimate, indeterminate, or illegible.[42] Socialist realist beauty was to reign unchallenged—an exhibition strategy utterly at odds with the "formalism and kitsch" showcase of Live Better—More Beautifully!

A rich tradition of native precedents was far more likely to have informed the Bauakademie's Chamber of Horrors. At the 1933 exhibition Away with National Kitsch, the newly Nazified Werkbund showed side-by-side living rooms: one a jumble of tawdry furniture and cheap political memorabilia; the other a dignified hearth worthy of a Teutonic *Zivilisation*.[43] This display of antipodes was followed four years later by the Degenerate Art (Entartete Kunst) exhibition in Munich, which seared the term *Schreckenskammer* into Western art history as a Nazi phenomenon.[44] The Degenerate Art Chamber of Horrors diagnosed avant-garde objects to be Bolshevist and Jewish; a generation later, Live Better—More Beautifully! declared them capitalist and American. The Bauakademie's unsavory conflation of pre- and postwar antimodernism may be explained by an article in its in-house journal, *Studienmaterial*, which featured German translations of Russian texts on "problems involving Marxist-Leninist aesthetics." The 1953 issue contained an

A socialist home's "general room" and a close-up of its study corner furnished with new neo-classical prototypes designed by a collective at VVB Sachsenholz, as seen at Live Better—More Beautifully! Deutsche Bauakademie, *Besser leben—schöner wohnen!*

article by the Stalin Prize–winning sculptor Vera Mukhina depicting the U.S. art scene as a "gangster world, in which anything is allowed." The headline above this excursus was rendered as *Entartete americanische Kunst*—"Degenerate American Art"—in German translation.[45] A presumed validation of the trope of degeneracy may have led Bauakademie officers to revive its associated Chamber of Horrors tactic in their struggle against modernism. East German spectators, however, would have been unaware of the arcane museological ancestry of Chambers of Horrors. For them, the obvious antecedent would have been a Nazi exhibition decrying non-Aryan cultural pathologies. The West's cold war propagandists delighted in drawing comparisons between the Third Reich and the communist East, a task made rather easy by their socialist realist counterparts.[46]

The Bauakademie paradigm of household consumption as cultural enlightenment made Live Better—More Beautifully! a dry and lifeless affair compared to the animated spectacle of the Better Life home. Lacking any human presence, the neotraditional interiors conveyed next to nothing about postwar lifestyles or activities. An especially curious omission, given the new working-class social order, was the lack of attention to the home as a site of domestic labor. Most of the room settings assembled for the exhibition depicted what was known in Soviet parlance as the "general room," which combined living, dining, and home study functions. Along with a few bedroom suites and a children's playroom, a single kitchen was shown: a compact Russian model named after its designer, architect Ivan Zholtovsky. The meager display perfectly illustrated the eclipse of the kitchen as a symbol of socialist reform. From the October Revolution until the close of Stalin's First Five-Year Plan in 1931, Soviet cultural revolutionaries lauded the communal kitchen as a "social condenser" capable of forging proletarian consciousness. Experience proved otherwise. Purpose-built collective kitchens sparked feuds and accusations of food theft, rather than a socialist utopia.[47] In the mid-1930s, with the advent of socialist realism, the emphasis in Soviet housing shifted from innovative programming to monumental packaging. The ideal resident changed as well. Failing to keep pace with peasant migration into newly industrialized cities, Stalin-era apartment construction targeted managers, engineers, and other "responsible cadres" as its primary clientele. Inside their new residences, a household maid was an unmentioned but popular amenity. The reality of a Soviet labor market for domestics, typically former

A state-of-the-art East German model kitchen of the mid-1950s. Heinz Hirdina, *Gestalten für die Serie. Design in der DDR 1949–1985* (Dresden: VEB Verlag der Kunst, 1988).

peasant girls, remained repressed from public discourse until the late 1930s, when cartoons and jokes about maids began to surface in satirical journals.[48] "Manned" as it sometimes was by an unmentionable class of female labor, the apartment kitchen was stripped of most representational duties, a fall from grace apparent in the Zholtovsky kitchen, which in terms of technology and space planning would have been considered state-of-the-art in Germany circa 1925.

A West German visitor to Live Better—More Beautifully! might have found its emblems of domestic culture—matched veneers, applied rosettes, high-gloss lacquer finishes—surprising for a socialist society. However, their transposition from bourgeois to proletarian contexts was what defined the emergent ideal of Stalin-era domesticity. In the 1930s, the word *kul'turnost'*, or "culturedness," entered common Russian usage. It denoted "the complex of behaviors, attitudes and knowledge that 'cultured' people had, and 'backward' people lacked."[49] As markers of the transformation of former peasants into disciplined workers, lace curtains, frilly lamp shades, and spotless tablecloths became totemic *kul'turnost'* artifacts. Stalinist socialism's rehabilitation of objects and behaviors formerly called bourgeois made the rough personal habits celebrated by a previous generation of Bolsheviks not only obsolete but also ideologically seditious.[50]

Ulbricht and his circle of German communists assimilated the concept of *kul'turnost'* while in Soviet exile during the war, as revealed a decade later in his praise for "furniture and decorative objects that lift the domestic culture of the working class to a higher level."[51] In its transmission to Germany, *kul'turnost'* was easily conflated with the native concept of *Bildung,* a term connoting intellectual and cultural development. Ulbricht's life story, in its official version, was a study of this transposition. Biographers fell silent when it came to Ulbricht's physical labors as an apprentice cabinetmaker but waxed poetic when relating his youthful trek through Italy. They scripted the future Party leader's road trip as a proletarian *Bildungsroman*—the chronicle of a journey to intellectual maturity—embellishing it with references to Goethe's Mediterranean pilgrimage.[52] Interiors shown at the Live Better—More Beautifully! exhibition expressed a similar synthesis of German *Bildung* and Soviet *kul'turnost'*. The neotraditional furnishings promoted by the Bauakademie invoked a family life characterized by decorous dining, quiet leisure, study, and self-improvement—socialist lifestyle ideals championed in the USSR as of the late 1930s. Socialist realist household furnishings allowed citizens to "buy into" the Party's colonization of everyday life, a form of managed consumption that advanced Stalinist identity politics by introducing templates for its behavioral ideals into the private sphere.[53]

The conference accompanying the Live Better—More Beautifully! exhibition took a militant line on aesthetic recidivism. Speakers denounced Western cultural influence and, more ominously, identified sources of internal subversion. Ulbricht's keynote address decried the lingering influence of modernism on the East German furnishings industry. "The attempt was made for decades to convince the laboring masses that the wretched and shabby novelties of capitalist profiteers also were beautiful!"—precisely the means by which formalism "exerted its harmful influence extensively throughout the population." Following in Ulbricht's footsteps, the president of the Bauakademie, Kurt Liebknecht, cited a specific East German manufacturer, Dresden's Hellerau Werkstätte, for flouting "democratic cultural objectives" and "lagging behind the demands of the working class." "In truth, the publicity for the crate-like furniture offered by the Hellerau Werkstätte is a hold-over from capitalist advertising," Liebknecht asserted, "which served the singular purpose of dumping the capitalist furniture industry's cheap novelties under the pretense of lifestyle reform."[54] Hellerau's Bauhaus-trained designers had earned scorn through market success. Sales were brisk at the Hellerau retail outlet in East Berlin. Institutional

The "cultured" home and family life of Stalin-era vintage, as depicted in *Soviet Life* magazine.

customers included the East German Ministry of the Interior, the Academy of Agricultural Economy, the Party's Karl Marx Academy, and, most embarrassing, the Bauakademie itself. The organization's cultural revolution had failed even among its own officials, a sin that could not go unpunished.[55] According to Liebknecht, the guilty parties were the designers, not the consumers.

Ulbricht proclaimed the Live Better exhibition and conference "a great step forward."[56] Others were not so sure. Shown a suite of furniture prototypes praised in the show's catalog for its "very spare but effective use of moldings," the East German prime minister, Otto Grotewohl, voiced his concerns, according to an industry sales representative:

> He found the suite of furniture lovely, but not for our working classes. It would be impossible for a worker to buy the suite, he said, first, as it is too . . . impractical, and second, far too expensive. Especially for families with children, the suite would not be recommended. . . . My own opinion is as follows: mass production of this suite of furniture would be hardly worth the effort, since it would be purchased only by a few enthusiasts, and not, by and large, by our working people.[57]

A Chippendale-style chair made in Dessau by Johann Andreas Irmer, ca. 1770, displayed at Live Better—More Beautifully! as a positive exemplar of German tradition. Deutsche Bauakademie, *Besser leben—schöner wohnen!*

East German citizens were just as skeptical. Each of the 67,727 visitors to the exhibition was supplied with a questionnaire, which less than 5 percent filled out. To supplement the survey data, members of the Bauakademie roved the exhibition floor noting conversations. The results were discouraging. According to survey feedback and overheard comments, the show's Chamber of Horrors had backfired. Rather than being repulsed by the modernist exemplars of "formalism and kitsch," seven out of eight survey respondents favored them. Worse yet, the main public criticism of the installation's furnishings by the Hellerau Werkstätte was their limited retail availability. Bauakademie analysts put the best face on the unwelcome feedback, concluding, "Only obstinate adherents of formalism were hardened in their viewpoint that these furnishings are beautiful because they are functional."[58] Officials maintained that when East German citizens looked at modernist storage units, they saw mere utility. Positive responses to Hellerau cabinetry were chalked up to cramped postwar living arrangements. This anomaly would correct itself once larger apartments like those along the Stalinallee became widely available, or so it was claimed.

displaying its wares in Leipzig would reduce the nation's export income, after Ulbricht's outburst it seemed a cost that the Bauakademie was willing to incur.

Over the ensuing six months, officials from the Bauakademie and the Ministry of Light Industry met repeatedly with Ehrlich and Selman Selmanagič, Hellerau's other Bauhaus-trained talent, to address the charge of discrimination against their firm. Knowing that their comments were being transcribed, the two designers mounted one of the most audacious defenses of modernism ever made in the face of an aesthetic dictatorship. Selmanagič called the Bauakademie just that: a "dictatorship" bent on exerting "monopoly status" over East German design. He described the organization's socialist realist prototypes as outmoded absurdities: "The musty reworking of national tradition undertaken here belongs back in the chest of moth-eaten hand-me-downs (*Mottenkiste*)." He denounced Bauakademie "shield-bearers" as unqualified to render criticism, despite their impressive titles—a barb undoubtedly directed at Liebknecht, who had received a Soviet Ph.D. in architecture during the war. Ehrlich was equally insolent, informing the committee that his remarks would be "especially sharp," since he expected them to be relayed "to a higher level." The "official opinion" promulgated by Bauakademie officers and pursued with "brute force" was utterly at odds with public opinion, Ehrlich asserted. Hellerau products could be found not only in the home of Johannes Becher, the East German minister of culture, but also in apartments of various Bauakademie officials: "two-faced" consumers of the very objects they condemned as formalist.[75] Just as at the "Issues of German Interior Design" conference in 1952, Bauakademie officers had structured the confrontation as a "criticism and self-criticism" session, and once again Ehrlich refused to play by the rules.

The Hellerau team's defiance of authority, attack on the integrity of Party industrial managers, and mockery of the Soviet cultural paradigm said to embody socialist progress were the raw materials from which show trials were spun. That potential outcome was clearly on the mind of the director of the Bauakademie Research Institute for Interior Design as he proposed the next step in reining in Hellerau's renegade designers:

They take a precarious position on many questions, and take issue with the party for its theory of Formalism. I therefore suggest that

these comrades be given an opportunity to set forth their
thoughts and designs before members of our Central Committee
and authorities among our comrade architects, and that we, closing ranks, demonstrate their views false. If it is then shown that
they have taken no self-critical position in regard to their errors,
this attitude, which is not useful to our development, must be
unmasked.[76]

"Unmasking" (in German, *Entlarvung*; in Russian, *razoblacheno*) was
the communist ritual used to expose citizens who while claiming to act
in the interest of socialism secretly subverted it, supposedly in collaboration with deposed class elements or imperialist agents. As Michael
David-Fox notes, an obsession with the "masked enemy" permeated
Stalinist daily life and became "a fundamental issue around which an
emergent Soviet political culture crystallized."[77] East bloc purge trials
portrayed the camouflaged subversive as the most treacherous of socialist subjectivities. Penetrating this false identity and revealing its betray-
als were highly refined Stalin-era skills, and had apparently survived
their patriarch's demise, as Jordan's letter of denunciation demonstrates.

As the presumptive agents of misconduct conducted at an industrial enterprise, Ehrlich and Selmanagič were "wreckers," in Stalinist
parlance. In retrospect, however, their behavior was not quite as reck-
less as it seemed. One month before the designers committed their initial round of cultural heresy before Bauakademie officers, Khrushchev
ridiculed "confectionary" architecture and its academic proponents
at Moscow's All-Union Building Conference, alerting Soviet design
professionals to an impending shake-up. By the second installment of
the Hellerau inquest, Soviet architectural journals were lampooning
Stalin-era "ornamentalism." Another top-down cultural revolution had
begun, and it repudiated the arcana of socialist realist form. Ehrlich and
Selmanagič, in their critique of the Bauakademie, had gambled that a
change was in the air—in fact, they had wagered their professional
future on it.

In March 1956, less than a year after the Bauakademie's last
attempt to subject Ehrlich and Selmanagič to the ritual of "criticism and
self-criticism," Hellerau's workshops hosted a visiting dignitary from
the Soviet Academy of Architecture's Institute of Interior Design. As
part of her visit to the Leipzig trade fair, comrade Manutscharova, the
institute's acting director, requested a stopover in Hellerau, the only

manufacturing firm on her itinerary. After meeting the firm's designers and seeing their work in factory production, Manutscharova joined her East German hosts in a roundtable discussion.[78] One of the USSR's leading authorities on furniture had come not to dictate socialist design principles to Hellerau's renegade talents but to learn from them. Before leaving East Germany, she sent a telegram to Moscow suggesting that product samples from Hellerau be shipped to the Soviet Union for exhibition there. Ehrlich and Selmanagič had won their wager and were on their way to becoming pioneers in the post-Stalinist avant-garde of socialist modernism.

People's Capitalism and Capitalism's People

International Style modernism completed its mutation from avant-garde icon to establishment orthodoxy over the course of the 1950s. Covering the opening of MoMA's 1953 Good Design exhibition, *New York Times* reporter Betty Pepis noted that furniture regarded as "extreme, even revolutionary" a few years earlier had become common-place, its familiarity neutralizing any lingering sense of "strangeness."[1] Equally striking was the extent to which this international aesthetic had become a marketplace convention. The 1952 Good Design show had revealed that "the points of origin are more widely spread than ever before—reinforcing the very positive impression that good contempo-rary designs for the home are international both in origin and appeal."[2] The U.S. State Department disseminated MoMA's gospel of global modernism abroad. American Home Furnishings, the exhibition devel-oped from MoMA's 1950 Good Design show, toured Stuttgart, Berlin, Munich, Amsterdam, Paris, London, Milan, and Trieste under Marshall Plan sponsorship.[3] Many of its featured furnishings took center stage at We're Building a Better Life, seen in Berlin, Stuttgart, Hannover, Paris, and Milan between 1952 and 1954. American Design for Home and Decorative Use, produced by MoMA for the U.S. Information Agency (USIA), visited cities in Finland, Sweden, Norway, Denmark, Belgium, and Italy from 1953 to 1955.[4] And thanks to federal start-up funding, Knoll International showrooms in Stuttgart, Paris, Milan, Brussels, Stockholm, and Zurich marketed many of the same pieces seen at Marshall Plan, MSA, and USIA exhibitions. MoMA's formula for a postwar modernism boasting broad points of origin deserved its International Style label, but export via U.S. cultural institutions, commercial enterprises, and propaganda campaigns proclaimed it an American-based franchise.

A straw poll conducted by Pepis in 1953 for the *New York Times* suggests the extent to which America had secured its reputation as a modernist superpower. Interviews with twenty foreign designers visit-ing Manhattan revealed a remarkable concurrence of opinion:

> They offered unanimous praise for the experimental attitudes and progressive machine production methods which prevail in our country. And, almost without exception, a single designer— Charles Eames of California—was mentioned as having made the

(facing page) Bud Weichers, sales manager at the Rollingwood devel-opment in San Pablo, California, holds an architectural rendering of one of the model homes visited by a Soviet delegation in 1955. U.S. National Archives, Still Pictures Division, RG306 PS (B) Subjects, Box 34, 56-16561.

> most remarkable contribution to creative designing both in his
> own country and in the visitors' native lands. [...] The work of
> several other American designers ... [was] considered impor-
> tant by those who came to observe from abroad. Ranking high
> on the lists was the furniture created by George Nakashima, Eero
> Saarinen, Edward Wormley, George Nelson, and the fabrics
> developed by Laverne Associates, Alexander Girard and Knoll
> Associates.[5]

Pepis concluded that "a visit to the United States these days is becoming as imperative for the serious interior designer from abroad as was a
period of study in Germany or France in the 'Twenties or Sweden in
the 'Thirties."[6] The fact that every American talent named by her poll's
respondents had been represented by work shown in at least one State
Department foreign exhibition was hardly a coincidence. Federal
investment in the International Style as a soft-power asset helped turn
America into the global epicenter of midcentury modernist design.

SHOWDOWN AT THE CONSUMPTION JUNCTION

International modernism's New World triumph may have inspired
European designers, but it was deeply unsettling to some Americans.
In 1953, Elizabeth Gordon, the editor of *House Beautiful,* electrified
readers with the promise of a revelation "never been put into print by us
or any other publication." Cultural propaganda emanating from "highly
placed individuals and highly respected institutions" was placing
democracy at risk. "Your first reactions will be amazement, disbelief
and shock," Gordon wrote. "You will say 'It can't happen here!'"[7] Her
editorial "The Threat to the Next America" told readers that they were
at a crossroads. *"Two ways of life stretch before us. One leads to the richness
of variety, to comfort and beauty. The other, the one we want fully to expose
to you, retreats to poverty and unlivability. Worst of all, it contains the threat
of cultural dictatorship"* (emphasis in original).[8] Gordon's unmasking of
lifestyle saboteurs, published just as East German authorities were
denouncing modernists as enemies of socialism, marked cold war
America's closest approximation to Stalinist aesthetic discourse.

As in standard socialist realist practice, Gordon provided a crash
course in art history to inform consumers why Bauhaus design undermined their national identity. She traced the origins of modern product

design to nineteenth-century American manufacturers. When the
New World's innovations crossed the Atlantic, European modernists
got them wrong. Bauhaus intellectuals "used these industrial forms as
ends in themselves, as art motifs for their own designs, not noticing—
probably not understanding—how they arose as practical forms solving
practical problems."[9] Upon immigration to the United States in the
1930s, Bauhaus masters brought with them an "intellectualized philosophy of design": the International Style. Its partisans, according to
Gordon, championed asceticism and mocked the postwar homes and
appliances crucial to an American Way of Life. "The continued
belittling of technology as 'gadgetry' will ultimately weaken the whole
structure of Western civilization and eventually lead to subsistence living and totalitarianism."[10] Modernists who preached "less is more" as "a
basis of judgment for the good life" were asking Americans to surrender
their common sense and free will:

> [I]f we can be sold on accepting dictators in matters of taste and
> how our homes are to be ordered, our minds are certainly well
> prepared to accept dictators in other departments of life. . . . So
> you see, this well-developed movement has social implications
> because it affects the heart of our society—the home. Beyond
> the nonsense of trying to make us want to give up our . . . conve-
> niences for what is *supposed* to be a better and more serene life,
> there is a threat of total regimentation and total control.[11]
> (emphasis in original)

What seemed a mere question of taste in home furnishings was in
reality a struggle for the nation's soul. "Freedom, your won freedom of
choice—and its consequences—is the only road to personal growth.
Your reason, your common sense, is the finest instrument you possess
for living. **Don't let them take it away**" (emphasis in original).[12] In a lecture at the Chicago Merchandise Mart, the cosponsor of MoMA's Good
Design shows, Gordon refuted charges that her *House Beautiful* essay
was an exercise in national chauvinism. She denied being "narrowly
nationalistic" but insisted that "just as there is such a thing as French
civilization, Japanese architecture, Italian music, German philosophy or
Russian fiction, so I believe that there is an American culture." Her
responsibility as the editor of a major American home journal was to
"help develop that culture by supporting it where I find it."[13] In telling
readers about the progress of American household design, Gordon

helped them formulate "their own declaration of independence against the frauds, the over-publicized phoneys, the bullying tactics of the self-chosen elite who would dictate not only taste but a whole way of life."[14]

Despite Gordon's pledge to describe America's cultural threat "in its bluntest terms," she identified its perpetrator only obliquely—albeit in a bold typeface: "**House Beautiful finally speaks up to point plainly at the nonsense that goes on in the name of 'good design.'**" Her excoriation of "non-rational objects that are chosen for glorification by *avant-garde* museums" (emphasis in original) and the code word "good design" pointed plainly to Edgar Kaufmann Jr. at MoMA. Gordon had reason to resent his Good Design project. Kaufmann's ambition to influence consumer behavior by inserting museum curatorship into the mechanisms of wholesale and retail trade reduced the value—both figuratively and literally—of Gordon's editorial advice to home-makers. Household journals situate themselves at a nexus of product information and consumer preference that Ruth Schwarz Cowan calls the "consumption junction."[15] Profit margins for *House Beautiful* were determined by its ability to translate loyal readership into advertising revenue: the price manufacturers pay to access a pool of promising customers. Gordon's expertise in matters of household design attracted and influenced readers, who in turn attracted advertisers. MoMA's innovation of displaying and conferring awards to objects of "good design" provided free publicity for manufacturers and usurped Gordon's role as an arbiter of taste, undermining her journal's revenue strategy. Worse yet, Kaufmann had cut deals with two *House Beautiful* competitors, *Interiors* and *House & Garden,* allowing them a sneak preview of MoMA's upcoming Good Design collections. What Gordon described as a "threat to America" also threatened her magazine's credentials among readers and advertisers, and ultimately its profits.

Both in terms of cultural politics and financial anxieties, Gordon overreacted. However brilliant Kaufmann was at promoting MoMA as an arbiter of good design, most American consumers were not buying it. Even an outside observer could read the writing on the wall, as revealed in the *New York Times* poll of foreign design professionals:

There was most disagreement among foreign commentators on the subject of American taste. "Underdeveloped," commented British ceramicist Bernard Leach, "faulty in evaluation of its own contemporary products." "Not firmly set," said his friend and student, Japanese potter Hamada. "In general, among the millions of people, not high," wrote Ilmari Tapiovaara of Helsinki, currently instructing at Chicago's Institute of Design. "But," added Mr. Tapiovaara, "fortunately there is a small but brilliant and influential group of those with good taste."[16]

With Kaufmann's departure from MoMA in 1955, the museum abandoned the Good Design project and its aspiration to reform consumer preference. The museum "had lost its bid to shape the taste of a nation," as historian Jeffrey Meikle observes.[17] Kaufmann's campaign was not without its victories, though. While failing to convert the masses, it had succeeded among elites, namely the captains of postwar industry who were reinventing international-style capitalism. Over the course of the 1950s, Knoll International established its modernist furnishings as the sine qua non of corporate elegance. In office headquarters, Knoll Barcelona chairs designed in 1929 by Mies van der Rohe "became a cliché of every new entrance lobby," as Florence Knoll later remarked.[18] Patterns of patronage differed in Western Europe, where State Department exhibitions had promoted International Style furnishings in a domestic context. There, as design historians Eric Larrabee and Massimo Vignelli point out, products from Knoll International were "far more often to be found in residences than in offices," making the brand "not so much a trade name as a generic term . . . signifying modern design."[19]

CULTURAL DIPLOMACY BESIEGED

Gordon's revelation of a conspiracy to subvert American taste in favor of a foreign "good design" dictatorship echoed the rhetoric and logic of McCarthy-era politics. Joseph McCarthy, a Republican senator from Wisconsin, used warnings of communist infiltrators to blaze a path to power. He denounced President Harry Truman, Secretary of State Dean Acheson and General George C. Marshall as "soft on communism," when in fact their Marshall Plan had neutralized communist agitation in Western Europe by triggering the fastest economic growth in its history. Truman authorized efforts to destabilize the Soviet bloc and facilitate "the emergence of the satellite countries as entities independent of the USSR," as stated in a 1948 National Security Council document, but kept the policy covert, committing publicly only to the containment of communism within its existing borders. McCarthy depicted containment as collaboration and alleged that communists had infiltrated federal agencies.[20] The Republican presidential candidate, General Dwight D. Eisenhower, capitalized on the concocted scandal. Asserting that the Truman administration had neglected the cold war's propaganda front, he pledged to abandon a "strictly defensive" foreign policy for one dedicated to Eastern Europe's liberation, a strategy that helped defeat Truman's Democratic Party in the 1952 presidential race.

As a reward for his election-year performance, McCarthy's party promoted him to the position of chairman of the Committee on Government Operations, a platform from which he denounced the State Department for harboring "socialists, misfits and perverts." His inseparable aides, Roy Cohn and G. David Schine, toured public libraries operated by the State Department on a European "clean-up expedition." They proclaimed the discovery of thirty thousand subversive books, including works by "some seventy-five different communist authors." The suspects included Albert Einstein, Ernest Hemingway, Helen Keller, Henry David Thoreau, and Frank Lloyd Wright. Librarians were dismissed; books were removed and in some cases burned.[21] West Germans perceived the carnival of censorship as a manifestation of the kind of totalitarian information control practiced in the USSR.[22] McCarthyism's transatlantic adventure degraded one of America's most strategic soft-power assets: the carefully cultivated perception that intellectual freedom was a fundamental aspect of U.S. democracy.

Stateside, the library scandal fueled taxpayer disenchantment with foreign cultural diplomacy, as expressed in a letter to Democratic Senator Lyndon B. Johnson from a member of his Texas constituency:

> Well, it looks like some should be a watch dog on $10,000,000 for U.S. Culture for Germans. Senator, such truck that the new Fair Deal is putting out, and spending the U.S. citizens hard earnings is nothing else than the stealing in the tax collection officials. [*sic*] Senator, you boys better wake up.[23]

Another accusation of fiscal extravagance came from a U.S. House of Representatives subcommittee examining the State Department's overseas building program. Its use of "impractical" Knoll furnishings for diplomatic offices was said to show "poor judgment." The subcommittee report claimed that in the new U.S. embassy in Brussels, "because of the modernistic furniture placed therein, the office of the Ambassador lacked the dignity which might be expected."[24]

American anticommunists, anti-intellectuals, and isolationists joined forces in their assault on U.S. cultural diplomacy, putting Eisenhower at odds with his party's congressional majority. As the former supreme commander of allied military forces in Europe, Eisenhower knew all too well the battlefield's wake of blood and rubble and regarded psychological warfare as the humane alternative.[25] Standing armies were also enormously expensive to maintain, absorbing capital that might otherwise flow into the consumer economy. The modernization of national security under Eisenhower proposed two substitutes for conventional warfare. A defense policy dubbed "the New Look" relied on nuclear warheads as a sobering and cost-effective deterrent to Soviet military aggression. Offense would be conducted through propaganda campaigns, which also received a New Look makeover. "Overt" federal propaganda dampened its anticommunist tone to focus on positive content. Far more important in terms of strategic value was information scrubbed clean of any attribution to State Department sources. Filtered through intermediaries ranging from independent news media to nongovernmental agencies, "camouflaged" propaganda was the new administration's preferred method to advance U.S. interests overseas.[26] No information strategy, covert or otherwise, could salvage Eisenhower's pledge to liberate the "captive nations" of Eastern Europe, however. The Red Army suppression of East Germany's 1953 uprising communicated the Kremlin's intent to defend its East bloc franchise with force. The popular insurrection's quick defeat shattered any illusion that U.S. propaganda could induce a "rollback" of communism. This reality was soon mirrored in a "new basic concept" for psychological warfare, which would attempt to "create and exploit troublesome problems for the USSR" while avoiding "incitement to premature revolt."[27] The Truman administration's policy of deterrence, publicly condemned by Eisenhower as "futile," was recycled as American propaganda's New Look within a year of his electoral triumph.[28]

The Eisenhower administration reorganized psychological warfare operations under a host of new agencies. To evade the gauntlet of McCarthy's public hearings, the new U.S. secretary of state, John Foster Dulles, insisted that overseas information programs be removed from his jurisdiction. In summer 1953, as the orchestrated hysteria over federally employed "communists, left-wingers, New Dealers, radicals and pinkos" came to a crescendo, Eisenhower announced the creation of the USIA (U.S. Information Agency).[29] Congress, swayed by McCarthy's allegations, responded by slashing the USIA personnel budget by one-third. As the United States reduced investment in the cold war's "battle for hearts and minds," the USSR poured in resources.[30] Stalin's successors announced a new goal of "peaceful coexistence" with the West, reversing previous Soviet policy and its ideological underpinnings. The "peace offensive" used international trade fairs to portray communism as technologically and economically advanced. Soviet bloc nations staged 60 foreign exhibitions in 1954, and 170 the following year. Meanwhile, the United States more often than not stayed home.[31]

Recognizing a foreign policy disaster in the making, Eisenhower established a five-million-dollar "President's Special Emergency Fund" in 1954 to subsidize U.S. trade fair participation. Responding to the Kremlin's use of exhibitions "as a means of disseminating propaganda and impressing the audience with the wonders of life in the Soviet Union," federal officials envisioned a new kind of display that would be perceived by foreign audiences as a "cultural exhibit" rather than a "pure trade fair project."[32] In what historian Robert Haddow calls a "McCarthy-proof" strategy for propaganda, Eisenhower created an Office of International Trade Fairs (OITF) within the Department of Commerce to manage U.S. trade fair participation. The agency would disassociate its operations from those of the beleaguered USIA, depicting its activities as a support service for U.S. private enterprise seeking foreign markets. American businesses would supply product displays and personnel for international exhibitions. OITF officials would ship the materials overseas, oversee their installation, and provide assistance to corporate sales agents abroad. OITF agents then assembled individual product displays into mosaics that related a narrative about American culture and values through material artifacts, an approach that camouflaged the efforts of federal propaganda specialists and successfully eluded the attention of McCarthy and his colleagues.[33] The novel arrangement also reflected Eisenhower's conviction that "the hand of government must be carefully concealed, and in some cases, I should say, wholly eliminated" when conducting psychological warfare.[34]

Trade fair diplomacy redeployed the suburban model home as an emissary of the American Way of Life. The OITF hired Peter Harnden,

who had produced the MSA's 1952 Better Life show, as director of its
Paris-based European Trade Fair Program. Harnden produced a new
generation of U.S. exhibitions on a shoestring budget by artfully editing
a grab bag of material donated by businesses into thematically coherent
installations. OITF operations employed a transatlantic division of
labor. Officials in Washington would choose a trade fair theme relevant
to the local venue and tied to a particular facet of American life. In
Paris, Harnden would review the stockpile of corporate displays, select
those that seemed appropriate, and integrate them into a cohesive
exhibit. Privatized cultural propaganda turned exhibition design into
a game of bricolage, and Harnden was soon its master. This novel genre
of installation art also came with unintended consequences. Since
exhibitions representing the United States were now assembled from
the "found" material of corporate donations, an unofficial federal
endorsement was suddenly available to any business willing to pay for
the privilege.

House Beautiful wasted no time in using the new system of trade
fair diplomacy to settle an old score. At Main Street USA, an exhibition
designed by Harnden's office for display in Paris, Barcelona, Milan, Bari,
and Valencia, MoMA relinquished its federal franchise on good design.
House Beautiful staffers at regional offices in Lafayette, Indiana, and
Toledo, Ohio, selected interiors and furnishings for two prefabricated
houses supplied by a consortium that included Scholtz Homes, the
National Homes Corporation, the National Association of Home
Builders, the Producer's Council, and the Prefabricated Home Manufacturer's Institute. The Main Street home interiors were assembled in
the United States, photographed for publication, dismantled and
shipped to Europe, and finally reassembled on site, where the original
arrangements were re-created down to the placement of ashtrays and
decorative accents.[35] Wall-hung photographs showed the home in use
by an American model family as it gathered in the living room listening
to music on the hi-fi, or greeted neighbors across the backyard.[36]
"Proudly *House Beautiful* shows Europe how Americans live," said
Gordon's article about the exhibit, boasting that the nation was moving
"*upward* culturally, so fast it is making the old conception of class vs.
mass as antiquated as the parlor."[37] The evidence presented for this
assertion included pastel-hued kitchens and rooms that combined sleek
contemporary furnishings with traditionally upholstered armchairs
amid a flurry of color-coordinated fabrics and knickknacks. Praised by

(above) The prefabricated home furnished by *House Beautiful* for display at European trade fairs. The original caption reads, "Visitors to the United States are often most struck by the fact that virtually every family, even in 'lower' income groups, had an automobile, and, hence, must have a garage or carport, as here." *House Beautiful* 97, no. 7 (July 1955): 93.

(above right) The living room of the *House Beautiful* model home shown at the Main Street USA exhibitions in Paris and Milan in 1955. *House Beautiful* 97, no. 7 (July 1955): 92.

Gordon as heralds of a "noticeable improvement in taste, as compared with interiors of only yesterday," the Main Street USA interiors would have been decried by modernism's partisans as better suited to Lafayette and Toledo than Milan or Paris. According to diplomatic historian Robert Haddow, they reflected a conscious exercise in down-market advertising in the belief that aiming low would yield increased exports.[38]

A year before its European debut, the *House Beautiful* aesthetic showcased at Main Street USA was market tested at the Texas State Fair and the Los Angeles County Fair, where visitor responses impressed Gordon as "hushed, pensive, sort of reverent, you might say."[39] What inspired on one side of the Atlantic could alienate on the other, however. A young Italian visiting the *House Beautiful* installation in Milan grumbled:

Americans show us beautiful refrigerators, and these only show us how poor and ugly our own are; Americans overwhelm us with displays of products based on an abundance of electricity— when in Italy we never know if the little costly current we have will operate at all. The exhibits don't relate to the reality of our life, nor do they offer positive help—and they seem, without meaning to, to cast a negative light on what we have struggled to accomplish.[40]

As the *House Beautiful* residences made the rounds of European trade fairs, a Better Life home produced by Harnden and updated with new furnishings by Knoll International and Herman Miller, traversed the same circuit. These divergent expressions of taste conveyed either America's aesthetic diversity or its cultural schizophrenia, depending on the observer's point of view.

As ideological conveyances, home installations at trade fairs took a decisive leap forward under Harnden's OITF management. By combining well-provisioned model homes with product displays, he developed more complex exhibition narratives representing the mechanics of American consumer capitalism as an integrated system. Technology in Daily Life, produced for a 1955 trade fair in Valencia, Spain, juxtaposed a furnished suburban residence with industrial research exhibits to demonstrate how American technological advances had changed lifestyle for the better.[41] In Paris, a supermarket mock-up alongside a model home clarified the relationship of the mechanized kitchen to its source of packaged industrially processed provisions. This additive approach to exhibiting the American Way of Life implied that its replication entailed importing an entire economic system, not just isolated products.[42] In effect, Harnden discovered how to fuse elements of the

The living room of a 1955 show home mock-up at the 1955 Frankfurt exhibition America at Home, based on Peter Harnden's 1952 West Berlin show We're Building a Better Life. Updated furnishings include Harry Bertoia's Diamond chair for Knoll, *center left*, and Allen Gould's "Cord and Iron" chair, *right. Die Innenarchitektur* 3, no. 7 (January 1956): 412.

wide range of exhibitions he had produced under the Marshall Plan and MSA into more elaborate and compelling variants.

A 1955 *New York Times* article applauded the OITF for creating an American presence at international trade fairs "for the first time in recent history."[43] A letter to the editor sent in response begged to differ. Its author maintained that absolutely nothing about the OITF program was particularly new, and noted that U.S. participation in West German trade fairs had begun years earlier as "a counter-attraction" to the East's Party propaganda. A furnished suburban home displayed in West Berlin had amazed Germans in 1951, the writer remembered. "At least one of the visitors was a teen-age Communist agitator who nearly succeeded in precipitating a fight in the American Sector, but wound up on a specially conducted tour of the model American home." The letter's author, Paul Shinkman, modestly avoided mentioning that as a former U.S. State Department official, he had been the communist teen's tour guide.[44] Anyone with Shinkman's knowledge of Marshall Plan exhibitions must have found the New Look in trade fair diplomacy strangely reminiscent of an antecedent dismissed by Eisenhower administration critics as "haphazard," "merely defensive," and "of little use."[45]

AT HOME WITH MR. AND MRS. CAPITALIST

Because they were unwilling to learn from Marshall Plan household propaganda, Washington's new ranks of psychological warriors were forced to reinvent it. The task fell to Ted Repplier, president of the Advertising Council, a voluntary industry organization that had orchestrated federal public relations campaigns during World War II. Funded by an Eisenhower Exchange Fellowship, Repplier embarked on a six-month study tour of U.S. propaganda methods in Asia, the Middle East, and Europe. He returned warning that America remained "terribly outgunned" in the "Idea War." To defend U.S. interests abroad, he insisted, "we desperately need a Crusade." It would spread the gospel of America's unique economic system, "which gives more benefits to more people than any yet devised." As a first step, Repplier devised a new brand name for the U.S. economic system. Its global trademark would be "People's Capitalism."[46]

Like many products, People's Capitalism was not as new as its ad campaign claimed. An unmentioned (and unwelcome) precedent was J. George Frederick's *The New Deal: A People's Capitalism*, which

on a tube of toothpaste or a can of dog food."[65] John L. Peters, the
president of World Neighbors, a global relief organization, took issue
with the portrayal of Ed Barnes as "an average wage earner," as did the
Washington correspondent for the *Deutsche Zeitung*, who called him "a
veritable labor aristocrat."[66] John Nuveen, a Department of Commerce
consultant, worried that "flaunting our abundance, fatness and luxury"
would alienate audiences in the developing world. "Are we selling pass-
ports or a way of life, and how do they get it?" he asked. "Where do
they send the box tops?"[67] On a more productive note, Warren Mullin,
a business analyst, thought that the Barnes home interiors looked "too
Madison Avenue." He wondered, "Could some orderly disorderliness
be managed?"[68] Repplier found Mullin's suggestion "perfectly wonder-
ful."[69] For showings of People's Capitalism abroad, used furniture
replaced the showroom-fresh interior displayed in Washington. Less
could be done to salvage the colonial home installation, which one
museum curator called "a conglomeration of erroneous ideas" assembled out of items from "a department store's basement counter."[70] In
the export version of People's Capitalism, the colonial shanty and its
mannequins were replaced with a reproduction of the historic log cabin
birthplace of Abraham Lincoln, an icon of U.S. patriotism irrelevant to
the exhibition narrative.

The photo gallery showing the Barnes family at work and play was
intended to convey the physical reality of their American Way of Life, a
task that was accomplished only too well. The racially segregated postwar community depicted in the images appalled some visitors. Reacting
to pictures of the Barnes children at school, John Gilhooley, an assistant
to the U.S. Secretary of Labor, asked, "If we really want to make the
point that America is classless, ought there not to be at least one Negro
and one woman in the picture?"[71] People's Capitalism portrayed an
apartheid America for good reason, according to a letter deploring the
civil rights record of the subdivision in which the Barnes family lived:

> The American Friends Service Committee, together with repre-
> sentatives of other national organizations . . . expressed their
> concern that, since Fairless Hills and the adjoining community
> of Levittown were built for workers at U.S. Steel, their Negro
> workers be included in these two communities. . . . No Negro has
> ever lived in either of these communities, although they total over
> 1,000 homes. This is the largest all-white community which has

The Barnes family, posed inside the "Madison Avenue" reproduction of their home living room initially displayed at People's Capitalism and subsequently changed for overseas showings. U.S. National Archives, Still Pictures Division, RG 306 PS Subjects 56-3109.

persistently refused all appeals to change its segregation policy, and this is widely known.[72]

Although this failing was disastrous for a soft-power asset developed for use in Asia and Latin America, the exhibit remained unchanged. People's Capitalism was stuck with its model home. As Repplier explained, "U.S. Steel gave us this and one doesn't look a gift horse too hard in the mouth."[73] The privatization of federal propaganda efforts had made it impossible to insulate the nation's reputation from that of a corporate donor.

Another intractable problem lay in communicating the notion of public ownership of the means of production through stock holdings. An effective graphic translation of this theory eluded Repplier and his Advertising Council volunteers. Their attempt, a display panel papered with ersatz stock certificates and explanatory notes, became mired in "the gobbledegook of economics," according to Conger Reynolds of the USIA. "I don't believe the latter will be understood by thousands upon thousands of people who view the exhibit."[74] Whether the dilemma was even worth resolving was debatable. Assertions of a "new capitalism" based on private stock ownership came under fire at a Yale University roundtable discussion sponsored by the Advertising Council in November 1956. Henry Wallach, a professor of economics, noted that only 15 percent of U.S. families were private shareholders. Reformulating theory to fit practice, the panel resolved that *widespread ownership need not be regarded as the most essential part of a people's capitalism* (emphasis in original).[75] A 1958 study in the *American Economic Review* revealed that the proportion of Americans holding shares had actually declined since the Great Depression, while clans like the DuPonts and Rockefellers "owned many times as much stock as all the wage earners in the United States." The claims behind "People's Capitalism" were "without substance," the report concluded, and the concept's rapid diffusion in news journals, business advertising, and stockholder reports had not reflected any true innovation in economic theory but rather "the effectiveness of organized propaganda."[76] A reexamination of the theory in 1964 concluded, "'Executives' capitalism' may be a more apt name for our corporate system than the overworked, largely unsupported slogan of 'people's capitalism.'"[77]

Text-heavy, graphically inept, and factually inaccurate, People's Capitalism shipped out in three different versions for its world tour in 1956. A copy of the Union Station exhibition modified in accordance with suggestions made at its preview headed south for stops in Guatemala City, Bogotá, Santiago, and La Paz. Setup and knockdown proved so cumbersome that entire sections were jettisoned in Bogotá, yielding an ad hoc abridgement that toured all remaining South American venues. Another stripped-down variant traveled to Colombo and Kandy in Ceylon (Sri Lanka), where the Barnes family's living room, amputated from the rest of the dwelling, was seen by fifty thousand visitors. In overseas settings, the exhibit's ponderous story was easily misinterpreted. According to a USIA observer, a local nun shepherding students through the show explained that the photos of the Barnes family proved that the saucy attire seen in Hollywood movies was, in fact, not worn by real Americans. Her exegesis, while devoid of the intended lesson on capitalism, perfectly illustrates the self-serving nature of soft power as

Colombian schoolchildren in line to see People's Capitalism at Bogotá's International Trade Fair in 1957. Headline captions on the two panels read, "No Economic System Is Perfect" and "Class Differences Are Disappearing." U.S. National Archives, Still Pictures Division, RG 306 PS Subjects 57-11089.

foreign cultural capital. The show's reliance on text to get its message across posed ongoing financial challenges. An anemic USIA budget forced American diplomatic outposts at each venue to foot the bill for translating and resetting display captions. Slated for a tour of India, People's Capitalism ran aground at its first stop, New Delhi, where it remained crated and warehoused for two years due to lack of funds.[78] The Barnes family home made its final appearance in 1956 at the America at Home trade fair exhibit in Zagreb, Yugoslavia.[79] "The fairgoer is supposed to get a rounded picture of a happy, contented Ed Barnes at work, at play, shopping, and at his do-it-yourself workshop," a journalist reported. "From that point on, the theme is lost."[80] Despite the efforts of leading ad industry talents, People's Capitalism was an unqualified failure, in large part because its creators ignored the wealth of experience gleaned in a previous generation of cold war household propaganda campaigns.

CULTURAL INFILTRATION INSIDE OUT

Participation at trade fairs in socialist nations like Yugoslavia only partially satisfied the Eisenhower administration's stated goal of "piercing the Iron Curtain."[81] An alternate cultural infiltration strategy involved bringing communists to America for intensive reorientation. The president's advisor on psychological warfare, C. D. Jackson, proposed that Washington "deluge Moscow with invitations," predicting that 90 percent of America's Soviet visitors would return, if "not necessarily convinced," then at least "profoundly perturbed" by their experience abroad.[82] The Kremlin seemed delighted to comply. At the Geneva summit of July 1955, Eisenhower and Khrushchev agreed to ease restrictions on bilateral exchanges. One month later, Soviet officials accepted an invitation extended through the U.S. State Department by Earl W. Smith of the National Association of Home Builders (NAHB), a construction industry coalition, to host Soviet housing officials on a cross-country tour of U.S. residential construction sites and materials manufacturers. A ten-member Soviet delegation headed by the USSR's Minister of Construction I. K. Kozuilia arrived in the United States on 3 October 1955. Over the next five weeks, the group visited dozens of building supply manufacturers and home-building sites in Virginia, New York, Massachusetts, Indiana, Illinois, Arizona, California, and Washington.[83]

It was not Kozuilia's first visit to the United States. A decade earlier, he had headed a delegation to the 1945 American-Soviet building
conference. Held in Manhattan during the waning days of wartime
alliance, the gathering marked the high tide of architectural knowledge
transfer between the superpowers. Sponsored by the Architects' Committee of the National Council of American-Soviet Friendship, a U.S.
voluntary organization, the conference brought together approximately
250 American participants and 50 Soviet counterparts to discuss the
future of housing in both nations. Soviet representatives arrived at the
talks with a shopping list in hand. They hoped to place an enormous
order for equipment that would make possible assembly-line construction of prefabricated housing.[84] Financing was to be one portion of a
six-billion-dollar reconstruction loan requested of the United States by
Soviet Foreign Minister Vyachselav Molotov. The scheme to harness
American cash and technology to Soviet postwar reconstruction was
stillborn, a casualty of collapsing foreign relations. A decade later,
Kozuilia seized the opportunity created by the Geneva Accords to
absorb the latest developments in American housing, albeit without
the prospect of U.S. lend-lease financing.

The visiting Soviet delegation of 1955 carefully documented
every construction and manufacturing process they saw, "their camera
shutters clicking almost as fast as they popped questions," according to
their U.S. hosts.[85] "At the [construction] site, the Reds swarmed over
the slab, dodging partitions and roofing sections as they came off the
truck, reaching up to gauge ceiling heights (which they considered
low), examining heating, plumbing and wire connections," an observer
reported.[86] American building industry officials knew that the Soviets
had devised their own prefabrication systems based on reinforced
concrete rather than wood-frame construction due to the limitations
of Soviet sawmills and the transport infrastructure needed to bring
timber to mills and lumber to construction sites. Nevertheless, American building methods were being evaluated for their relevance to
Soviet postwar reconstruction. As explained by delegate Aleksandr
Vlasov, Moscow's municipal architect, "In order to carry out this task
in the shortest time, our building industry is now switching to prefabri-
cating complete housing, and we are greatly interested in American
prefabrication."[87]

The contemporary American kitchen was another object of
Soviet fascination.[88] After hearing a keynote address by Vice President

The Soviet housing delegation visits a suburban construction site in North Springfield, Virginia, in 1955. Edward R. Carr *(center, gesturing)* explains building methods to I. K. Kozuilia, the delegation leader *(center)*. U.S. National Archives, Still Pictures Division, RG306 PS Subjects Box 301, 55-18364.

Richard Nixon at the inauguration of the National Housing Center in Washington, Kozuilia examined a model kitchen finished in pink enamel and outfitted with "pull down cooking units, ovens built into the wall, sliding panels that revealed cabinet space, even a built-in makeup kit." Bemused, the Soviet construction minister asked his hosts, "Can you also sleep here?"[89] Although a newfound spirit of consumer excess, expressed in chrome trim and push-button wizardry, haunted the American dream kitchen, Kozuilia maintained that it had undergone vast improvement since his last visit to the United States.[90]

The Soviet officials collected construction site souvenirs with an enthusiasm that amused and worried their American sponsors. "They wanted to know the price of everything, but not out of curiosity" an

NAHB tour guide reported. "One told me they were interested in buying things to take back to Russia."[91] At visits to manufacturing facilities, they placed orders for hundreds of products, ranging from spring-balanced windows and disposable paint rollers to ready-to-install door-and-jamb units. The delegation's voracious appetite for samples raised eyebrows in the industry, and its newsletter weighed the possible outcomes:

> This *could mean* big-ticket orders when the delegates get back to Russia—assuming that such export is determined to be consistent with U.S. interests. However, their penchant for sampling *could also mean* that the Russians will merely copy what they take back—dealing American manufacturers a slap in the face for their generous cooperation.[92] (emphases in original)

American builders had good reason to wonder about the acquisitive mania. Soviet reverse engineering—called the "Western option" by technology historian Raymond Stokes—had long been the USSR's tried-and-true method of achieving industrial parity with capitalist nations at a fraction of the cost of original research and development.[93] The Western option was a hallmark of the First Five-Year Plan of 1928–32, speeding Soviet industrialization through ready-made factory blueprints originally purchased (and later simply duplicated) from Albert Kahn Inc., the firm responsible for Ford's famed River Rouge plant outside Detroit.[94] Reverse engineering lived on during the cold war, as revealed by the mysterious resemblance of Soviet cars and appliances shown at international trade fairs to Western counterparts of previous model years. Soviet attempts to ship American building samples to Moscow for inspection had begun as early as 1935, architectural historian Richard Anderson has revealed.[95] As the Soviet housing delegation of 1955 devoured the latest advances in U.S. building technology, an American delegate to the Geneva foreign ministers conference, the follow-up to the Geneva summit, complained that the Kremlin "seemed to want exchanges supplying the Soviet Union with essential technical know-how without making corresponding concessions in the areas to which we attach importance."[96] The strategy of hijacking U.S. soft-power initiatives to accrue maximum Soviet benefit while thwarting American propaganda goals would reach its climax at the American National Exhibition in Moscow in 1959, a story told in the next chapter.

Of all the samples sought by Kozuilia and company for shipment back to Moscow, none astonished their hosts more than the completely furnished suburban house that they seemed determined to purchase. The first inquiry came in Fort Wayne, Indiana, during a facilities tour at General Industries, a prefabricated home manufacturer. "This is no joke," Kozuilia assured the firm's incredulous president, who demurred, citing his company's lack of export experience.[97] The prospective home buyers were more successful on the West Coast. At Rollingwood, a suburban development in San Pablo, California, the Soviet minister of construction discovered a three-bedroom, two-and-one-half-bath split-level that he found "delightful." The price tag was $13,750. Kozuilia requested that the home's unassembled components be shipped to the USSR, complete with heating and air conditioning equipment, GE electric kitchen, and all display model furnishings: dinette suite, sectional sofa and side chair, television set, occasional tables, beds, dressers, drapes, bathroom fixtures and ceramic tiles, floor coverings— everything but the bricks and mortar for the fireplace and chimney. Freight costs and optional extras brought the total cost to $40,000. "Just send the bill to the [Soviet] embassy in Washington," an unfazed Kozuilia told the developer.[98] Before heading back to his homeland, Kozuilia confessed to reporters that he too would like to live in a split-level.[99] The Soviet minister of construction had been ravished by an American suburban home.

Living room interior of the Rollingwood home purchased for export to the USSR. The building materials and furniture were shipped to Moscow in May 1956. U.S. National Archives, Still Pictures Division, RG306 PS B Subjects Box 346, 56-16562.

The Trojan House Goes East

People's Capitalism produced a rapid and unequivocal Soviet response. At the momentous Twentieth Party Congress of 1956, *Pravda* editor and Khrushchev protégé Dmitri Shepalov denounced the exhibition within days of its unveiling:

> In the United States the "new capitalism" myth has been elevated to an official state doctrine, and the propagation of this "people's capitalism" has been assigned to a special government information agency. . . . The information agency has even organized a special "People's Capitalism" exhibition that will be put on display at fairs all over the world. Yet "people's capitalism" is as absurd an idea as fried ice![1]

Party authorities rushed a counterpropaganda campaign into effect. Moscow's Foreign Language Publishing House issued *People's Capitalism?* a scathing critique created expressly for export. A *New York Times* reporter on assignment in the USSR photographed a billboard emblazoned with a cartoon depicting a well-dressed cadaver labeled "Capitalism" surrounded by business tycoons stitching a makeshift "People's" tag onto his lapel.[2] As irate Party leaders understood, capitalism's new trademark deliberately infringed upon communism's branding as the egalitarianism of working-class choice. For a brochure accompanying the Bogotá, Colombia, showing of People's Capitalism, Alberto Galindo, a former Pan-American conference president, encroached even further on Moscow's turf. Appropriating the Marxist orthodoxy of dialectical materialism, he wrote, "In the People's Capitalism of the United States, there is being forged the new, modern, liberal formula which, *if we are to apply the dialectic process,* could be the first step toward synthesis in the universal conflict [between communism and capitalism] which we are presently witnessing" (emphasis in original).[3] America's new and improved formula for capitalism had turned communism into a postwar "Brand X," according to the Advertising Council and its allies.

People's Capitalism failed to gain favor among members of the U.S. House and Senate, however, arguably its most crucial demographic. A year after the exhibition's Union Station debut, the House Appropriations Committee slashed Eisenhower's requested USIA budget by one-third.[4] The fiscal rebuke by a Congress controlled by the

(facing page) Anne Sonopol Anderson, an appliance "demonstration lady," expresses delight at the work of a robotic floor cleaner in the RCA/Whirlpool Miracle Kitchen at the American National Exhibition in Moscow, 1959. Library of Congress, Prints and Photographs Division, *Look* Collection—Job 59-8225 (color), LC-L901A-59-8225-2.

president's own party imperiled his most ambitious propaganda initiative to date: the cultural infiltration of Soviet bloc "captive nations."[5] Proposed trade fair participation for 1956 had included venues in Leipzig, East Germany, and Poznan, Poland—the goal being to strike "as close to Moscow as possible."[6] The administration went ahead with its plan for exhibitionist subversion with a minimum budget, attaining its ultimate goal in summer 1959 with the opening of the American National Exhibition in Moscow. The USIA's Moscow exhibition marshaled the persuasive power of two furnished homes (one inhabited by a model housewife), no less than four model kitchens, and a pavilion designed around the theme of a household products bazaar. Pundits celebrated the exhibition's Kitchen Debate between Nixon and Khrushchev as the victory of America's most audacious propaganda offensive. An alternate reading, uncolored by cold war triumphalism, has gone largely unexamined. The Kremlin had sanctioned an American consumer spectacle in Moscow, the Soviet capital and ideological hearth of global communism. Was this really a myopic blunder, or could it have been part of a Promethean scheme to steal the secrets of consumer modernity from its capitalist master?

ROMANCING THE BLOC

During Poznan's International Trade Fair in June 1956, Poles marked their homeland as a soft target for the Eisenhower administration's planned infiltration of Eastern Europe. Western exporters became accidental witnesses to history as workers took to the streets chanting, "We want bread!" The protest soon turned into a riot. Mobs attacked public buildings, including Party and police headquarters. Trade fair visitors used their hired cars to transport the wounded to hospitals.[7] Poznan's uprising raged out of control for three days. In the wake of the suppression, in an attempt to regain popular confidence, the Party rehabilitated Wladyslaw Gomulka, a former leader who had been denounced and jailed in the Stalin era. Sniffing an opportunity, U.S. foreign policy specialists called for an expansion of cultural diplomacy in Poland.[8] Offering Gomulka's government $95 million in loans and credits, Washington announced that it would sponsor a U.S. exhibition at Poznan's 1957 trade fair.[9] The theme of America's pavilion, Made in USA, divulged its propaganda strategy. A year after Poznan's bread riots, Polish citizens would be invited to a buffet of American abundance.

Before the U.S. exhibition even opened it doors, the Party newspaper *Gazeta Poznanska* deemed it a shameless provocation.[10] Upon seeing its wanton household extravagances being put on display to taunt the nation's proletariat, Polish construction workers walked off the site outraged, or so the story went. Journalists panned the upcoming exhibit as yet another demonstration of capitalism's disdain for the masses.[11] Days later, fairground visitors seemed to have a different opinion. They jammed the U.S. pavilion beyond capacity, prompting police to cordon off the entrance to constrain surging crowds. Beneath a translucent geodesic dome designed by Buckminster Fuller, socialist citizens examined sewing machines, listened to a jukebox blaring American hits, watched a nonstop fashion show featuring models outfitted in ready-to-wear apparel, and fed tokens (supplied courtesy of the sponsor) into vending machines stocked with candy and Coca-Cola. Echoing Riesman's "Nylon War" parody, *Time* magazine called the Poznan exhibit a "Nylon Wonderland."[12] Outside, a furnished three-bedroom suburban residence donated by *House and Home* magazine also exceeded visitor capacity. USIA exhibition planners attempted to open the entire home to foot traffic, but human gridlock made this untenable. After a brief circuit of the living room, visitors were shown the door and shunted along the home's perimeter walls for glimpses of the kitchen and other interiors, faces pressed to windows. To maximize views, USIA exhibitors removed the doors from all rooms. Tour guides explained that while the open kitchen was indeed a popular innovation in American homes, a complete lack of bathroom and bedroom privacy was, in fact, not customary.[13] The installation techniques developed by Peter Harden five years earlier for the MSA Better Life home, which had circumvented such crowd control problems, seemed to be a lost exhibition art.

One of the most popular Made in USA displays was the demonstration kitchen, donated and staffed by General Foods and its Birds Eye frozen foods subsidiary. Home economist Barbara Sampson more than fulfilled the model housewife role. Sampson was a "demonstration lady," one of the highly trained professionals employed by appliance and processed food manufacturers to introduce new products to American consumers.[14] In Poznan, she soon realized that her demonstrations of how to whip up a variety of hot meals from packaged, industrially prepared ingredients mystified an audience unfamiliar with supermarkets, electrical appliances, and convenience foods. To bridge the gap,

Polish spectators jam a model living room at the House and Home exhibit at the 1957 Poznan Trade Fair. The original caption claimed, "Starved for consumer goods, the visitors often tried to buy the displays." *House and Home* 12, no. 2 (August 1957).

she distributed individual frozen peas to thousands of onlookers who had never seen one. Invited home by one of her local assistants for a traditional Polish meal, Sampson's initiation into East bloc homemaking skills came as a revelation:

> The stove on which they cooked was a wretched two-burner affair with no knobs. To turn on the gas, they had to use pliers. The children's beds, ordinarily set up in the living room—they had only one bedroom—were moved to the kitchen so there would be space to serve dinner in the living room.

Sampson quickly realized that "refrigerators are as rare in Poznan as they are at the South Pole." Intending to take snapshots of her hosts cooking a Polish meal, she desisted. "They were so charming I couldn't do it." Looking back at the Birds Eye exhibit, she mused, "It was difficult to tell what most people thought about our display. They were friendly, but so awed they were speechless." The problem was neither new nor undiagnosed. USIA analysts knew that audiences overseas were predisposed to agree with the Soviet indictment of Americans as "a gadget-loving people produced by an exclusively mechanical, technological and materialist civilization." At a 1955 trade fair in Ethiopia, the USIA had nonetheless showcased a luxuriously equipped Ford Thunderbird, Dumont televisions, and a GE kitchen baking "typical American cakes" made from packaged mixes.[15] Of a 1956 exhibition in Syria, Jane Fiske Mitarachi in "Design as a Political Force," an assessment of U.S. trade fair diplomacy, noted: "the model kitchen . . . with its washers and disposals and mixers, might seem like a legitimate statement of American accomplishment in Paris; but in Damascus, an electric kitchen actually has no relation to middle-eastern cookery."[16] Similarly, demonstrations of how to reconstitute canned frozen orange juice in an electric blender were as alien to homemakers in Poznan as lessons on preparing Polish fermented rye soup would have been to U.S. suburban housewives.[17]

America's corporate food chain took center stage at the 1957 Zagreb trade fair in Yugoslavia, a nonaligned socialist nation presenting another opportune target for USIA infiltration operations. The Supermarket USA exhibition, sponsored by the National Association of Food Chains, featured a model self-service retail outlet within a glass-and-steel pavilion by the industrial design firm of Walter Dorwin Teague. The installation, which had debuted a year earlier as The American Way Supermarket at Rome's Third International Congress of Food

Distribution, boasted shopping carts, refrigerator cases, cash registers, and 2,500 food items supplied by some six hundred corporate donors.[18] The USIA employed young female students from the University of Zagreb as model shoppers. Their "demonstration effect" task involved wheeling a shopping cart down the aisles as spectators watched from an overhead catwalk similar to the one Harnden developed for West Berlin's Better Life exhibition. Loading the cart with cellophane-wrapped cuts of meat, canned goods, cake mixes, packaged frozen food, and fresh produce flown in from Philadelphia, they took their selections to a checkout stand to be rung up and bagged. The demonstration ended with the model shopper drawing a lottery ticket and awarding her trove of American groceries to a lucky audience member.[19] Merchandise showcased elsewhere within the pavilion included appliances, books, records, sporting goods, apparel, and the familiar battery of candy and soft-drink vending machines.[20] A furnished apartment displaced the usual suburban home representation of the American household. Visitors passed through the two-bedroom-plus-nursery, one-bath on their way out of the pavilion. Progressing from shopping spectacle to domestic idyll, the narrative sequence of The American Way Supermarket portrayed the consumer rather than the capitalist as the raison d'être for U.S. retail innovation.

Supermarket USA was a soft-power success story, advancing American prestige in ways that could be leveraged by local elites to benefit themselves. In his opening-day speech, Zagreb's deputy mayor announced, "This is not just a trade fair, but a great school, where the experience of other countries can be learned by our technical people and thus assist in the improvement of our own Yugoslav economy."[21] A Serbo-Croatian speaker hired by the USIA to track visitor responses overheard a worker telling a communist official, "If you install something like this here, all honors to you, and we will elect you for three more years."[22] Three days after the trade fair closed, Jugotechna, the state import-export organization, purchased the supermarket display for $30,000, a fraction of its initial cost.[23] Aided by the National Association of Food Chains, Belgrade opened Yugoslavia's first supermarket in April 1958.[24] Its debut prompted plans for ten more supermarkets in the Yugoslavian capital, and another sixty throughout the country.[25] Supermarket USA continued the project begun by the MSA's Caravan of Modern Food Service to spread the gospel of self-service shopping, first throughout Western Europe, and finally to the socialist world—

albeit in a nation embarked upon its own idiosyncratic path to a proletarian future. Whatever the ultimate impact on Yugoslav retailing, it was not simply the product of USIA machinations but also of choices made by the host nation's leaders in their own self-interest.[26]

DÉTENTE AND PSYCH WAR

After months of negotiation, on 28 January 1958 the United States and USSR endorsed the Soviet-American Cultural Agreement, paving the way for exchanges of performers, visiting delegations, films, broadcasts, and exhibitions as a "means of establishing mutual understanding." The accord also offered the United States a way to shift the tone and substance of superpower rivalry. Khrushchev's new policies of "peaceful coexistence" and "peaceful competition," announced at the Twentieth Party Conference in February 1956, overturned Party dogma concerning the inevitability of armed conflict between communist and capitalist camps. Without removing the threat of Soviet hard power, Khrushchev forged a "soft line" to extend communist influence internationally. In 1957, successful Soviet intercontinental missile and nuclear bomb tests established the relative parity of the USSR and United States in terms of cold war weaponry. The Soviets overtook America with the launch of the world's first orbital satellite, Sputnik. When the United States tried to launch its own satellite, its booster exploded upon ignition. A live telecast, intended to proclaim America's entry into the space race, broadcast the fiery miscarriage around the world. Newspapers dubbed the launch "Kaputnik."[27] CIA director Allen Dulles acknowledged the "very wide and deep impact" of the Soviet Union's propaganda in "relating their scientific accomplishments to the effectiveness of the Communist social system." Extravagant Soviet displays at international trade fairs leveraged satellite, missile, and nuclear reactor technology to burnish communism's progressive credentials, outshining the chronically underfunded U.S. competition, particularly in Asia and Latin America.[28] Given its record of "psych war" losses, America needed to regain ground.[29]

While the U.S. and Soviet delegations hammered out protocols for an exchange of national exhibitions, another U.S. venture in fairground diplomacy was foundering. In time-honored fashion, while the USIA was planning America's contribution to the 1958 Brussels World's Fair, Congress was eliminating the necessary funding. Despite estimates that the USSR would spend at least $50 million to build and operate its Brussels pavilion, an appropriations subcommittee reduced Eisenhower's requested $15 million budget by 20 percent. Howard Cullman, the exhibition's U.S. commissioner general, railed at the prospect of "a second-rate show for a first-class nation." One day before the Soviet-American Cultural Agreement of 1958 was signed, the *Washington Post* ran the headline, "We're Set to Be Shamed at Brussels."[30]

An air of crisis enveloped discussions of how to represent America in Brussels. An executive-branch council urged the USIA to abandon the People's Capitalism campaign and its "heavy, belabored" propaganda, encouraging a less deterministic approach that entrusted visitors to formulate their own positive views of the United States.[31] A second advisory panel concurred. The Cambridge Study Group, composed of USIA officials and academics from the Massachusetts Institute of Technology, convened a brainstorming session devoted to modernizing U.S. cultural diplomacy. With Peter Harnden as a participant, the group suggested exhibits emphasizing traditionally feminine roles like homemaking and fashion to counter negative stereotypes about American women. The USIA commissioned Harnden, assisted by Bernard Rudofsky, a frequent guest curator at MoMA, to devise installations for the Brussels pavilion. Harnden made the fateful decision to dispense with the usual American model kitchens, which he believed had lost impact both through overexposure at trade fairs and as the rising economic tide brought Western European household technology onto the market. Instead, the design team opted for a gallery of household objects displayed with playful panache. The proposal put Harnden and Rudofsky at odds with former Republican National Committee leader Katherine Graham Howard, appointed by Eisenhower as the U.S. exhibit's deputy commissioner. She implored Cullman, the event's commissioner general, to insist upon a more conventional installation:

> [T]he American kitchen has profound sociological and psychological implications. . . . It is one of the wonders of the world that Americans in every economic strata have kitchens with labor-saving devices which free the American woman from drudgery, which make the kitchen the heart of the home.

Even Khrushchev realized the broader portent of labor-saving household technology, Howard argued, citing his lingering visit to an

American kitchen display at a recent international trade fair, where he scrutinized the appliances.[32] Her pleas were ignored, paving the way for a litany of complaints that would make the Brussels commission Harnden's last major U.S. exhibition.

Cullman appointed a Committee of Selection and Procurement from Boston's Institute of Contemporary Art (ICA) to assemble household goods for display at Brussels. Composed of volunteers from the fields of industrial design, crafts, and interior decoration, the committee identified seven categories of products "peculiar to the American mode of living": mobility, portability, flexibility, disposability, outdoor living, toys, and the decentralized kitchen.[33] The committee's director, Joseph Carreiro, stated in a press release:

> We have made no effort to provide a complete story, or to convince or persuade anyone that our approach to living is the right one. We have tried through fragments, relationships, contrasts and the value revealed by the object, to point up our [national] diversity and uniqueness.[34]

After the sample collection's trial run at the ICA, Harnden and Rudofsky installed the full set of approximately six hundred objects on the mezzanine of Edward Durrell Stone's Brussels pavilion. Titled Islands for Living, the archipelago of clustered household objects was best known for its role in the pavilion's most popular event, a daily fashion spectacle. Before walking an atrium runway, European models in American outfits posed amid Harnden's Islands and their Eames leather and rosewood recliner, George Nelson desk, antique Shaker chair, and an assemblage of other domestic objects ranging from upscale to oddball.[35]

Although the fashion show attracted overflow crowds at every performance, critics in the United States bridled. Given the Soviet pavilion's emphasis on space-race triumphs, success at Brussels, they insisted, was not a simple popularity contest. Congressional detractors judged America's ready-to-wear triumph frivolous, and Harnden's wry installation pointless.[36] Islands for Living also attracted criticism from an alliance of U.S. home builders and housing officials who objected to its "Cinderella-type" portrayal of American life.[37] Far more serious, however, was the outrage ignited by Unfinished Work, a display presenting America's hot-button issues in problem-and-solution pairs: racial discrimination and desegregation, slums and urban renewal,

An "island" of contemporary furnishings at the Brussels World's Fair U.S. Pavilion, 1958. Photographer: Lucien Willems. Courtesy of the Ghent University Department of Architecture.

environmental degradation and conservation. Quarantined from the main pavilion and its showcase of American affluence, the Unfinished Work installation was housed in a jagged outbuilding that evoked the uncomfortable themes explored within. Photos of tenements in the shadow of the Capitol countered with images of new public housing and "a Negro couple in a modern, upper middle class kitchen in a Little Rock home" marked America's first international display of housing conditions at odds with the dream homes typically peddled at such exhibitions. Europeans were aware of America's ghettos, often from communist propaganda countering the claim of a "classless" U.S. democracy with sensational accounts of slums, poverty, segregation, and racial violence.[38] Soviet soft-power strategists understood that the global appeal of an American Way of Life could be neutralized, particularly in developing nations, by its portrayal as a "whites only" club. According to the testimony of American tour guides, Unfinished Work impressed European visitors as honest and courageous.[39] Segregationists like Democratic South Carolina Senator Olin Johnston, however, maintained that the display "could not have been more designed to reflect against the American nation if it had been made in Moscow by the Kremlin." Guards shooed press photographers away from Unfinished Work as USIA officials removed images showing black and white children playing together. Unconsoled, congressmen lobbied Eisenhower to close the exhibit entirely, which he did. Bruised pride and unrepentant racism had trumped effective cultural diplomacy, giving Soviet propagandists an uncontested field from which to attack.[40]

Unfinished Work and Islands for Living held difficult lessons for the USIA. Both had been favorably received by European audiences but were proclaimed fiascos by critics in the United States. A classified USIA document setting out the policy for a subsequent exhibition to be mounted in Moscow reflected the hard knocks taken in Brussels. It put an end to experiments with persuasion marked by "indirection," proposing "a clear thread of continuity leading the visitor in a logical fashion from one aspect of the American scene to another."[41] Adopting the Eisenhower administration's two-pronged approach to propaganda, exhibition development would proceed along twin tracks: one covert, the other concocted for media consumption. Critical planning decisions were to be reported to the public only "to the extent that this does not jeopardize the carrying out of the policy." The target audience for the Moscow show would be "university youths, people in cultural work and teaching, middle-level bureaucrats and skilled workers" considered by the USIA to be "potentially [the] most influential citizens of the Soviet Union." Displays highlighting "the unimpeded flow of diverse goods and ideas" would, it was hoped, increase "existing pressures tending in the long run toward a reorientation of the Soviet system in the direction of greater freedom."[42] To avoid snatching defeat from the jaws of victory as at Brussels, organizers of the American National Exhibition in Moscow would revert to tried-and-true ideological narratives, exert far greater control over information shared with the public, and rely far more heavily on corporate donations in the hope of circumventing budgetary constraints imposed by a Congress incapable of properly managing its soft-power investments.

AMERICA IN MOSCOW

In October 1958, one of America's acknowledged masters of midcentury modernism, George Nelson, was invited to Washington. His firm had been selected to coordinate the upcoming American National Exhibition in Moscow by Harold "Chad" McClellan, who had managed the Office of International Trade Fairs (OITF) as an assistant secretary of commerce, and Jack Masey, a USIA veteran. Nelson, with a gold medal already under his belt for the USIA exhibit at São Paulo's 1957

Biennial Exposition, was an inspired choice.[43] Advised of the federal offer, Nelson pondered its pros and cons:

> On the one hand, glamour plus realization that the exhibition could have an important effect on U.S.-USSR relations. On the other, the possibility of wrecking the office by taking on too large a project: the Government as a client, plus an impossible time schedule, offers fascinating possibilities of exposure to a scandal-loving press, with congressional investigation as possible jackpot.[44]

Glamour and historical significance defeated caution, and Nelson accepted the assignment.

After rejecting a series of inauspicious exhibition locations offered by Soviet authorities, McClellan secured a site in Sokol'niki Park, a northern Moscow suburb. Nelson gathered a brainstorming team that included Masey, Hollywood film director Billy Wilder, and the husband-and-wife design team of Charles and Ray Eames. During a marathon four-day meeting at the Eameses' iconic glass-and-steel house outside Los Angeles, the group developed a spatial and narrative sequence for the Moscow exhibition. Functioning as "a kind of 'information machine,'" a geodesic dome designed by Buckminster Fuller would open the visitor's tour. Inside, a multiscreen audiovisual spectacle produced by the Eames team would depict a typical week in the life of an American suburb.[45] The dramatized documentary was to establish credibility for the exhibition's ensuing representations of American abundance, as Nelson noted:

> An automobile, for instance, might be looked upon, if the Russians chose to do so, as a prototype made for display purposes. Twenty to thirty shots of the parking lots surrounding factories and shopping centers, traffic congestion in cities, and car movements on express highways could leave no possible doubt in the visitor's mind.[46]

Emerging from the hypnotic dazzle of the information dome, visitors would enter a glass-walled warehouse of goods. It was to be, according to Nelson, "a bazaar stuffed full of things, [the] idea being that consumer products represented one of the areas in which we are most effective, as well as one in which the Russians had already indicated they were most interested." His appraisal of Russian interest was confirmed weeks later

by Soviet first deputy premier Anastas Mikoyan during his diplomatic visit to the United States. Mikoyan and his entourage astounded suburban shoppers in White Oak, Maryland, who watched them make their way through aisles of packaged foods and household cleaners at the local Super Giant supermarket.[47] *This Week* magazine boasted, "He really went overboard for electric mixers, openers, fryers and other devices that make the American kitchen a complete contrast to its crude Russian counterpart," and quoted Mikoyan as exclaiming, "We have to free our housewives like you Americans! The Russian house-wife needs help!"[48] The American National Exhibition would serve up an assortment of household products to Soviet citizens, although Mikoyan's notion of help was not the intention.

A grueling round of bilateral negotiations finalized the terms of reciprocal U.S. and Soviet exhibitions slated for Manhattan and Moscow venues. A six-member Soviet delegation headed by Ivan Bolshakov, the USSR vice minister of foreign trade, scrutinized the U.S. proposal down to its details, challenging USIA plans to operate food concessions, distribute souvenirs and pamphlets, stage jazz concerts, and build fairground restrooms.[49] "I've been in many tough negotia-tions," McClellan noted, "and the moments put in by the Soviet team match the best."[50] The plot to seduce Soviet visitors with visions of household affluence may have been kept from the American press and public, but it was no secret to the Kremlin. A report to the Party Central Committee filed by its team of negotiators noted that "special attention will be paid to the demonstration of domestic appliances: electric kitchens, vacuum cleaners, refrigerators, air conditioners, etc."[51]

With Soviet permission finally granted, the scheme proposed by Nelson and company progressed to design development. "We have January, February, March and part of April to put together the most important of all United States exhibitions," Nelson jotted in his log-book.[52] He arranged consultations with Jane Fiske McCullough, who had analyzed previous OITF and USIA shows for the trade journal *Industrial Design,* and another authority on overseas exhibitions, Peter Harnden.[53] Of the thirty new employees Nelson hired, the most influ-ential was Philip George, a former associate at Harnden's Paris office, who was given responsibility for coordinating the exhibit and oversee-ing its assembly in Moscow.[54] Nelson's "bazaar" concept took the form of an enormous grid of steel shelving housed in a glass pavilion. His firm's design transformed the modular storage systems Nelson and other innovators had marketed for domestic use—a type of modernist furniture denounced as "formalist" by socialist realist ideologues—into a habitable, multistory structure accessed by stairways and mezzanine catwalks.[55] Visitors could literally wander the shelves to examine mer-chandise donated by hundreds of corporate sponsors, or gaze down from the elevated catwalks at demonstrations of American name-brand products. Given a relatively modest budget, Nelson stocked the pavil-ion with tried-and-true trade fair attractions. Barbara Sampson again

(facing page) American rush-hour imagery sprawls across seven screens in the audiovisual introduction produced by Charles Eames for the American National Exhibition in Moscow, shown within Buckmin-ster Fuller's domed pavilion. U.S. National Archives, Still Pictures Division, RG 306 PS-D Subjects, 70-2722.

conjured thousands of different meals from packaged products in her General Foods/Birds Eye demonstration kitchen.[56] Just as at Zagreb's Supermarket USA, a self-service shopping display revealed the source of the industrially processed ingredients used in Sampson's magic act. An RCA "Miracle Kitchen of the Future," previously displayed in 1958 at a trade fair in Milan, entertained visitors with high-tech enticements. A home workshop stocked with power tools for the do-it-yourselfer had debuted at a trade fair in Paris three years earlier, as had a Singer sewing machine demonstration. An RCA television studio, as first seen in West Berlin, represented American mass media and would unintentionally document the cold war's most famous soft-power showdown.[57] On a somewhat different note, Helena Rubenstein and Coiffures Americana sponsored beauty parlor makeovers for Soviet women selected from the audience. From labor-saving appliances to the chemistry of beauty, a grab bag of corporate presentations would combat Soviet technological triumphs with American consumer technology.

In designing the Moscow exhibition's model apartment—the narrative point of convergence for all goods and services on display—Nelson kept a far tighter reign. He envisioned the five-room residence, similar in concept to the unit shown in Zagreb, as that of an affluent family, with "children at play and the parents enjoying hi-fi, television and reading." The domestic stage set, designed by Lucia DeRespinis at

(facing page) Designers at George Nelson and Associates build a model of the modular display framework for the American National Exhibition in Moscow. Vitra Design Museum, Nelson Archive.

Watched by curious Soviet visitors, "demonstration lady" Barbara Sampson whips up a packaged cake mix in the General Foods/Birds Eye kitchen at the American National Exhibition in Moscow. U.S. National Archives, Still Pictures Division, RG 306 PS-D Subjects 59-14563.

Nelson's New York office, came with a model resident: the Russian-speaking wife of a U.S. press corps officer. She demonstrated the ease of laundry day with an automatic washer, answered visitor questions, and squelched comments by Party-line skeptics, such as "Isn't it true that rats bite your babies?"[58] Many of the furnishings were Herman Miller products—no surprise, given Nelson's rise to glory as the firm's design impresario—but the apartment interior also displayed the output of a virtual honor roll of American designers, including Florence Knoll, Paul McCobb, and Edward Wormley.[59] "We are assuming that the couple has pretty sophisticated taste and a pretty good income," Nelson remarked, estimating the model family's annual income at about $12,000—in 1959, over twice the national average.[60] Finding a single item from this sterling collection of midcentury modernism in the average U.S. home, much less the complete collection, would have been just as atypical.

A second American model home in Moscow conveyed a middle-of-the-middle-class life on the nation's suburban frontier, a display almost certainly included to rectify its omission at the Brussels fair.[61] Herbert Sadkin of All-State Properties, a Long Island developer of bedroom communities for Manhattan commuters, answered the USIA call for donations before Nelson and Masey were able to secure a home with better design credentials.[62] The All-State prefab, in comparison with the model apartment, reflected "less advanced taste," according to

Soviet visitors crowd an aisle of a model super-market display at the American National Exhibition in Moscow. U.S. National Archives, Still Pictures Division, RG 306 PS-D Subjects 59-14567.

Nelson, but was meant to display more affordable furnishings.[63] Exhibition organizers portrayed the home as belonging to "the Browns," a typical (albeit fictional) American family. Interior appointments, selected and donated by the New York headquarters of the Macy's department store chain, were budgeted at $5,000 to prove that the All-State home was no "privilegentsia" set piece.[64] Pale blue wall-to-wall carpeting and contemporary oil-finished walnut furniture, a closet filled with colorful towels and linens, and the consumer electronics said to be "indigenous to almost every modern American home" provided a sampler of affluence for the masses.[65]

Differences in press coverage launched the two model residences into divergent historical trajectories. Months before opening day, the Soviet news agency TASS derided the exhibition's "allegedly typical"

The apartment kitchen, designed by Lucia DeRespinis, at the American National Exhibition in Moscow. U.S. National Archives, Still Pictures Division, RG 306 PS-B Subjects 59-4995.

model homes, ridiculing the notion that "the Pennsylvania miner or Indiana metal worker always comes home to an apartment with deep fitted carpets, and that the textile workers of New England all have huge television sets, expensive radios, record players and tape recorders, all in fine cabinets."[66] The fulmination was hypocritical, and Party leaders knew it. Soviet international exhibitions like the recent one in Brussels regularly displayed residential stage sets "containing many facilities otherwise reported existing only in top-level Russian homes," as noted in the *Washington Post*.[67] *New York Times* Moscow correspondent Max Frankel nearly lost his Soviet visa for reporting of the USSR's 1959 show at Manhattan's Colosseum:

> Many a Russian would agree with the one who expressed a desire to come to the New York exhibit to find out how he lives. . . .
> [It] strives for an image of abundance with an apartment that few Russians enjoy, with clothes and furs that are rarely seen, and with endless variations of television, radio, and recording equipment, cameras and binoculars that are not so easily obtained in such quality or range in Soviet stores.[68]

Reports filed years earlier by the Soviet housing delegation visiting the United States had informed Party leaders that suburban American homes were often occupied by a working-class family of average income.[69]

It was Nelson's cosmopolitan apartment, and not Sadkin's suburban prefab, that grossly misrepresented an average American lifestyle. However, the former went all but unmentioned in Soviet press coverage, while the latter was the subject of furious denunciation. The Long Island dream home attracted attack not only as a propaganda threat but also as a soft target. Media space devoted to criticism of Nelson's luxurious apartment would have generated implicit comparisons with the cramped and poorly equipped Soviet units churned out by Khrushchev's mass housing program. With its wood-framed walls, the American suburban prefab struck many Russian visitors as insubstantial and temporary in construction. It was easy to depict as a Potemkin village cottage, and more alien than Nelson's city apartment, with its Russian-speaking hostess who entertained drop-in guests while doing her household chores.

Soviet vitriol directed at the All-State home captured the attention of American journalists, politicians, and entrepreneurs, who proceeded to create the script for its place in cold war history. Returning from Moscow, Sadkin told reporters that Russian officials had been "persistently cynical" in their attitude toward his model home, given the "drab and crudely finished" nature of their own housing stock.[70] With the gauntlet dropped, American journalists rushed to defend the virtue of the suburban Long Island prefab with patriotic fervor. Newspapers ran headlines like "Average American Home Jolts Red Propaganda," "Look at Building Here, Red 'Doubters' Invited," and "Nothing to Fear but the Truth."[71] Meanwhile, Sadkin's generosity in donating and shipping the home's components and assembly crew to Moscow garnered a bonanza in free publicity. All-State properties and the R. H. Macy Company sent reproductions of their Moscow exhibition home on a cross-country victory lap, with showings in Long Island venues, Joplin, Missouri, and on the rooftop of Macy's San Francisco store.[72] Eclipsed in the celebration of America's suburban sweetheart was Nelson's Moscow apartment, outfitted with modernist panache and all but ignored by journalists and later historians of the cultural cold war. The unkindest cut of all came from the *Washington Post,* which referred to the impeccably appointed interior as that of a "motel apartment."[73] With the gutting of city centers across the United States in the name of "urban renewal" and the attendant flight of affluent residents and their capital to the surrounding suburbs, a metropolitan home, no matter how upscale, had lost its ability to represent the American Way of Life both in the nation's popular imagination and its mass media reflection.

TRIUMPHALISM REVISITED

For six steamy midsummer weeks in 1959, crowds of stalwart Russians braved long waits and a gauntlet of Party agitators to enter the American National Exhibition at Sokol'niki Park. Just as planners and designers had hoped, Soviet citizens were captivated by the American commodity spectacle. They sampled Pepsi-Cola, examined automobiles with rocket-fin tail lamps, applauded rock-and-roll dance routines at an elaborately staged fashion show, and gazing at the performer apparel, asked, "Please, comrade, where can we buy it?" They pocketed souvenirs—some distributed free of charge, others surreptitiously 'liberated.' American tour guides turned a blind eye as toys, paperback novels, mail-order catalogs, and packaged food products disappeared from displays. By disregarding the summer's epidemic of petty theft,

U.S. corporate sponsors quietly circumvented a Soviet contract enjoining them from distributing free samples of any product other than Pepsi. Muscovites swarmed through the All-State home's central gangway, an innovation suggested by Philip George. The bisected floor plan overcame the problem of processing throngs within tight domestic spaces and earned Sadkin's prefab the nickname "Splitnik" in American newspapers. The home's multiple bedrooms impressed Soviets accustomed to communal apartments, often shared with one family per bedroom.[74] In a guest book, a visitor wrote, "At the first opportunity I would buy such a house. Meanwhile I have no house and live in a rented apartment and pay 300 rubles. I earn 700 rubles a month."[75] Domestic appointments like the hi-fi cabinet and convertible sofa bed were complete novelties for Soviets, provoking disbelief that such pieces were within reach of a typical U.S. worker.[76] Voting for the most interesting home life exhibit, visitors cast 22 percent of the ballots for Splitnik, and 26 percent for the fair's kitchen appliances.[77] Among the scraps of paper slipped to the crew of Russian-speaking tour guides recruited from across the United States, one read, "If the exhibition represents the American way of life, then it is the American way of life that we should overtake." The compliment echoed a vow made by Khrushchev proclaiming communism's capacity to not only replicate capitalist abundance but also outstrip it.[78]

Soviet authorities mobilized a rapid response to America's subversive consumer paradise. In the weeks that followed, the Party Central Committee convened a Moscow trade fair to sell hard-to-find goods and introduce a host of new products.[79] American diplomats noted that the city's shops seemed better stocked than usual. In the wake of the U.S. exhibition, Soviet state retailers adopted installment-plan financing—a purchasing system previously unknown in the USSR but which fairground tour guides were forced to clarify in order to explain how American workers could afford expensive household durables.[80] Officials in Washington proclaimed the Moscow exhibition "probably the most productive single psychological effort ever launched by the U.S. in any communist country."[81]

The U.S. media portrayed the Moscow exhibition as an American triumph, providing a needed success for the USIA and an international springboard for Republican presidential contender Richard Nixon. In the famous Kitchen Debate, Nixon, gesturing toward Splitnik's gleaming collection of appliances, proceeded to explain to Khrushchev that

in situ, as had the nation's 1955 housing delegation. For the USSR to accrue maximum benefit from America's commodity spectacle, its intelligentsia would require preferential access. Ironically, the classified USIA policy of targeting the "more politically alert and potentially most influential citizens of the Soviet Union" suited the goals of not only the U.S. State Department but also the Party Central Committee.[104]

As American officials surmised, the Party had indeed gone to great lengths to minimize the exposure of average citizens to the U.S. propaganda initiative. Byzantine admissions procedures created enormous waits to enter the Sokol'niki Park compound. Using a classic bait-and-switch routine, planted agitators worked the long queues, badgering would-be fairgoers with the question, "Why bother with the American exhibit? Go to our own 300 meters away.... We've got better things to see and you don't need a ticket."[105] Nearby, a collection of temporary structures, coated in metallic paint imitating the anodized aluminum sheen of Buckminster Fuller's geodesic dome, housed a rival exhibition. Titled All for You, Soviet Man, it showcased displays on housing, medical services, and other hallmarks of socialist progress. Visitors could examine photographs of a compact Soviet electric kitchen, as featured in *Izvestia* on the U.S. exhibition's opening day, captioned, "Our kitchen is as good as the American one shown at the exhibition in Sokol'niki." Depictions of a *novostroiki* apartment furnished "with taste, with a knowledge of the demands of our people" rounded out the glimpse of domestic artifacts plucked from a Soviet future.[106] Leslie Brady, counselor for cultural affairs at the American Embassy in Moscow, dismissed All for You, Soviet Man as a "ridiculous parody of the American exhibition": "Pretty girls demonstrate kitchen equipment and blood homogenizers. Glossy new cars stand resplendent on flower bedecked pedestals. A 'typical' apartment room displays tasteful Dutch furniture, etc., etc."[107] Brady was mistaken. The furnishings were not Western European imports but Soviet prototypes designed for the new apartment blocks under construction across the USSR.[108]

Fairground attendance and furniture provenance were not the only areas in which American and Soviet perceptions diverged. While Western journalists remained transfixed by Nixon and Khrushchev's verbal jousting in the All-State suburban home, Soviet newspapers focused on an alternate kitchen debate. Another dispute between the two leaders occurred at the Moscow exhibition's RCA Whirlpool

"Kitchen of the Future," a stage set outfitted with eye-popping appliances. Some were functioning prototypes, others mere dummies. A team of model housewives, headed by a Russian-speaking Ukrainian American, Anne Sonopol Anderson, demonstrated all of the appliances as if they actually worked. Created to promote the Whirlpool brand within the United States, RCA's display of smoke-and-mirrors miracles debuted in 1956. American audience response was so enthusiastic that the USIA drafted the futuristic kitchen into overseas service, amazing trade fair visitors in Germany, Italy, Yugoslavia, and Poland before its engagement in Moscow. A working prototype of a microwave oven turned out "110 varieties of edibles ranging from frozen beef pies to chocolate cake mixes" before the eyes of Soviet visitors.[109] The room's visionary conveniences included an adjustable-height sink, "mood lighting" that changed from bluish on hot days to reddish on cold for the homemaker's "psychological benefit," a dishwasher that traveled an "electronic track" to the dining table and back, a robotic "mechanical maid" that emerged from its baseboard garage to wander the floor on mop and polish missions, and a push-button "planning center" with a closed-circuit television to monitor baby's nap.[110] Unlike the mute collection of electric appliances that had provided the backdrop for the other Kitchen Debate, the Kitchen of the Future was inhabited by a human subject embodying the ideals of U.S. commodity culture, as advertised by RCA. Whether they were worth disseminating abroad was debatable. USIA position papers recognized the peril of reinforcing the international stereotype summarized by a newspaper in the Philippines: "Americans live in a cultural wasteland, peopled with gadgets and frankfurters and atom bombs."[111] RCA's use of a human subject embodying precisely this critique of the American consumer galvanized the Soviet media, just as the East bloc was attempting to define its own proprietary ethos of socialist mass consumption.

Because the Kitchen of the Future provided a case study of excesses said to be intrinsic to capitalism, it was of far greater consequence to Soviets than Splitnik's sunshine-yellow kitchen, both as a springboard for propaganda and as a foil against which an alternate model of consumer citizenship could be proposed. Casting a skeptical gaze at the kitchen's appliances, Khrushchev asked Nixon, "Don't you have a machine that puts food in the mouth and pushes it down?" His tone quickly moved from sarcasm to reproach. "Many things you've shown us are interesting," he admonished, "but they are not needed in

life. They have no useful purpose." A number of Soviet citizens went further, contending that America's Kitchen of the Future was not only irrational but also antisocial. In a letter to the newspaper *Izvestia*, Marietta Shaginian, a novelist, criticized the RCA kitchen for being overscaled and overmechanized, and enslaving the housewife rather than liberating her.[112] In the exhibition's visitor book, an engineer wrote:

> In the "miracle kitchen" a woman is just as free as a bird in a cage. The "miracle kitchen" shown at the exhibition demonstrates America's latest work in the field of perfecting obsolete forms of everyday living which stultify women.[113]

Another visitor added, "Is it possible to consider kitchens and cosmetics a cult . . . ?"[114] Whether contributed spontaneously or planted as

Sitting at a push-button control panel, home economist Anne Sonopol Anderson is seen through the open shelving of the RCA/Whirlpool Miracle Kitchen at the American National Exhibition in Moscow. Library of Congress, Prints and Photographs Division, *Look* Collection, Job 59-8225, LC-L917-59-8225-1.

propaganda, these remarks demonstrate the broad dissemination of Khrushchev's notion that excess—in domestic technology, just as in architectural ornament—was fetishistic and regressive, consuming resources without contributing to social purpose.

The Soviet economy was in no position to duplicate the kaleidoscopic selection of goods and mercurial shifts in taste associated with American consumer culture. Rather than attempting to replicate capitalist consumption, Soviet planned modernity proposed a more disciplined alternative. Accompanying the Party's 1959 proclamation that the USSR had embarked upon the "Advanced Construction of Communism," a new Five-Year Plan called for the introduction of appliances to "lighten the labor of housework." The electrification of Soviet housekeeping, as Susan Reid has observed, assumed a prominent role in the era's reformist ideology: "Machines in the home would not only make housework more efficient and liberate the housewife for active participation in political and economic life; regular use of new technology would also modernize users, inculcating the scientific consciousness requisite for the transition to communism."[115] Shortly after the close of the American National Exhibition, *Izvestia* surveyed the cornucopia of new Soviet consumer offerings, which included "washing machines, vacuum cleaners, electric floor polishers, and all kinds of kitchen machines for paring vegetables, beating egg whites and who knows what else. . . ."[116] The United States had shown analogous goods in its fairground pavilion, eliciting approval in guest book comments along with a claim that these items soon would have Soviet counterparts: "Small articles for everyday living are good, but we shall have them too," wrote an exhibition guest. "Apparently, the desire was to stun us only with these small articles. But ten years more and we will leave you behind."[117] Rather than the baroque extravagances of a proclaimed miracle kitchen, it was modest household technology that Party leaders had intended Soviet managerial cadres to inspect and reproduce after attending America's consumer goods spectacle in Moscow, a mode of technology transfer almost as effective as a transatlantic study tour (and far cheaper to arrange).

Over 2.5 million Soviet citizens visited the American National Exhibition in Moscow during its six-week run. U.S. officials observed that the four kitchens on display "were jammed with admiring Soviet women from morning until night. Even after the lights went out at night, they stood near the kitchens asking questions of demonstrators."[118]

On a final, unscheduled visit, Khrushchev ignored the throngs behind him, declaring, "Our people are not really interested in your exhibition."[119] One month later, during a first visit to the United States, his conflicting expressions of disdain and envy resurfaced. Beset by insecurity, the Soviet premier relied on diplomatic aides to investigate the surroundings and brief him on their findings. He refused to display curiosity or wonder when experiencing America firsthand, although he did express horror at the sight of rush-hour traffic jamming a highway during a helicopter flight with Eisenhower over Washington's suburbs—the real-life version of a virtual experience offered by the Eameses' seven-screen show in Sokol'niki Park.[120] As a boast of Soviet space race supremacy, Khrushchev presented the American president with a replica of the banner a Soviet vehicle had dropped on the moon just that week. But a different race piqued Khrushchev's competitive streak, as revealed in a brusque toast at a state dinner: "It is true that you are richer than we are at present. But tomorrow we will be as rich as you are. The next day? Even richer!"[121] His boast echoed one made to Nixon at the opening of the American National Exhibition: "In another seven years we will be on the same level as America. When we catch up with you, while passing you by we will wave to you."[122] Published in the USSR under the headline "We Will Overtake America!" Khrushchev's address revealed that a "politics of envy" had infected Soviet planning.[123]

Khrushchev's vow to beat the United States at its own game of consumer affluence represented the metastasis of an earlier and far more limited goal of surpassing American productivity. In 1955, a Soviet agricultural delegation visiting the U.S. Midwest had reported, "That which the Americans have taken decades to achieve we can manage to do in just a few years." Khrushchev pledged to surpass the United States in per capita production of meat, milk, and butter two years later, mocking economists who insisted that his goal could not be reached before 1975. These so-called experts had ignored the catalytic influence of socialist ideology upon human productivity, Khrushchev explained. He set 1960 as the date by which Soviet consumption, in the alimentary sense, would outstrip its American counterpart.[124] Escalation of the contest to other commodities followed suit. The Seven-Year Plan for 1959–65 pledged that the USSR would outdistance the West in productivity measures across the board. Industrial productivity would rise by 80 percent, despite the introduction of a seven-hour workday.[125] By 1980 certain basic consumer goods would be distributed free of charge.

Abundance for all, according to the USSR's Third Party Program, ratified in 1961, was a precondition for the full transition to communism, which would occur by 1980. This irrational exuberance contradicted the Party's concurrent goal of inventing an alternative commodity culture based on temperance. Soviet bloc citizens were being encouraged to embrace consumer discipline and simultaneously to imagine their homeland achieving parity with the West before overtaking it, a paradox neither addressed by Khrushchev nor recognized for its potentially destabilizing consequences.

WIR SCHAFFEN DAS BEISPIEL
für ein besseres Leben

ALLE KRAFT FÜR DIE LÖSUNG DER ÖKONOMISCHEN HAUPTAUFGABE

Consuming Socialism

In the dawning years of Khrushchev's Thaw, portents of a post-Stalinist citizen—the socialist mass-consumer—came to light. A descendant of the cultured proletarian of socialist realist pedigree, this novel subjectivity was the product of an international coproduction involving the East bloc. An early sighting reported in the East German advertising journal *Neue Werbung* occurred in the Czech city of Pilsen, which like East Berlin had witnessed a worker's uprising in June 1953. Four years later, a downtown department store staged a "showcase window pantomime" titled A Day at Home. This "new form of socialist advertising" employing live subjects was said to be "a realistic portrayal of a household day demonstrating an extensive assortment of products through a sequence of entertaining scenes." A male fashion model, two regional stage actresses, and three local children portrayed a family of modern consumers residing behind storefront windows. Sidewalk spectators watched as the model family demonstrated newly available appliances on a set depicting an unusually well-provisioned home. An offstage narrator lauded the products seen in use; loudspeakers carried his patter to crowds outside. A Day at Home, according to its sponsors, offered a lesson in "tasteful home furnishing." It was received by Czech audiences with "great interest," just as an analogous dream home had captivated crowds in divided Berlin five years earlier.[1] U.S. propagandists had staged their affluent household fantasy with a very different goal: to alienate socialist citizens from centrally planned privation. Among the uncanny parallels between the MSA's We're Building a Better Life exhibit and Pilsen's A Day at Home, the most apparent was the strategy of putting "consumers themselves in the store showcase, thereby turning them into objects of consumption and observation," in the words of historian Katherine Pence.[2] A Day at Home heralded a new era. An absence of objects, rather than the presence of socialist realist culture, would define the real-and-existing socialist home.

Despite similarities in exhibition strategy, We're Building a Better Life and A Day at Home showcased divergent approaches to product design. In Pilsen, roses bloomed across the surfaces of cups and saucers, florid upholstery covered bloated easy chairs, and appliances reminiscent of shop tools populated kitchen counters. That would soon change, however. In the late-1950s, Soviet and Eastern European designers jettisoned socialist realist cultural politics to restore modernism's socialist

(facing page) A 1959 poster for East Germany's "Main Economic Task" depicts an unhappy West German worker contributing to the production of atomic bombs *(left),* while his smiling East German counterpart stacks consumer goods beside a tranquil socialist family. The caption states, "We create the example for a better life." Deutsches Historisches Museum, Bildarchiv, P94/344.

Actors portray a modern consumer household for A Day at Home, a storefront exhibition staged in Pilsen (Plsen), Czechoslovakia, in 1957. *Neue Werbung* 4, no. 4 (April 1957).

credentials. Taste professionals aspired to achieve "world-class" (*Weltniveau*) standards in household design. Economists hoped that a new generation of contemporary consumer goods would encourage export sales of East bloc products, providing the hard currency needed for strategic Western imports. The construct of world-class design presumed a global marketplace, dismantling the Stalinist ideal of economic and cultural autarky. It also opened a portal to the West, inviting socialist citizens to imagine themselves on a convergence course with capitalist consumers, a notion as appealing as it was illusive. Rather than defining an emergent socialist modernity, "world-class" design and the stuttering attempts made to achieve it affirmed the instability of East bloc socialism as a historical formation.

THE REHABILITATION OF MODERNISM

In June 1957, USIA officials at the Poznan trade fair breached the iron curtain with a model home. Weeks earlier, the Bauakademie Research Institute for Interior Architecture had celebrated a similar achievement in the opposite direction. At the Munich exhibition How Does Europe Live Today? (Wie wohnt Europa heute?), sleek interiors designed in Belgium, Denmark, the Netherlands, Sweden, Switzerland, and West Germany were joined by an East German model apartment. With its open layout and contemporary furnishings, it pleased crowds and critics alike. A West German journal reported, "What was shown [by East Germany] in Munich was remarkable throughout, in the sense of a European standard: still somewhat timid and unsure in part, but obviously along the best route to the style of living that we in the German realism, Michel subtly redefined notions like formalism and national tradition in ways that were compatible with modernism. Because the resultant body of design theory remained built on Stalinist foundations, its critique was limited to oblique references, an epistemological weakness that, in terms of Party coexistence, was a *Realpolitik* strength.

The complexity of recycling antimodernist discourse in defense of modernism is evident in Michel's 1957 essay "Tradition or Novelty?" Starting from the familiar premise of capitalist commodity exchange as a corrupting influence, he condemned nineteenth-century profiteers and their flood of tawdry mass-produced novelties for the extinction of aesthetically virtuous domestic objects. However, in Michel's retelling of this socialist realist origin myth, the lost golden age was not neoclassical but vernacular. The simple forms and honest materials of preindustrial craft constituted the true East German tradition, according to Michel. His redirection of Stalinism's heritage fetish provided national roots for modernism while avoiding any mention of the Bauhaus, which in East Germany remained a politically ambiguous subject until the 1970s.[20] Michel also redefined beauty—a pivotal socialist realist construct—as the middle ground between ornamental excess and asceticism:

Model 53693 molded plywood armchair by Selman Selmanagič and a modular Model 602 cabinet by Franz Ehrlich, both manufactured by the Hellerau Werkstätten and introduced in 1957. *wie richte ich meine wohnung an?* (Leipzig: VEB Fachbuchverlag, 1961).

> One should not speak in favor of the primitive, functionalism, or Constructivism—however, one can invest purpose with grace. Between the superfluousness of . . . the dusty, gilded, and over-decorated "Baroque" porcelain service . . . and the penury of the battered, enameled steel pitcher, lies the purposeful beauty of household objects, reliant neither on pretense, invented form, nor rich decoration.[21]

According to Michel, "quality," "sobriety," and "appropriateness" would characterize a new generation of East German household objects. Echoing Werkbund arguments made a decade earlier, he declared the products of this new material culture crucial to the healthy development of postwar society:[22]

> Hand in hand with the sheer material harm of purchasing inferior manufactured goods comes a spiritual impact damaging to human character. The soulless and mendacious kitsch of our consumer goods exerts an influence as negative as that of inferior films and base literature, which are understandably countered through censorship.[23]

Convergence with the West was skin deep. Michel's commendation of censorship (presumably extending to the realm of household design) reveals the continuity with Stalinism's repression of cultural deviance that lurked beneath the streamlined surfaces of a socialist New Look.

A new magazine, *Kultur im Heim* (Culture at Home), popularized modernist home design in East Germany. The journal traced its origins to a March 1956 symposium sponsored by the Kulturbund (Cultural League), a voluntary association modeled on Soviet precedent and used as a "transmission belt" to relay Party initiatives to the public.[24] Its advisory panel proposed the founding of a "journal of housing culture" advancing national campaigns "to eliminate kitsch and petty-bourgeois habits from the homes of our citizens."[25] The recommendation was approved at the SED Third Party Conference. The editors of *Kultur im Heim* soon promised to provide the missing feedback link between socialist manufacturers and shoppers, thus breaking the "vicious circle" of East German retailing: shelves filled with unwanted products, made by firms whose designers ignored the needs of consumers, who in turn recoiled from the selection of available goods, leaving shop shelves filled with unwanted products. "If [the linkage] functions correctly, it modernism proclaimed loftier aspirations for "economic life . . . and human consciousness," according to *Kultur im Heim*.[29] The magazine's editors advocated pale colors and light veneers, portraying the shift in taste away from dark tones in Manichaean terms. They scolded East German retailers for consigning to "the darkest corner of the show-room" modern furnishings that were "optimistic" and "light in mood."[30] "Our times have shaped new people, and their consciousness grows and changes daily," another editorial proclaimed. "Life and living prefer-ences have also changed. From the conformist persuasions of a hypo-critical and unreal period, clear and optimistic living requirements emerge."[31] Modernism had emancipated socialist society from atavisms that were either petty bourgeois or Stalinist, depending on the reading.

WORLD-CLASS DESIGN

The SED Third Party Conference of 1956 exhorted East German industrial managers to "attain and overtake world-class technology standards." "Cultural Heritage and the World Class Standard," a *Kultur im Heim* article by the Bauakademie's Peter Bergner, transposed the Party mandate to household design. A quest for "the modern" implied adopting Western technology, he clarified, but not "the Western world's characteristic style."[32] Pictorials in *Kultur im Heim* carried a different message. Features like "International Review" and "Furniture from around the World" showed goods from West Germany, Sweden, Den-mark, Finland, Austria, England, and Japan. In stoking domestic desire for such products, editors hoped to goad East German industries to produce export-quality products—the overarching goal of the SED campaign. An internal Bauakademie memorandum declared that the "unsatisfactory model quality, on average, of furniture produced in the GDR" occurred because production was "almost never subjected to a serious comparison with the international benchmark."[33] "If we improve the quality of our furnishings," the editors of *Kultur im Heim* reasoned, "the balance of trade improves, as well as the standard of living of all workers—and with it, the cultural level of our citizens."[34] Modernist enlightenment and economic growth would go hand in hand—or so the theory went.

To reorient designers to international standards, the Bauakademie began sponsoring pilgrimages to West Germany, Switzerland, Denmark, and Sweden, where delegation members would collect data on the design and production of housewares.[35] The information was forwarded to the Ministry of Light Industry for analysis, then disseminated to East German manufacturers.[36] The continent's most spectacular exhibit of world-class home design, however, awaited at a site just two subway stops from the Bauakademie's East Berlin headquarters. West Berlin's International Building Exposition (Internationale Bau-Austellung) of 1957, known by the acronym Interbau, commissioned architects from Austria, Brazil, Denmark, England, Finland, France, Israel, Italy, Sweden, Switzerland, the United States, and West Germany to design a "city of tomorrow" displaying "the free world's technology and creative strength in its wide variety of forms."[37] West Berlin mayor Otto Suhr proclaimed that Interbau revealed "a new dwelling order" of nations "more allied to each other with respect to their aspirations for living than we ever realized," a comment evoking the Atlanticist lifestyle shown five years earlier at We're Building a Better Life.[38] Over the course of those five years, the Marshall Plan vision of barrier-free trade had crystallized as the European Common Market. The Treaty of Rome, endorsed in March 1957, eliminated tariffs between signatory nations, an economic development with potential consequences for household design. In "Design for European Trade," Peter Tenant of the Federation of British Industries declared that "six countries combining in one market and one area of production" would mean increased attention to export criteria.[39] With economic integration creating new conditions for European trade, East German officials were not alone in their quest for "world-class" consumer products.

Interbau marked a turning point in postwar reconstruction. West Germany's Second Housing Law of 1956 had abandoned the legislated egalitarianism of its predecessor.[40] The nation's flourishing advertising industry pitched yesterday's luxuries as today's necessities. Home budgets, no longer dominated by basics like food and clothing, could splash out on household durables like televisions and refrigerators. Installment purchases, once discredited as irresponsible, had become an accepted way of bridging the gap between desire and income.[41] West Germans, having largely satisfied and surpassed their fundamental needs, "consumed in order to achieve a more intangible result," as Ingrid Schenk notes.[42] Interbau trumpeted the nation's change in fortunes. One visitor recalled feeling so inspired by the model interiors that she quickly replaced her furniture with fresh pieces from Finland and Denmark, adding new Italian drapes and an assortment of American gadgets for the kitchen.[43] West Germany's economic miracle was making itself at home.

For those who knew where to look, Interbau revealed traces of a bygone propaganda campaign that, while popularizing America's household technology, had failed to improve the nation's cultural standing. In 1950, 58 percent of West Germans surveyed believed that

The "Giraffe" tower block designed by Klaus Müller-Rehm and Gerhard Siegmann looms over ticket booths and an international collection of banners at the 1957 Interbau housing exhibition in West Berlin. Landesbildstelle, Berlin.

(facing page) A model living room in the Werkbund's "City of the Future" Pavilion at the 1957 Interbau housing exhibition in West Berlin features furnishings by Knoll International, including Model 31 lounge chairs and sofa grouped around a T-angle coffee table, all by Florence Knoll; a "Womb" chair by Eero Saarinen; and, on the porch, a Butterfly chair by Hardoy, Kurchan, and Bonet. A Braun phonograph, designed by Hans Gugelot and Dieter Rams at the Ulm HfG, is displayed on the credenza. Karl Otto Archive, Akademie der Künste, Berlin.

Americans could teach them nothing about culture. Six years later, the proportion had risen to 70 percent.[44] American materialism, however, had provided lessons worth learning. The compact galley kitchens found throughout Interbau's model apartments were compared by a West German journalist to "the cooking niches and bar kitchens . . . that have proliferated first and foremost in the U.S., where the overwhelming majority of city dwellers quickly prepare meals from canned ingredients."[45] Another correspondent mused that "when deep-freeze menus are no longer limited to the freezers in commercial establishments and aircraft, then perhaps will the housewife of today's fantasy become

tomorrow's reality"—a notion advanced in U.S. exhibitions ranging from the Caravan of Modern Food Service to Supermarket USA.[46]

Proposals to display an American model kitchen at Interbau were turned down by the committee assembled to plan America's contribution.[47] With the United States bowing out of its traditional role as a purveyor of dream kitchens, the Werkbund took up the task. Its pavilion featured a model home by Vera Meyer-Waldeck designed around a great room surrounded with proprietary nooks for individual family members. Rather than marginalizing the housewife in an isolated kitchen, Meyer-Waldeck placed her at a central, freestanding hearth combining open fireplace, charcoal grill, and electric cooktop. Because "tomorrow's meal preparation will consist more of thawing than cooking," Meyer-Waldeck placed the cooktop on wheels, allowing the housewife to serve convenience foods wherever might be needed.[48] The ideal of nomadic domesticity advanced a decade earlier in Berlin by Alix Rohde-Liebenau had come full circle. Rather than eliminating the bourgeois practice of cooking as "a hobby, a pastime like playing the flute," Meyer-Waldeck's "wheeled camp kitchen" allowed the postwar family to pursue its migratory destiny as a leisure collective.

Interbau home interiors, seen by nearly one million visitors, displayed a remarkable homogeneity of style. Knoll International sponsored two model apartments, but its furnishings could be found throughout the exhibition. Products designed at Ulm's HfG, from Braun radios to record players and the modular shelving they perched upon, were also standard Interbau fare.[49] Although International Style modernism had conquered the design community, the same could not be said of West German consumers. A national survey conducted in 1957 found that only 13 percent of respondents favored Interbau's featured design mode. With a 51 percent approval rating, the plush 1930s "Gelsenkirchener Baroque" (named after a manufacturer in the town of Gelsenkirchen) was the most popular style. Middle-of-the-road decor took second place with 31 percent.[50] Marshall Plan and MSA assumptions that border-free trade implied a unitary product style had been profoundly misguided. As the miracle economy gained momentum, it did so without the benefit of a hegemonic modernist aesthetic. Traditional revival styles still held appeal, and not just in their nation of origin. "It is a sad fact that some of the worst examples of British goods find a ready market across the North Sea and the Channel, because for so many Continentals the pseudo-Jacobian, Byzantine and Gothic won't be long before your wishes are fulfilled," the magazine's editors pledged.[26]

Kultur im Heim taught readers to distinguish socialist modernism from its capitalist counterpart: space-age kitsch conforming to "the latest rage" but designed only to increase profit through planned obsolescence:

> This includes the epidemic of shrill, shrieking colors that have come into fashion; . . . the wild atomic curves of black area rugs; giant acid-green triangles on draperies; the bizarre and senseless forms of lamps, bowls, vases, etc. that are so often praised as being especially modern. There certainly are places in the world where the meaningless is modern, but the German Democratic Republic is not one of them.[27]

This caricature of West German design focused on a populist variant, called the Nierentisch style after its namesake object: the biomorphic, "kidney-shaped" coffee table. Exuberantly novel, derided even by Western critics as "applied Kandinsky," Nierentisch modernism betrayed the escapism of "a culture desperately seeking to rid itself of the past and to live *à la Picasso*," in Paul Betts's memorable formulation.[28] Socialist

The "Nierentisch" curves of a Knoll Butterfly chair are echoed by a bulbous armchair and an amoebic drapery print in a Werkbund showroom, 1963. Werkbund Archiv e.V.— Museum der Dinge, ABD 7-113/53.

unfortunate retail outcomes, including so-called shelf-warmers—products so undesirable, given their price, that they could not be sold—and what Polish shoppers termed *brakorobstwo*, a neologism applied to unused items that were unusable as sold. Socialism's byzantine regulatory system—negotiated by the Party, ministries, and manufacturers—set retail prices as determined by political expediency and complex systems of subsidy. Campaigns to improve the design and quality of goods, rationalize pricing, and develop efficient and courteous retailing were, in effect, cumbersome attempts to reverse engineer into socialism the qualities required for most market-driven businesses to survive.[75] East bloc shoppers may have been inured to their hardscrabble existence as retail hunters and gatherers, but having been invited to see themselves, rather than state industries, as socialism's sovereign consumers, the nation's lackluster economic performance—showcased by self-service retailing—helped disabuse any lingering faith in the Party's central planning skills.

The modular concrete residential districts built throughout the People's Republics also helped construct socialism's new consumer-citizen. The move into a new apartment unit, as historian Steven Harris notes, "was the first step many [socialist] citizens took in acquiring objects of mass consumption for the home, identifying themselves as consumers . . . and by extension comparing themselves with the wider consumer culture outside the Soviet Union and Soviet Bloc."[76] Standards for the new generation of housing blocks were set at the 1958 Union of International Architects' conference in Moscow. Multistory buildings assembled from industrially produced concrete panels were prescribed for urban peripheries; inner-city development was also a possibility, if accompanied by sweeping demolition to give heavy construction equipment free reign.[77] In East Germany, the SED's Main Economic Task called for building one hundred thousand new units per year through 1965.[78] Homemaking magazines and books showed flats furnished in skeletal wood furnishings of a style reminiscent of Nordic modernism. The similarity was by no means surprising, according to an East German design critic, since Scandinavia had successfully absorbed "the ideas of 'new dwelling' ('*neues Wohnen*') . . . developed in Germany during the 'Twenties.'"[79] According to this argument, the resemblance to foreign sources indicated a recovery of German tradition, not mimicry.

Dresden's Fourth German Art Exhibition, held in 1959, raised the ante for socialist consumption with television prototypes designed by

The "Atelier" model television, designed by Martin Kelm while still a graduate student, and subsequently put into production by the VEG Rafena Werke in 1957. Heinz Hirdina, *Gestalten für die Serie. Design in der DDR 1949–1985*. Photographer: Franziska Adebahr.

Martin Kelm, a former Mart Stam protégé, which received "justified applause from visitors." In his review of the exhibition, Horst Michel cited Marx (with a parenthetical amendment) to claim that the production of modern, tasteful furnishings presaged the creation of socialism's new citizens:

> Karl Marx says: "an object of art creates a public that has artistic taste and is able to enjoy beauty—and the same can be said of any other (artistically designed) product. Production accordingly produces not only an object for the subject, but also a subject for the object." [80]

Designers, then, had a pivotal role to play in shaping socialist consciousness. Michel's assertion gave them a renewed sense of self-importance and provided ammunition for their "battle for influence over the material environment of everyday life," as Susan Reid has noted of Soviet modernists.[81]

By the decade's end, however, plans to nurture an affluent socialist mass-consumer faltered as the East German economy stalled. A campaign to collectivize agriculture produced a harvest of food shortages. As market disruptions rippled outward, shoes, soap powder, even underwear vanished from stores.[82] Waiting lists ranged from two or three years for delivery of a television, to five for a refrigerator.[83] Residential construction fell far short of targets, with the Party blaming builders for their "lack of a clear socialist perspective." Whatever the reasons for failure, prospects for those seeking housing were grim. A 1961 survey by the Party Central Committee Council on Construction revealed that one-third of the nation's dwellings remained without running water, the same proportion shared toilet facilities with other units, and one out of ten units warranted demolition due to the severity of disrepair.[84] Another set of statistics was even more alarming. Every month in 1960, departures of citizens heading off for a new life in the West showed an increase of more than 100 percent over the same month in 1959.[85] East Germany was hemorrhaging its proletariat, especially skilled laborers. Given the West's booming economy and insatiable job market, many found it simpler to relocate than to remain.

On 3 August 1961, Ulbricht flew to Moscow for a secret meeting in Moscow. Khrushchev reluctantly approved a plan that would resolve East Germany's border problem but that would also confirm the SED's loss of popular support.[86] At the stroke of midnight on 13 August 1961, military commanders in East Berlin received instructions to rouse their troops and proceed to the border. The first Berlin wall consisted of soldiers and policemen standing side by side at two-meter intervals, backs to the east. Within hours the human wall was replaced by one built of posts and barbed wire. Three days later, masons began building a concrete divider. Adjacent houses were bricked shut and later demolished. Trip wires, lacerating traps, attack dogs, and watchtowers eventually sprouted along the cleared strip of urban land.[87] An official guide to East German architecture described the wall as a noteworthy piece of infrastructure: "The protective measures establish reliable conditions for the quick and successful economic, political and cultural development of the GDR and its capital city. It opens a new chapter in German history."[88] Ulbricht's "anti-Fascist protection wall" ended the nation's spontaneous evacuation, safeguarding the economy from a wholesale loss of labor and affording the Party a last chance to construct modern socialism.

"OVERTAKING WITHOUT CATCHING UP"

Two months after the wall sealed East Germany's socialist ecosystem, a Bauakademie design collective set out to revolutionize the nation's mass-housing program. Concrete panel apartment construction had begun three years earlier, but floor plans remained archaic, with all rooms opening off a windowless corridor. Charged with designing a cost-effective solution to the housing crisis, the collective proposed a new residential prototype, the P2, that reduced the size of the standard two-and-one-half room, four-person dwelling to 55 square meters (592 square feet). This feat of compression was accomplished by merging living and dining into a single open area and moving an adjacent galley kitchen far from exterior walls and windows, a formula advanced at Interbau four years earlier and roundly dismissed by the Bauakademie. Its apologists were forced to retract the propaganda of a previous decade, announcing, "A widely shared but mistaken idea is that, with the expanding construction of socialism, apartment size must also grow."[89] Horst Michel proclaimed, "Compactness, condensation of the essential does not imply impoverishment: quite the contrary—through the elimination of useless padding, value is added."[90] *Kultur im Heim* informed readers that in Sweden, where the smallest apartments were about the same size as P2 units, "mass-housing is built no larger than ours."[91] As formerly maligned *Existenzminimum* ideas were dusted off for real-and-existing socialist needs, the Party, taste professionals, and state media agreed: learning to think small was a big part of East German "world-class" design.

Completion of the first P2 prototype in East Berlin's Lichtenberg district prompted yet another Bauakademie model home show and domestic design conference. The new life–new dwelling (neues leben–neues wohnen) exhibition exuded modernity, from its lower-case title

to an open house featuring fifteen model units outfitted to "the international standard."[92] Interiors revealed the socialist rehabilitation of modular storage (*Anbaumöbeln*), a furniture type once so reviled that even its name had been synonymous with formalist excess. Times had changed. The P2's wall-mounted cabinets provided storage space for the new emblems of proletarian prosperity: "technical devices and hardware, such as the radio, phonograph, audio tape system, television, and film and slide projectors."[93] Furnishings were functional and rationally constructed, yet "free from modernistic effects."[94] "Considered all in all," Michel effused, "the new living–new dwelling exhibition demonstrates the progress, the great turning point, that has come to pass in the German Democratic Republic's style of living."[95]

The public seemed to agree. More than thirty-two thousand visitors, including a handful from West Berlin, toured the model units. One in a hundred recorded their impressions in the show's guest book. Most found the "apartments of the future" enchanting: "The exhibit shows how space can be put to better use than in the other [housing] types built in Berlin. I'd move into one of these beautiful apartments immediately." The compact kitchen, however, garnered several critical responses: "One can easily prepare a salad or mixed drinks in the little kitchen, but I think that a home-cooked dinner would leave it a mess." Built-in closets and drawers also raised eyebrows. "What is a family supposed to do with a complete bedroom suite and wardrobe when moving into such an apartment?" But the most common complaint stemmed from unrequited desire, plain and simple. "When will such furnishings finally appear on the market? When will officials in industry and retailing take into account the wishes and tastes of their customers?" "Once and for all, we want to put an end to being satiated only by exhibitions. We want the modern, rational way of life that is rightfully ours."[96] The project to cultivate an enlightened proletariat through the "demonstration effect" of socialist home exhibitions had become a finishing school for the disenfranchised. Prospects for consumer satisfaction seemed to recede as fast as home design made progress. The P2 prototype interior that received the greatest public acclaim, for example, was by a design collective associated with the Leipzig Trade Fair, an institution focused on export revenue, not domestic sales.[97] The national imperative to raise cash for strategic imports would force East German enthusiasts of "world-class design" to compete with foreign buyers wielding world-class currencies.[98]

(*facing page*) The P2 housing prototype in Berlin-Lichtenberg, designed by Wilfried Stallknecht, Achim Felz, and Herbert Kuschy. The building was the site of the new life–new dwelling (neues leben–neues wohnen) exhibition in 1962. Institut für Regionalentwicklung und Strukturplanung, Berlin-Erkner.

A three-day conference held in concert with new living–new dwelling assembled interior designers, architects, and furniture manufacturers from five East bloc nations. Ulbricht, whose presence at previous colloquiums had literally lent authority to the deliberations, was conspicuously absent. Delegates resolved that a "future socialist style" of housing would be international, involving a "radical standardization" of building parts. The same ideals would apply to furnishings: "the appointment of a dwelling is by no means a question of decoration, but rather an architectural task."[99] A "modular assembly system" (*Baukastensystem*) applied to furniture would "point the way toward design discipline . . . and distinguish itself fundamentally from the emphasis on individualism found in furnishings and interior design within capitalist nations."[100] Industrial production methods would reconstruct the designer as well, yielding the "furniture architect" (*Möbelarchitekt*), a title born during the conference proceedings.[101] Beneath the revolutionary rhetoric lay a thread of continuity. At an East German design conference of the previous decade (and cultural revolution), Hellerau's Franz Ehrlich had proposed a kit-of-parts approach allowing furnishings to be configured according to need, and was denounced as a formalist for his efforts.[102] The visitor who wrote, "Why not this ten years ago?" in the new living–new dwelling guest book hit the mark in more ways than she or he realized.

The model apartment interior designed by Horst Michel's design collective for the new life–new dwelling exhibition. SLUB/Deutsche Fotothek. Photographer: Friedrich Weimer, 1962 SLUB/DF 320995.

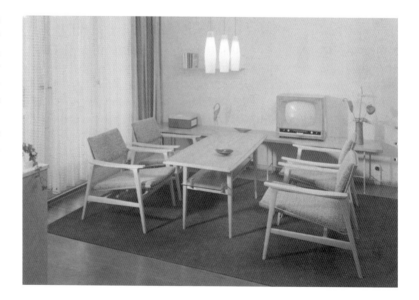

With modern interiors that would not have looked out of place at Interbau, new living–new dwelling seemed to announce the stylistic unification of East and West Germany. That impression would have been wrong, however. An ideological wall still divided the modern in its socialist guise, its functionalism officially characterized by "a clear and persuasive relation to mankind" and differentiated from the West's gratuitous use of "the 'modern' alone, solely formal in intended effect . . . pure charlatanism."[103] The claim that there were two German modernisms nearly indistinguishable in style, yet politically incompatible in content, was symptomatic of a late-socialist identity crisis. It was also expressed in the quixotic Party mandate *Überholen ohne Einzuholen* (literally "overtake without catching up"), which called for parity with the West without in any way emulating it. In adapting modernism to socialist ends, East bloc designers faced a similar impasse.[104] Photographic evidence of the dilemma can be found in an early East German guide to modernist home decor, published in 1961.[105] Its opening interior is a study outfitted with the new "world-class" furnishings and graced by a framed portrait of Karl Marx, heavily retouched to ensure reader recognition. Stripped of this socialist icon, the room's furnishings could easily have been mistaken for the offerings of any West

The opening illustration of an interior from an East German home decorating guide from 1961 shows a modern study displaying its socialist credentials with a conspicuously placed portrait of Karl Marx. *wie richte ich meine wohnung ein?*

German department store. As socialism adopted the design semiotics of its capitalist antipode, only an overdetermined identity statement would suffice in eliminating the resultant ambiguities.

STYLE AND INSTABILITY

Celebrating the official "conquest of late-bourgeois conceptions of art," Walter Ulbricht and over one thousand visiting elites opened Dresden's Fifth German Art Exhibition on 22 September 1962. Guiding the SED First Secretary through the Graphic and Applied Arts section, Horst Michel discovered himself having to defend the works on display. Three months later, Ulbricht issued his verdict in a public statement, which bears quoting at length:

> The color of the glassware there was grey. The color of curtains shown there was grey. . . . Certain "vases" were simple cylinders. One doesn't need a state-financed art institute for that. . . . Now, we understand that there are workers in the arts who want to advance standardization. . . . But here [in East Germany] we want rich color. And because most other countries also want the same, we need lively colors in glass made for export, so we can obtain good foreign currency sales. These issues have something to do with the battle against the Stalinist cult of personality. Some people think that, because we're against the Stalinist cult of personality, one has to grant freedom now for everything, including Western formalism and abstract art. No, we've said, that has nothing to do with Stalin. Stalin's view on the issue of socialist realism was incorrect, we know that. But that anyone would exploit the battle against the Stalinist cult of personality to smuggle formalism [into East Germany], that goes too far.[106]

"Left Behind by Life," an article by Karl-Heinz Hagen, the cultural editor of the Party newspaper *Neues Deutschland,* asserted that Dresden's "functional, industrial aesthetic" revealed "a politically illegitimate, West-oriented attitude on the part of its exponents."[107] A week later, the Cultural Commission of the Party Central Committee denounced "followers of the Bauhaus tradition" for their "ice-cold technics," "reduction of the color scale to merely black, white and grey tones," and "ongoing impoverishment of the applied arts."[108] Nearly a decade after Stalin's death, the color, form, and market viability of furnishings remained

The shift in East German modernism from skeletal asceticism to corpulent accumulation is illustrated in living room furnishings designed by Möbelkombinat Nord for display at Leipzig's fall 1974 trade fair. SLUB/Deutsche Fotothek. Photographer: Friedrich Weimer, 1974 SLUB/DF 752065.

a false front concealing economic stagnation. A 1989 report prepared by the Ministry of State Security, arguably four decades late, informed Party leaders that consumer goods were "increasingly becoming the basic criterion for the assessment of the attractiveness of socialism in comparison to capitalism."[121] At a crisis meeting of the Politburo, conducted as East German citizens flooded toward newly deregulated Western border crossings in Czechoslovakia, Hungary, and Poland, State Planning Commission Chairman Gerhard Schürer informed his colleagues: "Just to avoid further [national] indebtedness would mean lowering the standard of living for 1990 by around 25 percent to 30 percent, and would make the GDR ungovernable."[122] "There are poorer countries than the GDR with a much richer offering of goods in the stores," Schürer noted. "When people have a lot of money and can't buy the goods they want, they curse socialism."[123] The socialist command economy promising an equal distribution of wealth had proven incapable of eliminating periodic scarcity. As fantasized in Riesman's fictional "Nylon War," an unsustainable escalation of consumer desire, fueled by Western lifestyle comparisons at times explicitly promoted by Party leaders, bankrupted state socialism.[124]

Critical Masses

In 1966, two Soviet scientists, brothers Boris and Arkadi Strugatski, published the account of a catastrophic attempt to create "the universal consumer who desires everything." Their science fiction fantasy, *Monday Begins on Saturday*, takes place in a research compound located in Russia's far north. In the laboratory of Ambrosi Ambrusovitch Vibegallo, an "ideal man" gestates within a steel autoclave. Vibegallo describes his creation as "the model of our common ideal. . . . All of us, comrades, with due respect to us, are simply ciphers in comparison, because it desires such things as we cannot even conceive of."[1] A colleague, comrade Oira-Oira, fears that the release of a humanoid programmed with insatiable desire will pose hazards. "What happens when he consumes it all?" Vibegallo responds with disdain:

> What are you trying to say with your question, comrade Oira-Oira? That in the future of our scientific organization there will come a time of crisis, of regression, when our consumers will not have enough consumer products? That's not nice, comrade Oira-Oira![2]

Arrangements are made to decant the ideal man at an isolated test site. With the press ensconced behind protective barriers and cameras rolling to record the event, scientists open the autoclave by remote control. A glowing cloud shoots upward accompanied by a blast wave—not moving outward, as at an atomic bomb detonation, but inward, toward the ideal man. The roaring gust carries with it watches, wallets, wedding rings, cameras, boots, overcoats, necklaces, trousers, bottles of vodka, even Volga and Moskvich automobiles. The observers are saved from the same fate when Oira-Oira releases another laboratory creation brought along in case of an emergency: an evil djinn, the only entity capable of consuming the "universal consumer." As survivors pick through the wreckage and Vibegallo spouts his "demagogy about limitless and variegated needs," Oira-Oira mutters, "I told him a thousand times: You are programming a standard superegocentrist. He will gather up all the material goods he can lay his hands on, then . . . wrap himself in a cocoon and stop time."[3]

As cold war parody, *Monday Begins on Saturday* ranks with Riesman's "Nylon War" in prophetic accuracy. Both satires speculate about the role of consumption in deciding the fate of communism and

(facing page) Aleksandr Dmitrievich Romanychev, *By the Window*, 1968–71, oil on canvas. By the light of a window in a modern Soviet apartment block, a pregnant mother awaits her coming child, a member of the new generation of socialist consumer-citizens. Courtesy of Fieldstead and Company and The Museum of Russian Art, Minneapolis.

fantasize the deployment of material desire as an agent of destruction. Whereas Riesman imagines U.S. airdrops of household goods as the catalyst of subversion, the brothers Strugatski give credit where it is also due, depicting socialist consumption as a domestically engineered cataclysm. That possibility was foretold in a treasonous broadside seen posted in a Siberian city in December 1961: "You're a loudmouth, Khrushchev: where's that abundance you promised?"[4] Prescriptions for a socialist consumption regime were, in fact, marbled with contradictions. If Western appetites for commodities were pathologically inflamed by capitalist advertising, why would the USSR want to equal—and then surpass—the United States in measures of per capita consumption? How could Khrushchev's vow to "catch up" be reconciled with communism's reformist intentions?

Torn between promises of plenty and rationalizations for scarcity, the project to cultivate an enlightened socialist consumer instead became a finishing school for citizen alienation. The Khrushchev-era flats that Russians called "separate" apartments were the conflict's front line. Moving out of an ad hoc collective and into a proprietary housing unit gave residents new identities as socialist consumers, opportunities to become the "active engineers" of domestic modernization, and reason to compare their experiences with perceptions of "world-class" living standards outside the Soviet bloc.[5] Although domestic artifacts of the modern socialist home proliferated in magazines and public exhibitions, prospects for consumer satisfaction remained stuck in the future tense. Model apartment interiors presented to Muscovites at the 1961 exhibit Art into Life! provoked this visitor's book comment:

> Things done with great taste and very good. But as a whole, strange as it may sound, the exhibition leaves a painful impression of an organized mockery of the people. Do we still have to live in Potemkin villages from Catherine's time? . . . disgraceful, and again disgraceful. Simply so offensive it could make you weep![6]

A letter to the East German home journal *Kultur im Heim* regarding the publicity blitz promoting a new generation of "world-class" furnishings had this to say:

> I buy your magazine often. However, when I look through it . . . it seems to me that you don't live in this world. One sees very beautiful things there. . . . For most people, these home interiors

are an illusion. It seems to me that your world class exists only on paper (since its material foundation is, for most people, close to nil). . . . Please, don't answer from the perspective of the construction of socialism, giving yourselves an easy way out. . . . Drop your disgusting masquerade, which has no relation to reality.[7]

Rather than succumbing to America's Trojan house campaign, Party leaders had devised one of their own, with devastating consequences for public morale.

The conflicted project to create an East bloc analogue of the West's postwar consumer stimulated material desires and a sense of entitlement within an economy characterized by fluctuating shortages, destabilizing late-socialist societies. As Marshall Goldman, an expert on the Soviet economy, observed in a 1960 essay for the journal *Problems of Communism,*

> While life has materially improved for the Soviet citizen, there is every reason to believe that the increased supply of consumer goods has only whetted his appetite rather than satisfied his needs. The Russians have found that new apartments stimulate demand for new furniture, that new suits create a desire for new shoes. So goes the unending process of demand generation, a phenomenon well known in the consumer-oriented economies of the West.[8]

In the 1970s, East German economists belatedly adopted standard-of-living metrics like job security, child care, public education, and health care—alternatives to measures based simply on material acquisitions—to quantify the socialist reward system. Until then, however, "the SED . . . allowed itself to become fully and publicly beholden to a standard of well-being not of its own devising."[9] As Jeffrey Kopstein observes, the life span of state socialism undoubtedly contracted as communism defaulted on the creation of "its own unique understanding of modernity, its own vocabulary for it, its own discourse that would have enabled people to experience scarcity in a qualitatively different way."[10]

By establishing single-family occupancy as official policy, the socialist mass housing program launched by Khrushchev afforded unprecedented privacy, compared to previous East bloc living conditions, within which to construct an individual life. The implications for the Party's goal of constructing an overarching collective identity were assessed by an editorial in *Kultur im Heim:*

> If living space were only a repository of individual accents, subjective fantasies, and "tastemaking," there would be no need to treat it as a social issue—it would be purely a private affair. But its primary significance in the education of the human being, in the richer formation of socialist conditions of reality, as well as in its chief function within social psychology makes its form a paramount public affair.[11]

As design professionals pondered the modern home's potential to nurture collectivist subjectivity, the Soviet bloc's "universal consumer," as envisioned by the brothers Strugatski, was using privacy to administer communism's coup de grâce. Rather than producing socialist citizens committed to living out that role in the public realm, "separate" apartments became insular outposts of a "niche society" (in German, *Nischengesellschaft*). Wrapped in a cocoon of privacy, provisioned by a shadow economy generated by the inefficiencies of its centrally planned counterpart, residents withdrew from the public sphere, halting the flow of Marxist historical time and its teleological narrative of progress. Household consumption indeed proved fatal to communism, but rather than having been forced down the Party's throat, as depicted in Riesman's fantasy and triumphalist cold war histories, the poison pill was willingly ingested.

Socialism was not alone in grappling with the unexpected consequences of a program to breed ideal consumers. Just as the East bloc was commencing its foray into postwar prosperity, America entered a period of self-diagnosed malaise. The launch of Sputnik in 1957, followed by a parade of Soviet high-tech successes involving atomic weaponry, nuclear-powered ships and submarines, and intercontinental ballistic missiles, shocked the United States and its Western European allies. How could the Soviet Union, a nation previously regarded as educationally retrograde and industrially primitive, have outpaced the United States as technological front runner? Educators, cultural critics, and politicians faulted sybaritic materialism for distracting Americans from their destiny. George Kennan, one of the architects of the Marshall Plan and a former Soviet ambassador, blamed the "overwhelming accent of life on personal comfort and amusement . . . and a surfeit of privately sold gadgetry" for the "insufficient social discipline" he perceived in American postwar society.[12] Austrian-born essayist and Auschwitz survivor Jean Améry closed his 1961 *Preface to the Future* with the verdict: "Euro-American civilization, as seen at the end of the destiny-laden decade of 1950–1960, had only one point of reference— consumption. The rest is illusion."[13] The complaints that affluence had left its beneficiaries fat and complacent spread beyond intellectual circles. In a 1960 commencement address, President Eisenhower admonished a fresh crop of graduates that "freedom is imperiled where peoples, worshiping material success, have become emptied of idealism. Peace with justice cannot be attained . . . where opulence has dulled the spirit."[14] The abundance of an American Way of Life, promoted at home and abroad as the free world's future, appeared to be its Achilles' heel as well.

Prescriptions for a society grown fat varied. Educators demanded the improvement of public schools, increased funding, and more rigorous science and math courses, a curricular reform movement that crossed the Atlantic in West German warnings of an impending "education catastrophe."[15] Moral Re-Armament, a fiercely anticommunist evangelical movement, enjoined Americans to build national unity and spiritual discipline through regular churchgoing. The most striking indication of a crisis mentality, however, came with the mobilization of the Advertising Council, producer of the ill-fated People's Capitalism exhibition, to mount a campaign alerting Americans to the dangers of self-indulgence. Council leader Ted Repplier, whose 1955 "propaganda offensive" had celebrated America's consumer economy for giving "more people more benefits than any [other] yet devised," by 1960 had come to believe that the nation's strength was being sapped by "the attitudes of a people who have had it too good, too long." Repplier described the council's new initiative, "Challenge to Americans," as "the most difficult yet perhaps the most important project" the organization had ever undertaken. It would exhort citizens, in Repplier's words, "to pull up our socks, tighten our belts, [and redress] our current softness and ethical shabbiness." The widespread conviction that hedonism was eroding national resolve generated one of the oddest couplings imaginable, as capitalism's merchants of desire volunteered to promote consumer abstinence through ads imploring fellow citizens "to strike a balance between purpose and comfort in our private lives." Repplier's mission was antithetical to the established goals of his industry but oddly reminiscent of the attempt by the Advertising Workers of

WE ARE CHALLENGED: BE STRONG OR BE SPLIT

A fist-pumping Nikita Khrushchev represents communism's threat in the Ad Council's "Challenge to America" public service advertising campaign, 1964. Advertising Council Archives, University of Illinois, Repplier Papers, File 1180.

Socialist Countries to nurture a rational and disciplined East bloc shopper.[16]

As in the case of the "People's Capitalism" campaign a few years earlier, Repplier called on "the best minds in the United States" to participate in a symposium at an Ivy League venue to advance the new crusade. At the 1961 roundtable on "Moral Attitudes and the Will to Achievement of Americans" at Princeton, notables addressed "faults in our moral attitudes in relation to the demands of present world history" and "the most important deficiencies in American life." William F. Whyte, a pioneer in industrial sociology, deplored the pressures of a consumer society that imposed "an almost moral demand that we consume goods." Roger Starr, a union official, agreed. "Advertisers whet our appetites for a still higher standard of living and make us still softer and more the slaves of the things they have taught us to use," Starr lamented. "They cause us to insist on a standard of life utterly incomprehensible to the rest of the world."[17] His remark acknowledged a disconcerting reality that would ultimately subvert the Advertising Council initiative: its sponsors had the most to lose from their project's success.

By the time "Challenge to America" found its way into print and broadcast media in 1962, with the exception of a single reference to the peril of becoming "abnormally selfish and morally slack," all criticism of American self-indulgence had vanished. Instead, public service advertising alerted its audience to the peril of communism and presented a vague case for good citizenship and civic responsibility. Public service announcements proclaiming "We Are Challenged" appeared in magazines beside advertisements for "cars, mouthwash, and soft drinks," as historian Robert Zieger writes. "Two messages seemed to be conveyed, virtually simultaneously: national survival demanded resolute sacrifice, and 'things go better with Coke.'"[18] The conflict of interest associated with an advertising industry attack on profligate consumption virtually assured that the "Challenge to America" would be anything but that— not that an alternate sponsor would have made much difference. In a marketplace battle between spartan virtues and lifestyle hardware, there could be little question about the ensuing consumer preference, whether in the capitalist West or the socialist East.

Acknowledgments

Most people think of history writing as a solitary pursuit. In fact, it is a team effort. This book could not have been written without the enthusiasm of fellow scholars, the support of funding agencies, and the collaboration of a skilled publishing staff.

A postdoctoral fellowship from the Getty Foundation funded the archival explorations that made this book possible. Additional research funding came from the Woodrow Wilson Center's Kennan Institute and the University of Miami's Max Orovitz Award in the Arts and Humanities. The Faculty of Architecture, Planning and Design at the University of Sydney generously provided funds to purchase illustrations for this volume.

György Péteri of the Project on Eastern European Cultures and Societies (PEECS) at the Norwegian University of Science and Technology proposed that I write this book, and he has been both a friend and mentor through its protracted gestation. "Across the East–West Divide" and "Imagining the West," PEECS conferences at the Budapest Collegium and the University of Manchester, respectively, offered opportunities to present my findings for the first time. Participants Richard Anderson, John Connelly, Michael David-Fox, Danielle Fosler-Lussier, Catriona Kelly, Lars Peder Haga, Susan Reid, Tim Scholl, Vera Tolz, and Kiril Tomoff offered suggestions that greatly enriched this study. Two colloquiums sponsored by the Victoria and Albert Museum, "The Postwar European Home" and "Cold War Modern Exhibitions," also proved crucial in shaping this book. I am grateful to fellow conferees Paul Betts, David Crowley, Dennis Doordan, Jack Masey, and Jane Pavitt for their comments. The critical observations of Eleonory Gilburd, Susan Solomon, and Lynne Viola at the conference "Real Socialism and the Second World," sponsored by the Munk Centre for International Studies, were equally useful, as was feedback from Jusyna Jaworska, Ruth Oldenziel, Paolo Scrivano, and Karin Zachmann in conjunction with the symposium "Cold War Politics of the Kitchen" at the Zentralinstitut für Geschichte der Technik in Munich. Invaluable suggestions came from early readers of manuscript drafts, including Walter Hixson, Duanfang Lu, Gay McDonald, Emily Rosenberg, Paolo Scrivano, and Gwendolyn Wright. I am immensely grateful to them for sharpening and adding nuance to this study.

I am indebted to Theo Bowering, Rika Devos, Peter Gerlach, Chris Giampietro, Robert Haddow, Alexander Obeth, Anja Piekny, Suzanne Roberts, Jana Scholze, Ann Skillman, Wolfgang Vogt, Sheldon Weinig, and Karin Zachmann for helping procure illustrations for *Cold War on the Home Front*. No author could ask for a more enthusiastic or patient editor than Pieter Martin, who invited me to submit this project to the University of Minnesota Press. I also acknowledge the hard work of this book's editorial, production, and marketing team: Emily Hamilton, Mary Keirstead, Rachel Moeller, Daniel Ochsner, Heather Skinner, and Laura Westlund. In compiling the index, Sherri Barnes brought this book project to a close.

I owe a debt of love and gratitude to my partner, Gary Brown, who indulged my compulsive work habits with good humor and hot meals. This book is dedicated to my mother, Elsie, whose passion for teaching paved the way for my career in academia, and to my father, Carlos, who has been a paragon of grace in living with the consequences.

Notes

INTRODUCTION

1. David Riesman, "The Nylon War," in *Abundance for What? And Other Essays* (Garden City: Doubleday, 1964), 67. I wish to thank György Péteri for bringing this essay to my attention.
2. Ibid., 68, 69, 73.
3. Llewellyn Thompson, quoted in Walter L. Hixson, *Parting the Curtain: Propaganda, Culture, and the Cold War, 1945–1961* (New York: St. Martin's Griffin, 1998), 167.
4. Frederick Barghoorn, *The Soviet Cultural Offensive: The Role of Cultural Diplomacy in Soviet Foreign Policy* (Princeton, N.J.: Princeton University Press, 1960), 92.
5. I am grateful to György Péteri for sharing this insight into the competing exhibitions.
6. "Is This Typical?" *Pravda,* 10 April 1959, quoted in "Reds Belittle Exhibit of a Typical U.S. Home," *Washington Post and Times Herald,* 10 April 1959.
7. Walter Stern, "U.S. House for Moscow Exhibit to Be Mass-Built on L.I. Tract," *New York Times,* 15 March 1959.
8. Hixson, *Parting the Curtain,* 179.
9. James Reston, "A Debate of Politicians," *New York Times,* 25 July 1959.
10. William Safire, "The Cold War's Hot Kitchen," *New York Times,* 24 July 2009. A somewhat different account is given by Robert H. Haddow, *Pavilions of Plenty: Exhibiting American Culture Abroad in the 1950s* (Washington, D.C.: Smithsonian Institution Press, 1997), 216.
11. Hixson, *Parting the Curtain,* 181.
12. Malvina Lindsay, "U.S. Typical Home Enters Cold War," *Washington Post and Times Herald,* 20 April 1959.
13. Joseph S. Nye Jr., *Soft Power: The Means to Success in World Politics* (New York: PublicAffairs, 2004), 5–7.
14. Victoria de Grazia, *Irresistible Empire: America's Advance through Twentieth-Century Europe* (Cambridge, Mass.: Belknap Press/Harvard University Press, 2005), 555.
15. Barghoorn, *The Soviet Cultural Offensive,* 95.
16. Jessica C. E. Gienow-Hecht, "American Cultural Policy in the Federal Republic of Germany, 1949–1968," trans. Robert Kimberly and Rita Kimber, in *The United States and Germany in the Era of the Cold War, 1945–1990: A Handbook,* ed. Detlef Junker, Philipp Gassert, Wilfried Mausbach, and David B. Morris (Cambridge: Cambridge University Press, 2004), 1:406.
17. Kenneth Osgood, *Total Cold War: Eisenhower's Secret Propaganda Battle at Home and Abroad* (Lawrence: University of Kansas Press, 2006), 8–9.

18. Ibid., 218.
19. Bernard D. Nossiter, "Economic Aid Stressed in Ike Talk to Admen," *Washington Post and Times Herald,* 4 April 1956.
20. Hixson, *Parting the Curtain,* 26.
21. Don Slater, *Consumer Culture and Modernity* (Cambridge, Mass.: Polity Press, 1997), 35–36.
22. John Lewis Gaddis, *The Cold War: A New History* (New York: Penguin Press, 2005), 114.
23. Examples include Haddow, *Pavilions of Plenty*; Frances Stonor Saunders, *The Cultural Cold War: The CIA and the World of Arts and Letters* (New York: New Press, 1999); Reinhold Wagenleitner, *Coca-Colonization and the Cold War: The Cultural Mission of the United States after the Second World War* (Chapel Hill: University of North Carolina Press, 1994); and Ralph Willet, *The Americanization of Germany, 1945–1949* (London: Routledge, 1989).
24. Jessica Gienow-Hecht, "Shame on U.S.? Academics, Cultural Transfer, and the Cold War—A Critical Review," *Diplomatic History* 24, no. 3 (Summer 2000): 465–94. For a discussion of the scholarship on Americanization specific to the German context, see Frank Trommler, "A New Start and Old Prejudices: The Cold War and German-American Cultural Relations, 1945–1968—The Cold War as Culture," trans. Tradukas, in *The United States and Germany in the Era of the Cold War,* ed. Junker, Gassert, Mausbach, and Morris.
25. An important exception can be found in David Crowley and Susan E. Reid, "Style and Socialism: Modernity and Material Culture in Post-War Eastern Europe," in *Style and Socialism: Modernity and Material Culture in Post-War Eastern Europe,* ed. David Crowley and Susan E. Reid (Oxford: Berg, 2000), 1–24.
26. György Péteri, "Nylon Curtain—Transnational and Transsystemic Tendencies in the Cultural Life of State-Socialist Russia and East Central Europe," in *Nylon Curtain—Transnational and Transsystemic Tendencies in the Cultural Life of State-Socialist Russia and East Central Europe,* ed. György Péteri, Trondheim Studies on East European Cultures & Societies, vol. 18 (Trondheim: Program on East European Cultures and Societies, 2006), 6.
27. György Péteri, "Transfers—Centre for Historical and Cultural Studies," unpublished project proposal, October 2005, Trondheim, Norway: 2.
28. *Your Eighty Dollars, www.marshallfilms.org/filminfo.asp?id=YED-2,* accessed 27 November 2007. Over footage of monuments like the Acropolis, Colosseum, Notre Dame in Paris, and London's Tower Bridge, the narrator of *Your Eighty Dollars* intoned: "From the shadows of landmarks such as these, most Americans can trace their heritage and the roots of our nation. And we are proud to do so. . . . From this continent first came knowledge and science, the skills and culture on which the United States was built." Quoted in Hans-Jürgen Schröder, "Marshall Plan Propaganda in Austria and Western Germany," in *The Marshall Plan in Austria,* ed. Günther Bischof, Anton Pelinka,

and Dieter Stiefel (New Brunswick, N.J.: Transaction Publishers, 2000), 228–29.

29. Michael Vlahos, "Culture and Foreign Policy," *Foreign Policy* 82 (Spring 1991): 60.

30. On the postwar mobilization of the idea of Western Civilization, see Patrick Thaddeus Jackson, *Civilizing the Enemy: German Reconstruction and the Invention of the West* (Ann Arbor: University of Michigan Press, 2006).

31. Péteri, "Nylon Curtain," 6.

32. Sheila Fitzpatrick, *Tear Off the Masks! Identity and Imposture in Twentieth-Century Russia* (Princeton, N.J.: Princeton University Press, 2005), 24.

33. Péteri, "Transfers," 1–3.

34. Katherine Pence, "The Myth of a Suspended Present: Prosperity's Painful Shadow in 1950s East Germany," in *Pain and Prosperity: Reconsidering Twentieth-Century German History,* ed. Greg Eghigian and Paul Betts (Stanford, Calif.: Stanford University Press, 2003), 153.

35. Uta G. Poiger, *Jazz, Rock and Rebels: Cold War Politics and American Culture in a Divided Germany* (Berkeley and Los Angeles: University of California Press, 2000), 2–3.

36. Mark Landsman, *Dictatorship and Demand: The Politics of Consumerism in East Germany* (Cambridge, Mass.: Harvard University Press, 2005), 144.

37. Paul Steege uses the term "messy location," in the context of the cold war imperative to segregate ideological realms, to describe Berlin's geopolitical site. Paul Steege, "Making the Cold War: Everyday Symbolic Practice in Postwar Berlin" at the "Revising Alltagsgeschichte," paper presented at the German Studies Association Conference, New Orleans, 2003.

38. Ludwig Erhard, "Aktivere Berlin-Hilfe," quoted and translated in S. Jonathan Wiesen, "Miracles for Sale: Consumer Displays and Advertising in Postwar West Germany," in *Consuming Germany in the Cold War,* ed. David F. Crew (Oxford: Berg, 2003), 158.

39. "Marshall Plan Exhibit Brings Berlin Television," August 1951, press release, RG 286 MP Ger. 1061-1069, Visual records, U.S. National Archives, College Park, Md.

40. "Free Berlin Exhibits Draw Communist Youths," 24 August 1951, press release, RG 286 MP Ger. 1088-1106, Visual records, U.S. National Archives, College Park, Md.

41. Ulbricht's comments at a conference of regional secretaries of the SED, 4 June 1952, cited and translated in Michael Lemke, "Foreign Influences on the Dictatorial Development of the GDR, 1949–1955," in *Dictatorship as Experience: Towards a Socio-Cultural History of the GDR,* ed. Konrad H. Jarausch (New York: Berghahn Books, 1999), 102.

42. Aleksandr Fursenko and Timothy Naftali, *Khrushchev's Cold War: The Inside Story of an American Adversary* (New York: W. W. Norton and Company, 2006), 211.

43. On the mutually constitutive nature of East and West German self-representation, see Katherine Pence, "The Myth of a Suspended Present"; and Ingrid M. Schenck, "Scarcity and Success: The East according to the West during the 1950s," in *Pain and Prosperity,* ed. Betts and Eghigian, 137–59, 160–78.

44. On the changing scholarly topos of consumption, see Susan Strasser, "Making Consumption Conspicuous: Transgressive Topics Go Mainstream," *Technology and Culture* 43, no. 4 (October 2002): 755–70.

45. Crowley and Reid, "Style and Socialism," 9.

46. I use the term "cultural revolution" as defined by Michael David-Fox, as a "cultural program of modernity, in which not only society but culture itself becomes subject to active reconstruction." Michael David-Fox, "What Is Cultural Revolution," *Russian Review* 58, no. 2 (April 1999): 183. For a somewhat different approach to the concept, see Sheila Fitzpatrick, "Cultural Revolution Revisited," *Russian Review* 58, no. 2 (April 1999): 202–9.

47. The concept of a "state-private network" and its establishment by Marshall Plan supporters is argued by Scott Lucas in *Freedom's War: The U.S. Crusade against the Soviet Union, 1945–56* (Manchester, UK: Manchester University Press, 1999). The use of independent expertise from museum curators in American cultural diplomacy has a longer history, however, as documented in Frank Ninkovich, "The Currents of Cultural Diplomacy: Art and the State Department, 1938–1947," *Diplomatic History* 1, no. 3 (Summer 1977): 215–37.

48. Stefan Berger, *Inventing the Nation: Germany* (London and New York: Edward Arnold, 2004), 207.

49. Brendan M. Jones, "U.S. to Go behind Iron Curtain to Show American Way at Fairs," *New York Times,* 22 May 1956.

50. Beatriz Colomina, "The Exhibitionist House," in *At the End of the Century: One Hundred Years of Architecture,* ed. Richard Koshalek and Elizabeth A. T. Smith (New York: Harry Abrams, 1998), 139.

51. Alex Wilson and Jessica Boehland, "Small Is Beautiful: U.S. House Size, Resource Use, and the Environment," *Journal of Industrial Ecology* 9, no. 1–2 (Winter-Spring 2005): 278.

52. Lynette Evans, "Increasing Portion Size Not Just an Eating Problem," *San Francisco Chronicle,* 13 August 2005; Fred A. Bernstein, "Are McMansions Going Out of Style?" *New York Times,* 2 October 2005; Robert J. Samuelson, "Homes as Hummers," *Washington Post,* 13 July 2005; Kathleen Lynn, "Experts Predict Greener New Homes," *The Record,* 12 August 2007; Margot Adler, "Behind the Ever-Expanding American Dream Home," http://www.npr.org/templates/story/story.php?storyId=5525283, accessed 17 August 2007; U.S. Census Bureau, "Households by Type and Size: 1900–2002," no. HS 12, Statistical Abstracts of the United States, 2002.

53. Fredrich Bergström and Robert Gidehag, *EU versus USA* (Stockholm: Timbro, 2004), 24.

54. Australian Conservation Foundation, "Consuming Australia: Main Findings," http://www.acfonline.org.au, accessed 20 August 2007.

55. "Affluenza," http://www.pbs.org/kcts/affluenza/diag/what.html, accessed 17 August 2007.

1. HOUSEHOLD INFLUENCE AND ITS DISCONTENTS

1. Heinrich Hauser, *The German Talks Back* (New York: Henry Holt and Company, 1945), 2–3, 214–15. Hauser's book is analyzed in Michael Ermarth, "*The German Talks Back*: Heinrich Hauser and German Attitudes toward Americanization after World War II," in *America and the Shaping of German Society, 1945–1955,* ed. Michael Ermarth (Providence, R.I.: Berg, 1993), 124.

2. Konrad H. Jarausch and Michael Geyer, *Shattered Past: Reconstructing German Histories* (Princeton, N.J.: Princeton University Press, 2003), 277–81.

3. Frank Trommler, "A New Start and Old Prejudices: The Cold War and German-American Cultural Relations, 1945–1968—The Cold War as Culture," trans. Tradukas, in *The United States and Germany in the Era of the Cold War, 1945–1990: A Handbook,* ed. Detlef Junker, Philipp Gassert, Wilfried Mausbach, and David B. Morris (Cambridge: Cambridge University Press, 2004), 1:374; Alfred Andersch, "Das junge Europa formt sein Gesicht" (15 August 1946), reprinted in Hans Schwab-Felisch, ed., *Der Ruf: Eine deutsche Nachkriegzeitschrift* (Munich, 1962), cited in Keith Bullivant and C. Jane Rice, "Reconstruction and Integration: The Culture of West German Stabilization, 1945 to 1968," in Rob Burns, ed., *German Cultural Studies* (Oxford: Oxford University Press, 1995), 211.

4. David Gilgen, "Socialism and Democracy: The Debate about a New Social and Economic Order in West Germany after the Second World War," in *The Postwar Challenge: Cultural, Social, and Political Change in Western Europe, 1945–58,* ed. Dominik Geppert (Oxford: Oxford University Press, 2003), 117–19, 105–11.

5. "Aufruf der Kommunistischen Partei Deutschlands," 11 June 1945, quoted and translated in Eric D. Weitz, *Creating German Communism, 1890–1990: From Popular Protests to Socialist State* (Princeton, N.J.: Princeton University Press, 1997), 313. This remarkable document, drawn up under Soviet supervision, reflected Stalin's covert strategy of espousing a moderate line, untarnished by the rhetoric of state economic monopoly or class warfare, so that his highly placed "Teutons" might "instead zig-zag [following] opportunistic politics towards socialism." Colonel Sergei Tiul'panov (information officer of the Soviet Military Administration in Germany) orders to the Socialist Unity Party (SED), March 1948, quoted and translated in S. J. Ball, *The Cold War: An International History, 1947–1991* (London: Arnold, 1998), 30.

6. In fact, the synthetic socialism that German intellectuals believed was their postwar *Sonderweg* was anything but unique to their nation. Across Eastern Europe, communist leaders returning to their home countries from wartime

exile in Moscow were instructed to collaborate with other antifascist parties, and to backpedal the commitment to reproduce Stalinist systems of governance in their native land. See Charles Gati, *Hungary and the Soviet Bloc* (Durham: University of North Carolina Press, 1986).

7. Alix Rohde-Liebenau, "Neuordnung des Tagesablaufs und der Innenrichtung," entry 212 in a competition held in conjunction with the exhibition Berlin Plant in August 1946. Premiated entries were displayed in July 1947 in the famed White Hall of Berlin's Schloß. Rohde-Liebenau's manifesto is reproduced in Johann Freidrich Geist and Klaus Kürvers, *Das Berliner Mietshaus 1945–1989* (Munich: Prestel, 1989), 444–48.

8. Hermann Henselmann, "Lebensgestaltung an der Arbeitstätte," *Neue Bauwelt,* no. 7 (1949): 25–29.

9. Anna Di Biagio, "The Marshall Plan and the Founding of the Cominform, June–September 1947," in *The Soviet Union and Europe in the Cold War, 1943–1953,* ed. Francesca Gori and Silvio Pons (New York: St. Martin's Press, 1996), 217, 215.

10. Jeffrey Kopstein, *The Politics of Economic Decline in East Germany, 1945–1989* (Chapel Hill: University of North Carolina Press, 1997), 25–29.

11. On the imbrication of Constructivism and Stalinist labor politics, see Greg Castillo, "Stalinist Modern: Constructivism and the Soviet Company Town," in *Architectures of Russian Identity: 1500 to the Present,* ed. James Cracraft and Daniel B. Rowland (Ithaca, N.Y.: Cornell University Press, 2003), 135–49.

12. Trommler, "A New Start and Old Prejudices," 374–75.

13. Vera Meyer-Waldeck, "Die Werkbund-Ausstellung 'Neues Wohnen' Köln 1949," *Architektur und Wohnform* 57, no. 6 (July 1949): 121.

14. On the emergence and early history of the German Werkbund, see John V. Maciuika, *Before the Bauhaus: Architecture, Politics, and the German State* (Cambridge: Cambridge University Press, 2005); and Fredric J. Schwartz, *The Werkbund: Design Theory and Mass Culture before the First World War* (New Haven, Conn.: Yale University Press, 1996).

15. Paul Betts, *The Authority of Everyday Objects: A Cultural History of West German Industrial Design* (Berkeley: University of California Press, 2004), 29–32, 64–65.

16. Alfons Leitl, "Anmerkungen zur Zeit," *Baukunst und Werkform* 1 (1947): 8, quoted and translated in Betts, *The Authority of Everyday Objects,* 76.

17. Sonja Günther, *Die fünfziger Jahre. Innenarchitektur und Wohndesign* (Stuttgart: Deutsche Verlags-Anstalt, 1994), 23.

18. Alfons Leitl, "Kritik und Selbstbesinnung. Ein Nachwort zur Werkbund-Ausstellung 'Neues Wohnen' in Köln," *Baukunst und Werkform* 2, no. 2 (1949): 61.

19. Martin Heidegger, "Building Dwelling Thinking," in *Basic Writings: From Being and Time (1927) to The Task of Thinking (1964)* (San Francisco: HarperSanFrancisco, 1993). On Werkbund's connection to Heidegger, see Betts, *The Authority of Everyday Objects,* 85–87.

20. Rudolf Schwarz, *Neues Wohnen: Werkbund-ausstellung. Deutsche Architektur seit 1945* (Cologne: n.p., 1949), unpaginated.

21. Erik Nölting, *Neues Wohnen*, unpaginated.

22. Hans Schmidt, *Neues Wohnen*, unpaginated.

23. Ellen Furlough and Carl Strikwerda, "Economics, Consumer Culture, and Gender: An Introduction to the Politics of Consumer Cooperation," in *Consumers Against Capitalism? Consumer Cooperation in Europe, North America and Japan, 1840–1990*, ed. Ellen Furlough and Carl Strikwerda (Lanham, Md.: Rowman & Littlefield, 1999), 1–2.

24. Ibid., 94–95.

25. Leitl, "Kritik und Selbstbesinnung," 57–58.

26. Hauser, *The German Talks Back*, 18.

27. Jarausch and Geyer, *Shattered Past*, 277.

28. Don Slater, *Consumer Culture and Modernity* (Cambridge, Mass.: Polity Press, 1997), 135.

29. Schütte-Lihotzky quoted in Lore Kramer, "Rationalisierung des Haushaltes und Frauenfrage—Die Frankfurter Küche und zeitgenössische Kritik," in *Ernst May und das neue Frankfurt 1925–1930* (Berlin: Ernst, 1986), 166.

30. On the rationalization of the German *Hausfrau*, see Martina Heßler, "The Frankfurt Kitchen: The Model of Modernity and the 'Madness' of Traditional Users, 1926 to 1933," in *Cold War Kitchen: Americanization, Technology, and European Users*, ed. Ruth Oldenziel and Karin Zachmann (Cambridge, Mass.: MIT Press, 2008), 163–84.

31. Kramer, "Rationalisierung des Haushaltes," 77–84.

32. Fritz Weichert, "Die neue Baukunst als Erzieher," *Das neue Frankfurt* 11/12 (1928).

33. Adelheid von Saldern, *The Challenge of Modernity: German Social and Cultural Studies, 1890–1960* (Ann Arbor: University of Michigan Press, 2002), 93–114. On Frankfurt's social housing program, see also Christoph Mohr and Michael Miller, eds., *Funktionalität und Moderne: Das Neue Frankfurt und Seine Bauten 1925–1933* (Cologne: Rudolf Müller Verlag, 1984).

34. Victoria de Grazia, *Irresistible Empire: America's Advance through Twentieth-Century Europe* (Cambridge, Mass.: Belknap/Harvard, 2005), 107.

35. Christian Borngräber, "The Social Impact of the New Architecture in Germany," *Architectural Association Quarterly (AAQ)* 2, no. 1 (1979): 40; Mary Nolan, *Visions of Modernity: American Business and the Modernization of Germany* (New York: Oxford University Press, 1994), 215; Nicholas Bullock, "Housing in Frankfurt and the New *Wohnkultur*," *Architectural Review* 163, no. 976 (June 1978): 341.

36. Karen Kirsch, *The Weissenhofsiedlung: Experimental Housing Built for the Deutscher Werkbund, Stuttgart, 1927* (New York: Rizzoli, 1989), 17.

37. Dennis Sharp, introduction to *Pel and Tubular Steel Furniture of the Thirties*, ed. Dennis Sharp, Tim Benton, and Barbie Campbell Cole (London: Architectural Association, 1977); Tim Benton, "A Visual Chronology of

Tubular Steel," in *Pel and Tubular Steel Furniture,* ed. Sharp, Benton, and Cole, 3–4, 5–7.

38. Kirsch, *The Weissenhofsiedlung,* 17.

39. Ibid., 78, 33. Kirsch defends the architects of the 1927 Werkbund housing exhibition, writing that "neither the exhibition directorate nor the architects themselves ever mentioned the idea of building housing for the oppressed, exploited German people" (33), an argument that overlooks the Werkbund's original project brief.

40. Kurt Schwitters, quoted in Karin Schulte, "The Weißenhof Estate in Stuttgart," in *Mies van der Rohe: Architecture and Design in Stuttgart, Barcelona, Brno,* ed. Alexander von Vegesack and Mattias Kries (Milan: Skira, 1998), 140.

41. Kirsch, *The Weissenhofsiedlung,* 19.

42. Jarausch and Geyer, *Shattered Past,* 291.

43. Kirsch, *The Weissenhofsiedlung,* 33.

44. Hubert Hoffmann, "die wiederlebung des bauhauses nach 1945," in *Bauhaus und Bauhäusler,* ed. Eckhard Neumann (Bern: Hallweg, 1971), 206. On Hoffmann's attempt to revive the Bauhaus in the service of postwar German socialism, see Greg Castillo, "The Bauhaus in Cold War Germany," in *Bauhaus Culture: From Weimar to the Cold War,* ed. Kathleen James-Chakroborty (Minneapolis: University of Minnesota Press, 2006), 172–76.

45. Paul Overy, "Visions of the Future and the Immediate Past: The Werkbund Exhibition, Paris 1930," *Journal of Design History* 14, no. 4 (2004): 337.

46. Arthur Rüegg, "From Utopia to Concrete Fall," in *Swiss Furniture and Interiors in the Twentieth Century* (Basel: Birkhäuser, 2002), 95.

47. Hannes Meyer, "Die Neue Welt," in *Hannes Meyer 1889–1954: Architekt, Urbanist, Lehrer,* ed. Werner Kleinerüschkamp (Berlin: Ernst, 1989), 72.

48. Betts, *The Authority of Everyday Objects,* 80.

49. Volker Berghahn, *America and the Intellectual Cold Wars* (Princeton, N.J.: Princeton University Press, 2001), xvii.

50. Paul G. Hoffman, *Peace Can Be Won* (Garden City, N.Y.: Doubleday, 1951), 105.

51. OMGUS "Report of Staff Conference," 27 September 1947, Microfilm M1075, Roll 3, U.S. National Archives, College Park, Md. A later volley in the campaign against Western modernism was fired off by Vladimir Semenov, the political advisor to the commander-in-chief of the Soviet Military Administration in East Germany. Under the pseudonym N. Orlov, Semenov authored a two-part broadside titled "Wege und Irrwege der modernen Kunst," *Tägliche Rundschau,* 20 and 23 January 1951. Semenov revealed that the pseudonym "N. Orlov" was his in the autobiography, *Von Stalin bis Gorbatschow* (Berlin: Nicolai, 1995).

52. The origins and ideological underpinnings of a Fordist consumer economy are traced in Susan Strasser, *Satisfaction Guaranteed: The Making of the American Mass Market* (New York: Pantheon, 1989).

53. Hoffman, *Peace Can Be Won*, 87.

54. "A Potential Danger," RG 286 MP Ger. 1695, Still Pictures Division, U.S. National Archives, College Park, Md.

55. On the experiences of Germany's postwar "expellees" and displaced persons, see Jörg Echernkamp, *Nach dem Krieg: Alltagsnot, Neuorientierung und die Last der Vergangenheit* (Zurich: Pendo Verlag, 2003).

56. Charles McGovern, "Consumption and Citizenship in the United States, 1900–1940," in *Getting and Spending: European and American Consumer Societies in the Twentieth Century,* ed. Susan Strasser, Charles McGovern, and Mattias Judt (Cambridge: Cambridge University Press, 1998), 56–57.

57. Ibid., 58.

58. George Lipsitz, "Consumer Spending as State Project: Yesterday's Solutions and Today's Problems," in *Getting and Spending,* ed. Strasser, McGovern, and Judt, 131–32.

59. Donald Albrecht, introduction to *World War II and the American Dream: How Wartime Building Changed a Nation,* ed. Donald Albrecht (Washington, D.C.: National Building Museum; Cambridge, Mass.: MIT Press, 1995), xxii.

60. Greg Hise, "The Airplane and the Garden City: Regional Transformations during World War II," in *World War II and the American Dream,* ed. Albrecht, 152–55.

61. Lizabeth Cohen, "The New Deal State and the Making of Citizen Consumers," in *Getting and Spending,* ed. Strasser, McGovern, and Judt, 125.

62. Hoffman, *Peace Can Be Won*, 134–36, 141–43, 147–49.

63. On the Marshall Plan as a "New Deal synthesis," see Michael J. Hogan, *The Marshall Plan: America, Britain, and the Reconstruction of Western Europe, 1947–1952* (New York: Cambridge University Press, 1987), 22, 427. A critique of his analysis can be found in Charles S. Maier, "American Visions and British Interests: Hogan's Marshall Plan," *Reviews in American History* 18, no. 1 (March 1990): 102–11.

64. U.S. Army Intelligence, "Russian Propaganda Regarding the American Way of Life" (Project 3869), 10 October 1947, RG319, 270/9/23/7 Box 2900, U.S. National Archives, College Park, Md.

65. Patricia van Delden, "Housing Publicity," 5 May 1949, RG 260 390/42/21/3 Box 323, U.S. National Archives, College Park, Md.

66. Hoffman, *Peace Can Be Won*, 148.

67. A biographical sketch of Harnden's achievements can be found in Jordi Marlet, "Recoregut per la historia de la galeria Cadaqués: Una porta d'entrada a l'art contemporani," *Avui* 910 (July 2003). Marie Harnden's diary of life during the war was published as Marie Vassiltchikov, *Berlin Diaries, 1940–1945* (New York: Knopf, 1987).

68. Rudolf Pfister, "So Wohnt Amerika. Eine Betrachtung über das Fertighaus," *Baumeister,* no. 10, 1949, quoted in Werner Durth, "Architektur als Medium der Politik," in *Die USA und Deutschland im Zeitalter der Kalten Krieg,* ed. Detlev Junker (Stuttgart: Deutsche Verlags-Anstalt, 2001), 1:733.

69. Donald W. Muntz to Patricia van Delden, "Special Report re America House Publicity Efforts on Behalf of the *So Wohnt Amerika* Exhibition, 24 August 1949, RG260, 390/42/21/3 Box 323, OMGUS Information Control, Records of Information Centers and Exhibits Branch, 1945–49, U.S. National Archives, College Park, Md.

70. Kenneth J. Arrow, review of *Income, Saving, and the Theory of Consumer Behavior* by James S. Duesenberry, *American Economic Review* 40, no. 5 (December 1950): 906.

71. James S. Duesenberry, *Income, Saving, and the Theory of Consumer Behavior* (Cambridge, Mass.: Harvard University Press, 1949), 27.

72. David W. Ellwood, *Rebuilding Europe: Western Europe, America, and Postwar Reconstruction* (London: Longman, 1992), 161–62.

73. Brian Angus McKenzie, *Remaking France: Americanization, Public Policy, and the Marshall Plan* (Oxford: Berghahn Books, 2005), 165–66.

74. Telegram, Dean Acheson to Paul Shinkman, 18 August 1950, RG59 862A.191 (Internal Affairs of State Relating to Exhibitions and Fairs in Germany), Box 5225, U.S. National Archives, College Park, Md.

75. Memorandum, Bruce Buttles to John McCloy, ibid.

76. Telegram, John McCoy to U.S. Secretary of State, 22 September 1950, ibid.

77. *Amerika zu Hause. Deutsche Industrie Austellung, Berlin,* 1950 (n.p.), unpaginated.

78. Ibid.

79. Memorandum, Paul A. Shinkman to Henry J. Kellermann, 3 November 1950, RG59 862A.191 (Internal Affairs of State Relating to Exhibitions and Fairs in Germany) Box 5225, U.S. National Archives, College Park, Md.

80. "Model U.S. Home at West Berlin Fair No. One Attraction for Awed Germans," undated newspaper clipping, ibid.

81. H. B. McCoy to John McCloy, 16 August 1950, ibid.; Ellwood, *Rebuilding Europe,* 137; Jennifer A. Loehlin, *From Rugs to Riches: Housework, Consumption and Modernity in Germany* (Oxford: Berg, 1999), 52; Michael Wildt, "Changes in Consumption as Social Practice in West Germany during the 1950s," in *Getting and Spending,* ed. Strasser, McGovern, and Judt, 305.

82. Telegram, Page to U.S. Secretary of State, 17 October 1950, RG59 862A.191 (Internal Affairs of State Relating to Exhibitions and Fairs in Germany), Box 5225, U.S. National Archives, College Park, Md.

83. Paul Shinkman, "Trade Fair Participation," *New York Times,* 20 June 1955.

84. Memorandum, Paul A. Shinkman to Henry J. Kellermann, 3 November 1950, RG59 862A.191 (Internal Affairs of State Relating to Exhibitions and Fairs in Germany), Box 5225, U.S. National Archives, College Park, Md.

85. Ibid.

86. Paul Shinkman to Secretary of State, 15 October 1950, ibid.

87. Telegram, John McCoy to U.S. Secretary of State, 22 September 1950, ibid.

88. Telegram, Webb to John McCoy, 26 September 1950, ibid.

89. Webb, Frankfurt Office of the U.S. High Commander for Germany (HICOG) to HICOG Berlin, 12 September 1950, ibid.

2. CULTURAL REVOLUTIONS IN TANDEM

1. John Kenneth Galbraith, "Is There a German Policy?" *Fortune* 35, no. 1 (January 1947): 187, 195.
2. Isabel Cary Lundberg, "World Revolution, American Plan," *Harper's* 197, no. 1183 (December 1948): 39–40.
3. David M. Potter, *People of Plenty: Economic Abundance and the American Character* (Chicago: University of Chicago Press, 1954), 134–40. I am grateful to Dennis Doordan for having brought Potter's study to my attention.
4. One can only speculate as to the reasons for Potter's surprising oversight. Because the Smith-Mundt Act, a federal law passed in 1948, stipulated that the U.S. government abstain from directing its foreign propaganda—including Marshall Plan publicity concocted for European distribution—at its own citizens, Potter had less access to evidence of the tenor of U.S. overseas public diplomacy efforts than one might presume today. It is also possible that Potter was influenced by the defamation of the Truman administration's foreign policy efforts as ineffectual, a campaign unleashed by Republican politicians like Senator Joseph McCarthy in a successful attempt to secure majority status for his party, a development discussed in chapter 5.
5. On the initial processes of cultural revolution in East Germany, see David Pike, *The Politics of Culture in Soviet-Occupied Germany* (Stanford, Calif.: Stanford University Press, 1992); Norman M. Naimark, *The Russians in Germany: A History of the Soviet Zone of Occupation, 1945–1949* (Cambridge, Mass.: Harvard University Press, 1995); and Wolfgang Schivelbusch, *In a Cold Crater: Cultural and Intellectual Life in Berlin, 1945–1948*, trans. Kelly Barry (Berkeley: University of California Press, 1998). On the cultural revolution in East bloc educational institutions, see John Connelly, *Captive University: The Sovietization of East German, Czech, and Polish Higher Education, 1945–1956* (Chapel Hill: University of North Carolina Press, 2000).
6. Pike, *The Politics of Culture*, 315–18, 226–30.
7. Kiril Tomoff, "A Pivotal Turn: Prague Spring and the Soviet Construction of a Cultural Sphere," in *Nylon Curtain: Transnational and Transsystemic Tendencies in the Cultural Life of State-Socialist Russia and East-Central Europe*, ed. György Péteri, Trondheim Studies on East European Cultures and Societies, vol. 18 (August 2006), 56.
8. John Connelly, "Ulbricht and the Intellectuals," in *Intellectual Life and the First Crisis of State Socialism in East Central Europe, 1953–1956*, ed. György Péteri, Trondheim Studies on East European Cultures and Societies, vol. 6 (November 2001), 88.
9. As Connelly notes, "Unlike counterparts elsewhere in the region, the East German intelligentsia had no existence separate from the Party," a point that

helps describe East German intellectuals' general lack of support for Khrushchev's de-Stalinization reforms at their inception; ibid., 81, 104.

10. Ibid., 82, 101, 103.

11. Victoria de Grazia, *Irresistible Empire: America's Advance through Twentieth-Century Europe* (Cambridge, Mass.: Belknap/Harvard, 2005), 106.

12. Volker Berghahn, "Conceptualizing the American Impact on Germany: West German Society and the Problem of Americanization," paper for the German Historical Institute conference on "The American Impact on Western Europe," March 1999, www.ghi-dc.org/conpotweb/westernpapers/berghahn.pdf.

13. Interpretations of the motives underlying the Marshall Plan range from triumphalist narratives canonizing American efforts to rescue postwar Europe to revisionist accounts stressing U.S. economic self-interest. For a review of this debate, see William Diebold Jr., "The Marshall Plan in Retrospect: A Review of Recent Scholarship," *Journal of International Affairs* 4 (Summer 1988): 421–35.

14. "Import Aid Urged to Revive Bizonia," *New York Times*, 1 April 1949.

15. *"Germany 49" Industry Show in New York* (Frankfurt am Main: Exhibition Committee for the German Industrial Show, 1949), 5.

16. "German Exhibits Draw Picket Line," *New York Times*, 10 April 1949.

17. "German Exhibit Here Receives Clay's Message," *New York Herald*, 9 April 1949; "Gen. Clay Extols German Fair Here," *New York Times*, 9 April 1949; "German Exhibits to Greet Buyers, *New York Times*, 11 April 1949.

18. Herwin Schaefer, quoted in Jupp Ernst, "So fing es wieder an," in *Der deutsche Werkbund, 1907, 1947, 1987*, ed. Ot Hoffmann (Berlin: Wilhelm Ernst & Sohn Verlag, 1987), 45. I am grateful to Paul Betts for bringing the Ernst essay to my attention. Ernst mistakenly attributes Schaefer's report to an article in the *New York Herald*; Schaefer remembers writing the critique for a German Werkbund publication and receiving "nasty stares" upon his arrival in Bavaria for having made the caustic comments (Herwin Schaefer to Greg Castillo, undated).

19. Jennifer Jenkins, "Domesticity, Design and the Shaping of the Social," *German History* 25, no. 4 (2007): 478–79.

20. Vera Meyer-Waldeck, "Die Werkbund-Austellung 'Neues Wohnen,' Köln 1949," *Architektur und Wohnform* 57, no. 6 (July 1949): 20.

21. Cristopher Oestereich, *"Gute Form" in Wiederaufbau. Zur Geschichte der Produktgestaltung in Westdeutschland nach 1945* (Berlin: Lukas Verlag, 2000), 180; Sonja Günther, *Die fünfziger Jahre: Innenarchitektur und Wohndesign* (Stuttgart: Deutsche Verlags-Anstalt, 1994), 102.

22. Oestereich, *"Gute Form" in Wiederaufbau*, 284, n. 112.

23. For a detailed discussion of the formation of the German Design Council and its politics, see Paul Betts, *The Authority of Everyday Objects: A Cultural History of West German Industrial Design* (Berkeley: University of California Press, 2004), 178–211.

41. Maddrell, *Spying on Science,* 127–28.

42. Donald Monson to Joseph Heath, 31 October 1952, RG469/250/79/28/03-04 Box 3 (Consumption, Housing, Propaganda Strategies; Records of the U.S. Foreign Assistance Agencies 1948–61, Special Representative in Europe, Office of Economic Affairs, Labor Division, Country Files Related to Housing), U.S. National Archives, College Park, Md.

43. Michael Harris to Joseph Heath, undated, ibid.

44. Robert G. Moeller, "Reconstructing the Family in Reconstruction Germany: Women and Social Policy in the Federal Republic, 1949–1955," *Feminist Studies* 15 (1989): 131.

45. Bertram Schaffner, *Father Land: A Study of Authoritarianism in the German Family* (New York: Columbia University Press, 1948), 34; quoted in Hanna Schissler, "German and American Women between Domesticity and the Workplace," in *The United States and Germany in the Era of the Cold War, 1945–1990: A Handbook,* ed. Detlef Junker, Philipp Gassert, Wilfried Mausbach, and David B. Morris (Cambridge: Cambridge University Press, 2004), 1:559.

46. Nancy Reagin, "Comparing Apples and Oranges: Housewives and the Politics of Consumption in Interwar Germany," in *Getting and Spending: European and American Consumer Societies in the Twentieth Century,* ed. Susan Strasser, Charles McGovern, and Mattias Judt (Cambridge: Cambridge University Press, 1998), 245–48. See also Nancy Reagin, *Sweeping the German Nation: Domesticity and National Identity in Germany, 1870–1945* (Cambridge: Cambridge University Press, 2007), 72–109.

47. Mary Nolan, *Visions of Modernity: American Business and the Modernization of Germany* (New York: Oxford University Press, 1994), 120–27.

48. "Ewerbsätigkeit und Hausfrauengeist," *Die Deutsche Hausfrau* 13 (1928): 50–52, quoted and translated in Reagin, "Comparing Apples and Oranges," 254.

49. Ibid., 254.

50. Ibid., 252.

51. Ibid., 253.

52. Axel Schildt and Arnold Sywottek, "'Reconstruction' and 'Modernization': West German Social History during the 1950s," in *West Germany under Construction: Politics, Society and Culture in the Adenauer Era,* ed. Robert G. Moeller (Ann Arbor: University of Michigan Press, 1997), 427.

53. Lyon to Secretary of State, 22 September 1952.

54. "Current Informational Report," HICOG Bonn Foreign Service Dispatch, 9 February 1953, RG 59, 511.62A, Box 2246 (International Informational and Educational Relations between U.S. and Germany), U.S. National Archives, College Park, Md.

55. Moeller, "Reconstructing the Family," 126.

56. Volker R. Berghahn, "Recasting Bourgeois Germany," in *The Miracle Years: A Cultural History of West Germany 1949–1968,* ed. Hanna Schissler (Princeton, N.J.: Princeton University Press, 2001), 328.

57. Jonathan Woodham, "Design and Everyday Life at the *Britain Can Make It* Exhibition, 1946: 'Stripes, Spots, White Wood and Homespun versus Chintzy Armchairs and Iron Bedsteads with Brass Knobs,'" *Journal of Architecture* 9 (Winter 2004): 468–69.

58. Ingrid M. Schenk, "Scarcity and Success: The East according to the West during the 1950s," in *Pain and Prosperity: Reconsidering Twentieth-Century German History,* ed. Greg Eghigian and Paul Betts (Stanford, Calif.: Stanford University Press, 2003), 172.

59. Moeller, "Reconstructing the Family," 117–18, 110.

60. Ibid., 112.

61. Schissler, "German and American Women between Domesticity and the Workplace," 564.

62. Moeller, "Reconstructing the Family," 112.

63. Walther von Hollander, "Mann in der Krise: Anklage von Frauen," *Constanze* 1 (1948): 22, quoted and translated in Dagmar Herzog, "Desperately Seeking Normality: Sex and Marriage in the Wake of War," in *Life after Death: Approaches to a Cultural and Social History of Europe during the 1940s and 1950s,* ed. Richard Bessel and Dirk Schumann (Cambridge: Cambridge University Press, 2003), 187.

64. H. H., "Hut ab vor unseren Frauen!" *Constanze* 2 (1948): 4–5, quoted and translated in Herzog, "Desperately Seeking Normality," 187.

65. Herzog, "Desperately Seeking Normality," 187.

66. See, for example, anonymous, *A Woman in Berlin: Eight Weeks in the Conquered City—A Diary,* trans. Philip Boehm (New York: Metropolitan Books, 2005).

67. Boris Groys, *The Total Art of Stalinism: Avant-Garde, Aesthetic Dictatorship, and Beyond,* trans. Charles Rougle (Princeton, N.J.: Princeton University Press, 1992), 51.

68. Georgii Malenkov, quoted in N. Dmitrieva, "Das Problem des Typischen in der bildenden Kunst," *Kunst und Literatur,* no. 1 (1953): 100; cited in Groys, *The Total Art of Stalinism,* 50.

69. Michael Schudson, *Advertising: The Uneasy Persuasion* (New York: Basic Books, 1984), 215.

70. Erica Carter, *How German Is She? Postwar West German Reconstruction and the Consuming Woman* (Ann Arbor: University of Michigan Press, 1997); in particular see chapter 1, "Postwar Identity and the West German Woman," 19–43.

71. Article in *Neue Zeitung,* 20 September 1952, translated and quoted in Lyon to Secretary of State, 20 September 1952, RG59 862A.191 (Internal Affairs of State Relating to Exhibitions and Fairs in Germany), Box 5225, U.S. National Archives, College Park, Md.

72. Article in *Tagesspiegel,* 20 September 1952, translated and quoted in Lyon to Secretary of State, 20 September 1952, ibid.

73. Carter, *How German Is She?* 225.

74. Arne Andersen, *Der Traum vom guten Leben* (Frankfurt/Main: Campus, 1999), 92.

75. Schildt and Sywottek, "'Reconstruction' and 'Modernization,'" 429.

76. Lizabeth Cohen, *A Consumer's Republic: The Politics of Mass Consumption in Postwar America* (New York: Knopf, 2003), 123; Ludwig Erhard, "Einen Kühlschrank in jeden Haushalt," *Welt der Arbeit*, 16 June 1953, trans. J. A. Arengo-Jones and D. J. S. Thompson in *The Economics of Success* (London: Thames and Hudson, 1963), 145–48.

77. Andersen, *Der Traum vom guten Leben,* 97.

78. Cohen, *A Consumer's Republic,* 123.

79. Ibid., 93–94. On the Nazi "people's products" program, see also Wolfgang König, *Volkswagen, Volksempfänger, Volksgemeinschaft. 'Volksprodukte' im Dritten Reich: Vom Scheitern einer nazionalsozialistischen Komsumgesellschaft* (Paderborn: Ferdinand Schöningh Verlag, 2004).

80. Wiesen, "Miracles for Sale," 152.

81. Rainer Gries, "Help Yourself! The History and Theory of Self-Service in West and East Germany," in *Selling Modernity: Advertising and Public Relations in Modern German History,* ed. Pamela Swett, Jonathan Wiesen, and Jonathan Zatlin (Chapel Hill: University of North Carolina Press, 2007), 310.

82. Michael Wildt, "Changes in Consumption as Social Practice in West Germany during the 1950s," in *Getting and Spending,* ed. Strasser, McGovern, and Judt," 307–8.

83. Walter Dirks, "Der Neid auf den Kühlschrank," *Frankfurter Hefte* 10 (April 1955), quoted and translated in Jennifer A. Loehlin, *From Rugs to Riches: Housework, Consumption, and Modernity in Germany* (New York: Berg), 74.

84. Sharon Zukin, *Point of Purchase: How Shopping Changed American Culture* (New York: Routledge, 2004), 29.

85. Loehlin, *From Rugs to Riches,* 92.

86. Ibid.

87. Don Slater, *Consumer Culture and Modernity* (Cambridge, Mass.: Polity Press, 1997), 113.

88. Wildt, "Changes in Consumption as Social Practice," 310–11; Loehlin, *From Rugs to Riches,* 91–93.

89. Wildt, "Changes in Consumption as Social Practice," 310.

90. Ibid.; Loehlin, *From Rugs to Riches,* 93.

91. "Caravan of Modern Food Service," RG 286, Gen 1935-1970, 1982–1998, Still Pictures Division, National Archives, College Park, Md.

92. Victoria de Grazia, *Irresistible Empire: America's Advance through Twentieth-Century Europe* (Cambridge, Mass.: Belknap Press/Harvard University Press, 2005), 377–87.

93. "Maison Sans Frontieres," Gen 2400-2406, Still Pictures Division, National Archives, College Park, Md.

94. Pierre Bourdieu, "Habitus," in *Habitus: A Sense of Place,* ed. Jean Hillier and Emma Rooksby (Aldershot: Ashgate, 2002), 27–34; and Kim Dovey, "The Silent Complicity of Architecture" in *Habitus,* 267–80.

4. STALINISM BY DESIGN

1. Theo Harych, "Stalinallee," typescript, Mappe 7, Nachlaß Theo Harych, Literarische Abteilung, Akademie der Künste, Berlin.
2. East Berlin's Stalinallee has accrued an extensive post-unification body of scholarship. The short list includes Werner Durth, Jörn Düwel, and Niels Gutschow, *Ostkreuz/Aufbau. Architektur und Städtebau der DDR,* 2 vols. (Frankfurt: Campus Verlag, 1998); Bruno Flierl, "Stalinallee in Berlin," *Zodiac* 5 (March 1991): 76–115; Helmut Engel and Wolfgang Ribbe, eds., *Karl-Marx-Allee. Magestrale in Berlin* (Berlin: Akademie Verlag, 1996); Tilo Köhler, *Unser die Strasse—Unser der Sieg. Die Stalinallee* (Berlin: Transit, 1993); and Herbert Nicolaus and Alexander Obeth, *Die Stalinallee. Geschichte einer deutschen Straße* (Berlin: Verlag für Bauwesen, 1997).
3. On the Stalinallee's model of socialist commercial culture, see Johanna Böhm-Klein, "Wohnen, Geschäftsleben und Infrastruktur der Stalinallee," in *Karl-Marx-Allee. Magistrale in Berlin,* ed. Helmut Engel and Wolfgang Ribbe (Berlin: Akademie Verlag, 1996); Katherine Pence, "Schaufenster des sozialistischen Konsums: Texte der ostdeutschen 'consumer culture,'" in *Akten. Eingaben. Schufenster. Die DDR und ihre Texte,* ed. Alf Lüdke and Peter Becker (Berlin: Akademie Verlag, 1997), 91–118; and Katherine Pence, "'You as a Woman Will Understand': Consumption, Gender and the Relationship between State and Citizenry in the GDR's Crisis of 17 June 1953," *German History* 19, no. 2 (2001): 218–52.
4. Greg Castillo, "Peoples at an Exhibition: Soviet Architecture and the National Question," in *Socialist Realism without Shores,* ed. Thomas Lahusen and Evgeny Dobrenko (Durham, N.C.: Duke University Press, 1997), 91–100.
5. Johanna Böhm-Klein, "Wohnen, Geschäftsleben und Infrastruktur der Stalinallee," in *Karl Marx Allee,* ed. Engel and Ribbe, 146.
6. Herbert Riecke, *Mietskasernen im Kapitalismus, Wohnpaläste im Sozialismus* (Berlin: Verlag Kultur und Fortschritt, 1954), 7.
7. Jakob Jordan, "Über einige Aufgaben des Instituts für Innenarchitektur der Deutschen Bauakademie," *Deutsche Architektur* 3, no. 1 (1954): 12; R. Walde, presentation typescript, "Fragen der deutschen Innenarchitekten und des Möbelbaues," Bundesarchiv SAPMO, DH2 DBA A 141; Nicolaus and Obeth, *Die Stalinallee,* 240.
8. Eric Larrabee and Massimo Vignelli, *Knoll Design* (New York: Harry Abrams, 1981), 19.
9. "Stellungnahme zum Referat zur Innenarchitektur-Konferenz," 2 December 1953, DH2 VI/61/8, SAPMO, Bundesarchiv Berlin-Lichterfelde.

10. Hans Hopp, Gegen den Formalismus – für eine fortschrittliche Innenarchitektur"; R. Walde, presentation typescript, "Fragen der deutschen Innenarchitekten und des Möbelbaues," Bundesarchiv SAMPO, DH2 DBA A 141.

11. Daniela Berghahn, *Hollywood behind the Wall: The Cinema of East Germany* (Manchester: Manchester University Press, 2005), 130.

12. R. Walde, "Unser klassisches Erbe und die heutige Situation. Erläuterungen zum folgenden Bildteil," in "Fragen der deutschen Innenarchitekten und des Möbelbaues," Bundesarchiv SAMPO, DH2 DBA A 141.

13. Photographers were sent to the Staatliche Kunstsammlung Dresden, Stadtmuseum Cottbus, Stadtmuseum Potsdam, Stadtmuseum Bautzen, Landesgalerie Sachsen Anhalt (Halle/Salle), Stadt- und Bergmuseum Freiburg, Stadtmuseum Wurzen, Stadtmuseum Görlitz, Gothe-Museum and Schlossmuseum Weimar, Stralsundisches Museum Ostmecklenburg, Rostocker Museum, Stadtmuseum Zittau, Städtisches Museum Glauchau, Grassi-Museum Leipzig, and stately homes (*Schloßmuseen*) in Wernigerode, Quedlinburg, Wörlitz, Mosigkau, and Chemnitz, along with other private homes. Bundesarchiv SAMPO, DH2 DBA VI/07/29.

14. Paul Mebes, *Um 1800. Architektur u. Handwerk im letzten Jarhundert,* 3rd ed. (Munich: E. Bruckman, 1920). I am grateful to Richard Anderson for bringing the parallels between Mebes's work and the Bauakademie's postwar neoclassical revival to my attention.

15. The holdings of the former DBA library are housed at the Institut für Regionalentwicklung und Strukturplanung (IRS), Berlin-Erkner.

16. Mebes, *Um 1800*, 3.

17. Walter Curt Behrendt, introduction to the 3rd ed., *Um 1800,* by Mebes, 7–12.

18. Ibid., 10, 11.

19. "Reisebericht," 20 October 1953, DH2 VI/61/8, SAPMO, Bundesarchiv Berlin-Lichterfelde.

20. Christian J. Emden, *Walter Benjamins Archäologie der Moderne. Kulturwissenschaft um 1930* (Munich: Wilhelm Fink Verlag, 2006), 12.

21. The archival paper trail of this project, aside from its initial formulation, is unfortunately lost or misfiled—or in the wake of Stalin's death and Khrushchev's subsequent "Thaw," the research initiative may have come to nothing.

22. Hope M. Harrison, "The New Course: Soviet Policy toward Germany and the Uprising in the GDR," in *The Cold War after Stalin's Death: A Missed Opportunity for Peace?* ed. Klaus Larres and Kenneth Osgood (Lanham, Md.: Rowman and Littlefield, 2006), 195.

23. Rainer Gries, "Westliche Markenprodukte waren die schlimmsten Provokateure," *Das Parlament* no. 25–26 (12–19 June 1992): 9.

24. Christian Oestermann, "New Documents on the East German Uprising of 1953," Bulletin 5 (Washington, D.C.: Cold War International History Project, Woodrow Wilson International Center for Scholars).

25. Jeffrey Kopstein, *The Politics of Economic Decline in East Germany, 1945–1989* (Chapel Hill: University of North Carolina Press, 1997), 35. For the GDR's attempts to ameliorate its "provisioning chaos" prior to the 1953 uprising, see Pence, "'You as a Woman Will Understand,'" 218–52.

26. The East German uprising has generated a substantial literature. Introductions include Arnulf Baring, *Uprising in East Germany: June 17, 1953* (Ithaca, N.Y.: Cornell University Press, 1972); Gary Brice, *Resistance with the People: Repression and Resistance in Eastern Germany, 1945–1955* (Lanham, Md.: Rowman and Littlefield, 2003).

27. Gries, "Westliche Markenprodukte waren die schlimmsten Provokateure," 9.

28. Harrison, "The New Course," 204.

29. "Der neue Kurs und die Aufgaben der Partei," quoted and translated in Anne Kaminsky, "'True Advertising Means Promoting a Good Thing through a Good Form,'" in *Selling Modernity: Advertising in Twentieth-Century Germany,* ed. Pamela Swett, S. Jonathan Wiesen, and Jonathan R. Zatlin (Durham, N.C.: Duke University Press, 2007), 264.

30. John Connelly, "Ulbricht and the Intellectuals," in *Intellectual Life and the First Crisis of State Socialism in East Central Europe, 1953–1956,* ed. György Péteri, Trondheim Studies on East European Cultures and Societies, vol. 6 (November 2001), 90.

31. Kurt Liebknecht, "Die Architektur der Wohnung für die Werktätigen unter besonderer Berüchsichtigung des Möbels," in *Besser Leben—schöner wohnen! Raum und Möbel,* ed. Deutsche Bauakademie and Ministerium für Leichtindustrie (Leipzig: VEB Graphische Werkstätten, 1954), 7.

32. "Protokoll über die Sitzung—Möbelausstellung—Konferenz," 19 October 1953, DH2 VI/61/8, SAPMO, Bundesarchiv Berlin-Lichterfelde.

33. "Aktennotiz, Werbung für Ausstellung," 19 October 1953, DH2 VI/61/8, SAPMO, Bundesarchiv Berlin-Lichterfelde.

34. Walde, DBA Forschungsinstitut für Innenarchitektur, to Schloß Wörlitz, Heimatsmuseum Potsdam and Städtisches Museum Glauchau, 24 September 1953, DH2 VI/61/8, SAPMO, Bundesarchiv Berlin-Lichterfelde.

35. "Thema: Innenarchitektur im Wohnungsbau," 20 September 1953, DH2 VI/61/8, SAPMO, Bundesarchiv Berlin-Lichterfelde; "Besser leben—schöner wohnen" (typescript), p. 103, DBA-DH2 A43, SAPMO, Bundesarchiv Berlin-Lichterfelde. A similar message is advanced in *Besser leben—schöner wohnen!* 13; "Protokoll über die vorberritende Besprechung zur Konferenz über Fragen der Innenarchitektur," 2 June 1953, DH2 VI/61/8, SAPMO, Bundesarchiv Berlin-Lichterfelde.

36. Liebknecht, "Die Architektur der Wohnung," 54, 15.

37. Ibid., 14, 15, 16.

38. Denes Holder, "Zweifamilienhaus am Rande einer Großstadt," *Architektur und Wohnform* 61, no. 3 (1952/53): 86.

39. Suga Yasuko, "Designing the Morality of Consumption: 'Chamber of Horrors' at the Museum of Ornamental Art, 1852–53," *Design Issues* 20, no. 4

(Autumn 2004): 47. I am grateful to David Crowley for sharing this and the following reference with me.

40. Adam Jolles, "Stalin's Talking Museums," *Oxford Art Journal* 28, no. 3 (2005): 429–55.

41. Ibid., 443.

42. Boris Groys, *The Total Art of Stalinism: Avant-Garde, Aesthetic Dictatorship, and Beyond,* trans. Charles Rougle (Princeton, N.J.: Princeton University Press, 1992), 49–50.

43. On the Away with National Kitsch exhibition, see Paul Betts, *The Authority of Everyday Objects: A Cultural History of West German Industrial Design* (Berkeley: University of California Press, 2004), 32–34.

44. On the Nazi Degenerate Art exhibition of 1937, see Peter-Klaus Schuster, ed., *Nationalsozialismus und "entartete Kunst": die "Kunststadt" München 1937* (Munich: Prestel, 1998).

45. Wera Muchina, "Thema und Gestaltung in der dekorativ-monumentalen Bildhauerkunst," *Studenmaterial* 7 (1953): 23–24. The article was translated from *Sovietskaia Iskustvo.*

46. On the survival of this trope into the post–cold war era, see Paul Betts, "The New Fascination with Fascism: The Case of Nazi Modernism," *Journal of Contemporary History* 37, no. 4 (October 2002): 544–45.

47. Steven Kotkin, *Magnetic Mountain: Stalinism as a Civilization* (Berkeley: University of California Press, 1995), 174; Anne D. Rassweiler, *The Generation of Power: The History of Dneprostroi* (Oxford: Oxford University Press, 1988), 105.

48. Sheila Fitzpatrick, *Everyday Stalinism: Ordinary Life in Extraordinary Times: Soviet Russia in the 1930s* (New York: Oxford University Press, 1999), 99–100.

49. Ibid., 79–80.

50. Vadim Volkov, "The Concept of *Kul'turnost'*: Notes on the Stalinist Civilizing Process," in *Stalinism: New Directions,* ed. Sheila Fitzpatrick (London: Routledge, 1999), 210–30; Vera Dunham, *In Stalin's Time: Middleclass values in Soviet Fiction* (Cambridge: Cambridge University Press, 1976), 41–54.

51. Volkov, "The Concept of *Kul'turnost',"* 220–22.

52. Liesellote Thomas, Hans Vieillard, and Wolfgang Berger, *Walter Ulbricht. Arbeiter, Revolutionär, Staatsman* (Berlin: Staatsverlag, 1958), 14. See also Johannes R. Becher, *Walter Ulbricht. Ein deutscher Arbeitersohn* (Berlin: Dietz Verlag, 1962).

53. Catriona Kelly and Vadim Volkov, "Directed Desires: *Kul'turnost'* and Consumption," in *Constructing Russian Culture in an Age of Revolution: 1881–1940,* ed. Catriona Kelly and David Shepherd (Oxford: Oxford University Press, 1998), 300.

54. Kurt Magritz, "Wohnkultur mit Kastenmöbeln," *Tägliche Rundschau,* 27 November 1953.

55. Dominique Krössin, "Kultur ins Heim. Geschemckserziehung versus Eigensinn," in *Fortschritt, Norm und Eigensinn. Erkundungen im Alltag der DDR,* ed. Andreas Ludwig (Berlin: Ch. Links Verlag, 2000), 152; Heinz Hirdina, *Gestalten für die Serie. Design in der DDR 1949–1985* (Dresden: VEB Verlag der Kunst, 1988), 48; Anna Minta, "The Authority of the Ordinary: Building Socialism and the Ideology of Domestic Space in East Germany's Furniture Industry," in *Constructed Happiness: Domestic Environment in the Cold War Era,* ed. Mart Kalm and Ingrid Ruudi (Tallinn: Estonian Academy of Arts, 2005), 155; Magritz, "Wohnkultur mit Kastenmöbeln."

56. Jordan, "Über einige Aufgaben des Instituts für Innenarchitektur der Deutschen Bauakademie," 14.

57. Brigette Monk to Jakob Jordan, 3 November 1953, DH2 VI/61/8, SAPMO, Bundesarchiv Berlin-Lichterfelde.

58. "Auswertung der Ausstellung am Alexanderplatz vom 15.11.—29.11.53" DH2 VI-61-3, SAPMO, Bundesarchiv Berlin-Lichterfelde.

59. "Eine Wende in der Möbelindustrie," *Berliner Zeitung,* 6 December 1953.

60. Ibid.

61. "Bitte nicht setzen!" *Berliner Zeitung,* 14 February 1953; "Jetzt zusammensetzen und Mängel beseitigen," *Tribüne,* 14 June 1954.

62. Liebknecht, "Die Architektur der Wohnung," 50. See also "Aus dem Ministerratsbeschluß über die neuen Aufgaben der Innenarchitektur und der Möbelindustrie vom 21. Januar 1954," *Neues Deutschland,* 28 January 1954.

63. Liebknecht, "Die Architektur der Wohnung," 49; Hirdina, *Gestalten für die Serie,* 48.

64. Liebknecht, "Die Architektur der Wohnung," 51.

65. "Beschluß über die neue Aufgaben der Innenarchitektur und der Möbelindustrie vom 21. Januar 1954," DH2-DBA A/79, SAPMO, Bundesarchiv Berlin-Lichterfelde. An abbreviated version of the resolution was published in the SED's national newspaper as "Für eine neue Wohnkultur unserer Werktätigen. Aus dem Ministerratsbeschluß über die neue Aufgaben der Innenarchitektur und der Möbelindustrie vom 21. Januar 1954," *Neues Deutschland,* 28 January 1954.

66. *Neue Berliner Illustrierte,* 48 (1953): 4; quoted in Ina Merkel, "Eine andere Welt. Vorstellungen von Nordamerika in der DDR der fünfziger Jahre," in *Amerikanisierung. Traum und Alptraum im Deutschland des 20. Jahrhunderts,* ed. Alf Lüdke, Inge Marßolek, and Adelheid von Saldern (Stuttgart: Franz Steiner, 1996), 249.

67. Dr. Brandes, DEFA VEB Studio für populärwissenschaftliche Filme, to DBA Institüt für Innenarchitektur (and attached draft of response), 12 October 1954, DH2 DBA A/79, SAPMO, Bundesarchiv Berlin-Lichterfelde.

68. Kotkin, *Magnetic Mountain,* 198–237.

69. Liebknecht, "Die Architektur der Wohnung," 11.

70. "Besprechsprotokoll, Ausstellung Straßmannstraße von 10 Mai 1954," DH2 VI/61/3, SAPMO, Bundesarchiv Berlin-Lichterfelde.

71. On the Leipzig trade fairs, see Katherine Pence, "'A World in Miniature': Leipzig Trade Fairs in the 1950s and East German Consumer Citizenship," in *Consuming Germany in the Cold War*, ed. David Crew (Oxford: Berg, 2003), 21–50.

72. "Niederschrift über den Rundgang des Stellvertretenden Ministerpräsidenten der DDR durch die Stände der zentralgeleiten Industrie und des Handwerks," 11 November 1954, DH2 DBA A/79, SAPMO, Bundesarchiv Berlin-Lichterfelde.

73. Jakob Jordan, "Wie müssen wir unsere Innenarchitektur verbessern?" *Neues Deutschland,* 5 November 1954.

74. Jakob Jordan to Kurt Liebknecht, 9 December 1954, DH2 DBA A/79, SAPMO, Bundesarchiv Berlin-Lichterfelde.

75. "Zusammenfassende Niederschrift über die bisher in der Innen- und Möbelarchitektur geführten Diskussionen speziell mit den Architekten der Deutschen Werkstätten Hellerau," 7 June 1955, DH2 DBA A/79, SAPMO, Bundesarchiv Berlin-Lichterfelde.

76. Jordan to Liebknecht, 9 December 1954.

77. Michael David-Fox, *Masquerade: Sources, Resistance, and Early Soviet Political Culture. Trondheim Studies on East European Cultures and Societies,* no. 1 (Trondheim: Norwegian University of Science and Technology, 1999), 2; Sheila Fitzpatrick, *Tear Off the Masks! Identity and Imposture in Twentieth-Century Russia* (Princeton, N.J.: Princeton University Press, 2005), 65–69; Katerina Clark, *The Soviet Novel: History as Ritual* (Chicago: University of Chicago Press, 1985), 186.

78. Heinrichs, "Bericht über die Reise gemeinsam mit Frau Manutscharowa," 6 March 1956, DH2 DBA A/79, SAPMO, Bundesarchiv Berlin-Lichterfelde.

5. PEOPLE'S CAPITALISM AND CAPITALISM'S PEOPLE

1. Betty Pepis, "Selected for Good Design," *New York Times,* 8 February 1953.

2. Betty Pepis, "New Range Shown for 'Good Design,'" *New York Times,* 20 June 1952.

3. "American Home Furnishings Exhibit in Stuttgart," RG 286 MP Gen 893-1012, Still Pictures Division, U.S. National Archives, College Park, Md.

4. The exhibition also was displayed under the title Design for Use, USA. Museum of Modern Art, "Internationally Circulating Exhibitions," *www.moma.org/international/PDF/icelist.pdf,* accessed 10 September 2006.

5. Betty Pepis, "Ideas for Export," *New York Times,* 16 August 1953.

6. Ibid.

7. Elizabeth Gordon, "The Threat to the Next America," *House Beautiful* 95, no. 4 (April 1953): 126.

8. Ibid.

9. Ibid., 130.

10. Elizabeth Gordon, "The Responsibility of an Editor," speech at the Chicago Furniture Mart, 22 June 1953, 25–26. Thomas Church Papers, Environmental Design Archives, University of California, Berkeley.

11. Gordon, "The Threat to the Next America," 126–27.

12. Ibid., 251.

13. Gordon, "The Responsibility of an Editor," 28–29.

14. Gordon, "The Threat to the Next America," 251.

15. Ruth Schwarz Cowan, "The Consumption Junction: A Proposal for Research Strategies in the Sociology of Technology," in *The Social Construction of Technological Systems: New Directions in the Sociology and History of Technology,* ed. Wiebe E. Bijker, Thomas P. Hughes, and Trevor Pinch (Cambridge, Mass.: MIT Press, 1987), 261–80.

16. Pepis, "Ideas for Export," 36.

17. Jeffrey L. Meikle, *Design in the USA* (Oxford: Oxford University Press, 2005), 150.

18. Eric Larrabee and Massimo Vignelli, *Knoll Design* (New York: Harry Abrams, 1981), 36.

19. Ibid., 178.

20. Kenneth Osgood, *Total Cold War: Eisenhower's Secret Propaganda Battle at Home and Abroad* (Lawrence: University of Kansas Press, 2006), 39–40.

21. Louise S. Robbins, "The Overseas Libraries Controversy and the Freedom to Read: U.S. Librarians and Publishers Confront Joseph McCarthy," *Libraries & Culture* 36, no. 1 (Winter 2001): 28; Osgood, *Total Cold War,* 295–96; Jessica C. E. Gienow-Hecht, "American Cultural Policy in the Federal Republic of Germany, 1949–1968," trans. Robert Kimberly and Rita Kimber, in *The United States and Germany in the Era of the Cold War, 1945–1990: A Handbook,* ed. Detlef Junker, Philipp Gassert, Wilfried Mausbach, and David B. Morris (Cambridge: Cambridge University Press, 2004), 1:405.

22. Frank Trommler, "A New Start and Old Prejudices: The Cold War and German-American Cultural Relations, 1945–1968—The Cold War as Culture," trans. Tradukas, in *The United States and Germany in the Era of the Cold War,* ed. Junker, Gassert, Mausbach, and Morris, 379–80.

23. Charlie M. Cook to Lyndon B. Johnson, 14 February 1952, RG 59 511.62A Box 2246, Files on International Informational and Educational Relations between the United States and Germany, U.S. National Archives, College Park, Md.

24. Jane C. Loeffler, *The Architecture of Diplomacy: Building America's Embassies* (New York: Princeton Architectural Press, 1998), 67–68.

25. For a comprehensive account of Eisenhower's psychological warfare strategy, see Osgood, *Total Cold War,* 46–103.

26. Ibid., 71–72, 77–78.

27. Walter L. Hixson, *Parting the Curtain: Propaganda, Culture, and the Cold War, 1945–1961* (New York: St. Martin's Griffin, 1998), 92.

28. Osgood, *Total Cold War,* 79–80.

29. Ibid., 89.

30. Hixson, *Parting the Curtain,* 122.

31. Osgood, *Total Cold War,* 216–17; Jane Fiske Mitarachi, "Design as a Political Force," *Industrial Design* 4, no. 2 (February 1957): 38. Assistant Secretary of Commerce H. Chad McClellan sounded the alarm on Soviet efforts at an Argentinean exhibition: "The Russians had built their own building, and it seemed to me to be the best lighted building in the entire city of Buenos Aires. The exhibit was principally of machinery, machine tools and equipment, consumer goods such as textiles, fabrics, furs, clothing, etc. [...] I doubt that the show could have been put on for less than $350 - $400,000." H. C. McClellan to T. S. Repplier, 22 February 1956, 13/2/205 Folder 729, Ted Repplier Papers, Advertising Council Archives, University of Illinois at Champaign-Urbana.

32. Osgood, *Total Cold War,* 220.

33. Hixson, *Parting the Curtain,* 40.

34. Osgood, *Total Cold War,* 77.

35. Joseph A. Barry, "Proudly House Beautiful Shows Europe How Americans Live," *House Beautiful* 97, no. 7 (July 1955): 86–94, 115–16; Peter Harnden, "Ausstellungen der USA in Europa," *die Innenarchitektur* 3, no. 7 (January 1956): 408.

36. Robert H. Haddow, *Pavilions of Plenty: Exhibiting American Culture Abroad in the 1950s* (Washington, D.C.: Smithsonian Institution Press, 1997), 44.

37. Elizabeth Gordon, "How High Is Up?" *House Beautiful* 97, no. 7 (July 1955): 110.

38. Haddow, *Pavilions of Plenty,* 44.

39. Ibid., 113.

40. Mitarachi, "Design as a Political Force," 52–53.

41. Harnden, "Ausstellungen der USA in Europa," 406–8.

42. Haddow, *Pavilions of Plenty,* 60–61.

43. Brendan M. Jones, "Official U.S. Role in Trade Fairs Set," *New York Times,* 4 January 1955; "U.S. to Participate in 20 Trade Exhibits," *New York Times,* 28 January 1955.

44. Paul Shinkman, "Trade Fair Participation," *New York Times,* 20 June 1955.

45. Shawn J. Parry-Giles, "The Eisenhower Administration's Conceptualization of the USIA: The Development of Overt and Covert Propaganda Strategies," *Presidential Studies Quarterly* 24 (1994): 265.

46. Theodore S. Repplier, "Transcript (edited) of Report on U.S. Propaganda Overseas," 30 June 1955, 13/2/207 Folder 729, Ted Repplier Papers.

47. J. George Frederick, *The New Deal: A People's Capitalism* (New York: Business Bourse, 1944); Eric Allen Johnston, *America Unlimited* (Garden City, N.Y.: Doubleday, Doran and Co., 1944).

48. John MacCormac, "Crusader for 'A People's Capitalism,'" *New York Times,* 23 April 1944.

49. John H. Crider, "Eric Johnston Accepts Stalin Bid to Visit and Study Soviet Russia," *New York Times,* 22 March 1944, 1. On Johnston's 1944 visit to the USSR, see William Lindsay White, *Report on the Russians* (New York: Harcourt, Brace and Co., 1945).

50. Russell Porter, "Free-Enterprise Way Here Much Understood Abroad," *New York Times,* 11 May 1947.

51. "People's Capitalism," *Stet* no. 184 (January 1956): 1–3.

52. Paul G. Hoffman, *Peace Can Be Won* (Garden City, N.Y.: Doubleday, 1951), 152.

53. Ibid., 141. Much of Hoffman's platform for an American "free world doctrine" reappeared in the "new Magna Carta of freedom" proposed by Allen Dulles before the Eisenhower administration's Council of Foreign Relations in 1953; see Osgood, *Total Cold War,* 288–322.

54. "Capitalism Show Seen by 25,000," *Washington Post,* 23 February 1956.

55. Osgood, *Total Cold War,* 272.

56. "Copy for People's Capitalism Exhibit," 13/2/305, Folder 126, Ted Repplier Papers.

57. Roger Stuart, undated dispatch for Scripps-Howard newspapers on the People's Capitalism exhibit, 13/2/205 Folder 729, Ted Repplier Papers.

58. Haddow, *Pavilions of Plenty,* 125.

59. Lizabeth Cohen, *A Consumer's Republic: The Politics of Mass Consumption in Postwar America* (New York: Knopf, 2003), 295.

60. Ibid., 121–23.

61. Ibid., 294–95.

62. Don Slater, *Consumer Culture and Modernity* (Cambridge, Mass.: Polity Press, 1997), 190–91.

63. Wendell R. Smith, "Product Differentiation and Market Segmentation as Alternative Marketing Strategies, *Journal of Marketing,* 21, no. 7 (July 1956): 7.

64. "Makins Lauds Capitalist Show," *Washington Post,* 3 April 1956.

65. Ralph Bugli, "'People's Capitalism!' Rah! Rah! Rah!" *Intercom* 3 (February 1956), unpaginated, 13/2/205 Folder 729, Ted Repplier Papers.

66. John L. Peters to Theodore Repplier, 24 February 1956; Henry M. Pachter to Theodore Repplier, 23 February 1956, 13/2/205 Folder 729, Ted Repplier Papers.

67. John Nuveen to Theodore S. Repplier, 29 February 1956, 13/2/205 Folder 729, Ted Repplier Papers.

68. Warren Mullen to Theodore S. Repplier, 16 February 1956, 13/2/205 Folder 729, Ted Repplier Papers.

69. Theodore S. Repplier to Warren Muller, 21 February 1956, 13/2/205 Folder 729, Ted Repplier Papers.

70. Jean White, "Changes Ike Suggested to Be Made in Exhibit," *Washington Post,* 16 February 1956.

71. John J. Gilhooley to Robert Mullen, 7 March 1956, 13/2/205 Folder 729, Ted Repplier Papers.

93. For example, the Tu-4—the first Soviet bomber capable of delivering an atomic bomb—was an exact copy of the American B-29, three of which were confiscated by the USSR after having made emergency landings in Siberia during World War II. On the East bloc practice of imitation as a means of technology transfer, see Raymond Stokes, "In Search of the Socialist Artefact: Technology and Ideology in East Germany, 1945–1962," *German History* 15, no. 2 (1997): 221–39.

94. On Albert Kahn Inc. and Stalin's Five-Year Plan, see Federico Bucci, *Albert Kahn, Architect of Ford* (New York: Princeton Architectural Press, 1993); Grant Hildebrand, *Designing for Industry: The Architecture of Albert Kahn* (Cambridge, Mass.: MIT Press, 1974).

95. Richard Anderson, "1939 and the Soviet House of Tomorrow," unpublished paper, August 2006.

96. Hixson, *Parting the Curtain,* 106.

97. Stetson, "Enroute with the Russians."

98. "Russia Buys a House," *New York Times,* 30 October 1955; Harrison E. Salisbury, "Touring Soviet Aide Pictures U.S. as Christmas Dream Come True," *New York Times,* 29 October 1955; Charles E. Egan, "Somebody 'Sold' in Russian Deal," *New York Times,* 11 March 1955.

99. Untitled article, *Washington Post and Times Herald,* 5 November 1955.

100. "5 Building Experts Arrive from Russia," *New York Times,* 11 May 1956.

101. "Russians to Get a U.S. Dwelling," *New York Times,* 23 July 1956.

102. USIA 306 - PS Subject 56-16610, 16611; Still Pictures Division, National Archives, College Park, Md.

103. Amanda Wood Aucoin, "Deconstructing the American Way of Life: Soviet Responses to Cultural Exchange and American Information Activity during the Khrushchev Years" (Ph.D. diss., University of Arkansas, 2001), 57–58.

6. THE TROJAN HOUSE GOES EAST

1. Henry Loomis to Theodore Repplier, 29 February 1956, 13/2/205 Folder 729, Ted Repplier Papers, Advertising Council Archives, University of Illinois at Champaign-Urbana. For excerpts from speeches by Khrushchev denouncing People's Capitalism, see Harry Schwartz, "The America in Khrushchev's Mind," *New York Times,* 16 August 1959.

2. Jack Raymond, "Russian People's Friendliness toward the U.S. Is Counteracted by Official Propaganda," *New York Times,* 5 May 1956.

3. Alberto Galindo, *People's Capitalism: The Process of Its Realization* (New York: Advertising Council, undated), 9–10.

4. John D. Morris, "President Scores Cut of 37 Million in U.S.I.A. Budget," *New York Times,* 18 April 1957.

5. Walter L. Hixson, *Parting the Curtain: Propaganda, Culture, and the Cold War, 1945–1961* (New York: St. Martin's Griffin, 1998), 110.

6. Brendan M. Jones, "U.S. to Go behind Iron Curtain to Show American Way at Fairs," *New York Times,* 22 May 1956.

7. "Polish Artillery Reported Ending Revolt in 3d Day," *New York Times,* 1 July 1956.

8. Hixson, *Parting the Curtain,* 78–79, 111.

9. Robert H. Haddow, *Pavilions of Plenty: Exhibiting American Culture Abroad in the 1950s* (Washington, D.C.: Smithsonian Institution Press, 1997), 63; "U.S. Expands Role in Trade Exhibits," *New York Times,* 3 January 1957.

10. "U.S. Pavilion Designed for Poznan Fair in June," *New York Times,* 8 March 1957; Sydney Gruson, "Polish Folk Laud an Exhibit by U.S.," *New York Times,* 9 June 1957.

11. Gruson, "Polish Folk Laud an Exhibit by U.S.," 40; Sydney Gruson, "Poles at Fair Jam U.S. Display Called Rich Man's Show by Reds," *New York Times,* 10 June 1957.

12. "Nylon Wonderland: U.S. Exhibit in Poland's International Trade Fair," *Time,* 1 June 1957, 31–32.

13. Edgar Clark, "U.S. Builder's Model House Is the Biggest Hit for 500,000 Polish Fair-goers," *House and Home* 12, no. 2 (August 1957): 98–101.

14. Carl Nolte, "Mary Jean Kelly—Promoter of Modern Appliances," *San Francisco Chronicle,* 6 August 2005.

15. Kenneth Osgood, *Total Cold War: Eisenhower's Secret Propaganda Battle at Home and Abroad* (Lawrence: University of Kansas Press, 2006), 217, 222.

16. Jane Fiske Mitarachi, "Design as a Political Force," *Industrial Design* 4, no. 2 (February 1957): 54.

17. June Owen, "Food: Home Economist's Poznan Trip," *New York Times,* 15 July 1957.

18. Fiske Mitarachi, "Design as a Political Force," 52. On the Italian adoption of U.S.-style supermarkets, see Victoria de Grazia, *Irresistible Empire: America's Advance through Twentieth-Century Europe* (Cambridge, Mass.: Belknap, 2005), 376–415.

19. Djuka Julius, "Supermarket 'Stars' at the Zagreb Fair: Especially the Meat Counter," *Washington Post,* 8 December 1957.

20. "U.S. Plans Exhibit at Yugoslav Fair," *New York Times,* 17 July 1957; "U.S. Supermarket Soon Will Invade Tito's Domain," *New York Times,* 24 July 1957; "Showcase for American Business and Industry Rises in Yugoslavia," *New York Times,* 1 September 1957.

21. Elie Abel, "Gomulka Avoids U.S. Show at Fair," *New York Times,* 15 September 1957.

22. Elie Abel, "Typical American Supermarket Is the Hit of the Fair in Yugoslavia," *New York Times,* 8 September 1957.

23. "Yugoslav Unit Buys Model Supermarket," *New York Times,* 25 September 1957.

24. "Supermarket U.S.A. in Belgrade," *Washington Post,* 21 February 1958.

25. Elinor Lee, "Shopping Plan Goes into Orbit," *Washington Post,* 15 August 1958.

26. "U.S. Supermarket Soon Will Invade Tito's Domain."

27. Osgood, *Total Cold War,* 342.

28. "Discussion at the 339th Meeting of the National Security Council, Thursday, 10 October 1957," Eisenhower Presidential Papers, NSC Series, Box 9, Eisenhower Library; quoted in James Schwoch, "The Cold War, the Space Race, and the Globalization of Public Opinion Polling," paper presented at the International Studies Association Conference, New Orleans, March 2002, 11.

29. Hixson, *Parting the Curtain,* 152–53.

30. Warren Unna, "We're Set to Be Shamed at Brussels," *Washington Post,* 26 January 1958.

31. Hixson, *Parting the Curtain,* 141.

32. Haddow, *Pavilions of Plenty,* 158. The anecdote cited by Howard was from a conversation she had with Robert Warner of the USIA exhibits program division; she did not identify the trade fair at which Khrushchev's kitchen visit occurred.

33. "Boston to Get World's Fair Preview," *Boston Globe,* 24 November 1957; Cynthia Kellogg, "An American Brussels Fair Designer Gives French Home Modern Look," *New York Times,* 4 December 1957.

34. "American Design Preview: Brussels World's Fair," undated press release, Institute of Contemporary Art archives, Boston.

35. Marjorie J. Harlepp, "U.S. Revises Home Show at Fair Site," *New York Times,* 6 June 1958.

36. Haddow, *Pavilions of Plenty,* 148–58.

37. Misha Black, "The Nations Displayed," *Design* (London) 117 (September 1958): 24; Hugh L. Morris, "Overseas Home Exhibits Scorned as Non-Typical," *Washington Post,* 21 March 1959.

38. On the use of U.S. racial inequality in Soviet propaganda, see Amanda Wood Aucoin, "Deconstructing the American Way of Life: Soviet Responses to Cultural Exchange and American Information Activity during the Khrushchev Years" (Ph.D. diss., University of Arkansas, 2001), 224–59; and Laura A. Belmonte, *Selling the American Way: U.S. Propaganda and the Cold War* (Philadelphia: University of Pennsylvania Press, 2008), 159–77.

39. Michael Krenn, "'Unfinished Business': Segregation and U.S. Diplomacy at the 1958 World's Fair," *Diplomatic History* 20 (Fall 1996): 591–92.

40. Hixson, *Parting the Curtain,* 145–47.

41. Cristina Carbone, "Setting the Stage for the Kitchen Debate: Architecture at the American National Exhibition in Moscow of 1959," paper presented at the "Cold War in the Kitchen" conference, Munich, 2005. Carbone cites the title of this document as *Secret Basic Policy Guidance for the U.S. Exhibit in Moscow in 1959* (RG 306, Box 7, FOIA, National Archives, College Park, Md.).

110. Pence is wrong, however, to consider this demonstration a vehicle for a "GDR-specific version of 'consumer culture,'" as the exhibit was mounted in Czechoslovakia.

3. "Wie wohnt Europa heute," *Innenarchitektur* 5, no. 1 (July 1957): 33–34.

4. Peter Bergner, "Teilnahme auf Aufforderung durch den BDIA an der Sonderschau 'Wie wohnt Europa heute.'" Bundesarchiv SAPMO, DH2 VI/61/2.

5. Jacob Jordan to Muggelberg, Bergner, and Witte, 10 May 1955; Jordan to Paulick, 5 September 1955; Bundesarchiv SAPMO DH2 VI/61/2.

6. "Ein Bravo der gelungenen Möbelaustellung," *Berliner Zeitung,* 5 February 1956.

7. Trautvetter, "Aktennotiz," 19 October 1956, Bundesarchiv SAPMO DH2 VI/61/2.

8. Jacob Jordan to Duntz, "Beteiligung der Forschungsinstituts für Innenarchitektur an der Internationalen Handwerkmesse im Mai 1957," 22 November 1956, Bundesarchiv SAPMO, DH2 VI/61/2.

9. "Aktennotiz Betr.: Aussprache im Zentralkommitte am 26.11. 56," Bundesarchiv SAPMO, DH2 VI/61/2.

10. "Vorlage zur Durchführung jährlicher Sonderaustellungen schöner Industrieerzeugnisse auf den Frühjahrmessen in Leipzig: Erste Sonderschau im Frühjahr 1957," undated, Bundesarchiv SAPMO DF7 Inst.132.

11. "Aktenvermerk," 29 November 1956, Bundesarchiv SAPMO, DH2 VI/61/2.

12. "Wie wohnt Europa heute," *Innenarchitektur* 4, no. 12 (June 1957); continued in 5, no. 1 (July 1957): 790, 33–34.

13. Dominique Krössin, "Kultur ins Heim. Geschemckserziehung versus Eigensinn," in *Fortschritt, Norm und Eigensinn. Erkundungen im Alltag der DDR,* ed. Andreas Ludwig (Berlin: Ch. Links Verlag, 2000), 153.

14. "Moderne Möbel bestellt," *Berliner Zeitung,* 9 November 1956.

15. It would take the GDR decades to address the problem of adequate domestic supply of consumer hardware, as indicated by a comment made at the 1960 Leipzig Trade Fair: "A great step toward our goal for 1965 would be if for once the appliances shown in the Fair halls would come into retail trade in sufficient numbers." Katherine Pence, "Leipzig Trade Fairs in the 1950s," in *Consuming Germany in the Cold War,* ed. David F. Crew (Oxford: Berg, 2003), 38.

16. "Stellungnahme des Präsidiums der Deutschen Bauakademie vom 9.6.1955," cited in Andreas Schätzke, *Zwischen Bauhaus und Stalinallee: Architekturdiskussion im östlichen Deutschland, 1945–1955* (Braunschweig: Vieweg, 1991), 162.

17. Eli Rubin, "The Form of Socialism without Ornament: Consumption, Ideology, and the Fall and Rise of Modernist Design in the German Democratic Republic," *Journal of Design History* 19, no. 2 (Summer 2006): 156, 158. Horst Michel also proposed vernacular German household objects of the Middle Ages as native exemplars of "good design" in an attempt to link contemporary functionalism to Stalin-era discourses focused on national

tradition. Petra Eisele, "Ist Geschmack Glücksache?" in *Horst Michel, DDR-Design,* ed. Petra Eisele and Siegfried Gronert (Weimar: Bauhaus University, 2004), 31–34. Michel, in fact, deserves credit for East German modernism's first westward push. Design prototypes he exhibited with his Weimar colleagues at Leipzig's 1955 spring trade fair garnered praise from West German visitors, landing his institute an invitation to display faculty work a few months later in Darmstadt. Horst Michel to Jacob Jordan, 16 September 1955, Bundesarchiv SAPMO, DH2 VI/61/2; Eisele, "Ist Geschmack Glücksache?" 43; Horst Michel, "Aus der Arbeit des Instituts für Innengestaltung in Weimar," *Bildende Kunst* 2 , no. 3 (1957): 338.

18. Heinz Hirdina, *Gestalten für die Serie, Design in der DDR 1949–1985* (Dresden: VEB Verlag der Kunst, 1988), 51.

19. Ibid., 56; Heinz Köster, "Horst Michel: Biographie und Zeitgeschichte," *form + zweck* 10, no. 5 (1979); quoted in Eisele, "Ist Geschmack Glücksache?" 40–41.

20. On the long process of rehabilitating Bauhaus design ideology in the GDR, see Greg Castillo, "The Bauhaus in Cold War Germany," in *Bauhaus Culture: From Weimar to the Cold War,* ed. Kathleen James-Chakraborty (Minneapolis: University of Minnesota Press, 2005), 188–93.

21. Horst Michel, "Tradition oder Neuheit?" *Deutsche Architektur* 6, no. 1 (1957): 31–32.

22. Horst Michel, "Das Angemessene," *Bildende Kunst* 1, no. 11/12 (1956): 594.

23. Ibid., 32.

24. Mark Landsman, *Dictatorship and Demand: The Politics of Consumerism in East Germany* (Cambridge, Mass.: Harvard University Press, 2005), 15.

25. "An die 3. Parteikonferenz der Sozialistischen Einheitspartei Deutschlands," undated, Bundesarchiv SAPMO, DH2 DBA/A79.

26. "Antwort auf Tausende Briefe," *Kultur im Heim* 2, no. 1 (1957): 1. Rhetoric used in this editorial is strikingly similar to that of the Kulturbund in its recommendations to the SED Third Party Congress.

27. Vertiko, "Ästhetik—für jeden verstänlich! Kultur und Mode," *Kultur im Heim* 3, no. 4 (1958): 12.

28. Paul Betts, *The Authority of Everyday Objects: A Cultural History of West German Industrial Design* (Berkeley: University of California Press, 2004), 138, 129.

29. Vertiko, "Ästhetik—für jeden verstänlich!" 12.

30. *Kultur im Heim* 2, no. 1 (1957): 3; cited in Dominique Krössin, "Kultur ins Heim," in *Fortschritt, Norm und Eigensinn. Erkundigen im Alltag der DDR* (Berlin: Links, 1999), 157. Other articles calling for reform in socialist retailing include "Einige Betrachtungen zur Lage auf dem Möbelmarkt," *Kultur im Heim* 2, no. 4 (1957): 9, 43; "Uns fehlen einige Elefanten um in den Porzellanläden einmal richtig 'aufzuräumen,'" *Kultur im Heim* 4, no. 2 (1959): 42–44.

31. *Kultur im Heim* 2, no. 2 (1957): 43, 9; cited in Krössin, "Kultur ins Heim," 157, 153–54.

72. Alma S. Scurlock to Theodore Streiber, 28 February 1956, 13/2/205 Folder 729, Ted Repplier Papers.

73. Theodore S. Repplier to Warren Muller, 21 February 1956, 13/2/205 Folder 729, Ted Repplier Papers.

74. Conger Reynolds to Theodore Repplier, 22 February 1956, 13/2/205 Folder 729, Ted Repplier Papers.

75. David M. Potter, *The American Round Table Discussions on People's Capitalism*, part 1 (New York: Advertising Council, 1957), 7, 13, 8.

76. Victor Perlo, "'People's Capitalism' and Stock Ownership," *American Economic Review* 48, no. 3 (June 1958): 333–47. The theory of people's capitalism spread to Germany in the early 1960s, generating studies including Oskar Klug, *Volkskapitalismus durch Eigentumsstreuung, Illusion oder Wirklichkeit?* (Stuttgart: G. Fischer, 1962); and Heinz-Dietrich Ortlieb, *Die Legende von Volkskapitalismus* (Berlin: K. Vogt, 1963).

77. Michael D. Reagan, "What 17 Million Shareholders Share," *New York Times,* 23 February 1964.

78. Jean White, "'Derailed' Capitalism Exhibit Re-Emerges," *New York Times,* 2 September 1958.

79. Elie Abel, "Zagreb Puzzled by West's Shows," *New York Times,* 10 September 1956.

80. Elie Abel, "U.S. 'Soft Sell' Is Hard Pressed by Red Hucksters at Zagreb Fair," *New York Times,* 8 September 1956; Mitarachi, "Design as a Political Force," 46.

81. Osgood, *Total Cold War,* 219.

82. Hixson, *Parting the Curtain,* 101–2.

83. "Soviet Housing Men Due in Washington," *New York Times,* 2 October 1955.

84. On the activities of the Architects Committee of the National Council of American-Soviet Friendship, see Greg Castillo, "Constructing the Cold War: Architecture, Urbanism, and the Cultural Division of Germany, 1945–1957" (Ph.D. diss., University of California at Berkeley, 2000), 61–79.

85. Don Stetson, "Enroute with the Russians," unpaginated, undated news release, National Association of Home Builders library, Washington, D.C.

86. Ibid.

87. Ibid.

88. Roy Meachum, "Russian Housing Experts Impressed by Our Kitchens and Bathrooms," *Washington Post and Times Herald,* 31 October 1955.

89. "Soviet Builders Due October 11th," *Chicago News,* 5 October 1953; Richard Lyons, "10 Russian Officials Start Housing Tour," *Washington Post and Times Herald,* 5 October 1955.

90. Untitled article, *New York Times,* 22 October 1955; untitled article, *Washington Post and Times Herald,* 5 November 1955.

91. Meachum, "Russian Housing Experts Impressed by Our Kitchens."

92. Stetson, "Enroute with the Russians."

32. Peter Bergner, "Neue Möbel für 1957," *Deutsche Architektur* 5, no. 12 (1957): 590; "Das kulturelle Erbe und das Weltniveau," *Kultur im Heim* 2, no. 4 (1957): 1, 43; reprinted from *Form und Zweck.*

33. Memorandum, Sektor Raumausstatung der DBA, 24 July 1959, SAPMO DH2 III/21/16.

34. Michel, "Tradition oder Neuheit?" 33. Michel's advocacy of export trade as a goad to national design reform dominated his presentation at the 1956 Leipzig Conference on Questions of Design and Production of Standardized and Modular Furnishings: "We at last should take pains to manufacture some new, better, *German* products for export. So that the foreign customer doesn't say: 'I'd like to buy this primitive set of furniture because I can get it cheaper than I can in my own country'; rather, we must attain, I think, the production of things good enough that the foreign customer asks: 'May I please obtain that from you?' Other nations must demand products from us that are better than those than they have wanted from us before." "Discussionsbeitrage," 27 February 1956, Bundesarchiv SAPMO, DH2 VI/61/12.

35. Jordan to Leutoff, "Betr.: Sudienreisen im kapitalistischen Ausland 1957," 4 October 1956, Bundesarchiv SAPMO, DH2 VI/61/12.

36. Hoffmann to Jordan, 23 October 1957, Bundesarchiv SAPMO, DH2 DBA/A79.

37. Vittorio Magnano Lampugniani, "The 'Zero Hour': Reconstruction's Goals and Premises," *Domus* 21, no. 685 (July-August 1987): 96.

38. "Die Welt Baut in Berlin," *Bauwelt* 48, no. 28 (1957): 705.

39. Peter Tennant, "Design for European Trade," *Design* (London), no. 107 (November 1957): 21–23.

40. Alexandra Staub, "*Einmal im Leben*: Rooting the 'Little Man' to Conservative Values in Postwar West Germany," in *After Fascism: Society, Political Culture, and Democratization in Europe since 1945,* ed. Matthew Berg and Maria Mesner (Manchester: Manchester University Press, forthcoming).

41. Michael Wildt, "Continuities and Discontinuities of Consumer Mentality in West Germany in the 1950s," in *Life after Death: Approaches to a Cultural and Social History of Europe during the 1940s and 1950s,* ed. Richard Bessel and Dirk Schumann (Cambridge: Cambridge University Press, 2003), 161–92.

42. Ingrid Schenk, "Producing to Consume Becomes Consuming to Produce: Advertising and Consumerism in German American Relations," in *The United States and Germany in the Era of the Cold War, 1945–1990: A Handbook,* ed. Detlef Junker, Philipp Gassert, Wilfried Mausbach, and David B. Morris (Cambridge: Cambridge University Press, 2004), 1:582–83.

43. Nikolaus Bernau, "Geschichte des Hansaviertels. Die 'schöne, luftigere' Stadt als Gegenstück zur Stalinallee," *Der Tagesspiegel* (Berlin), 15 December 1999.

44. Axel Shildt and Arnold Sywottek, "'Reconstruction' and 'Modernization': West German Social History during the 1950s," in *West Germany under Construction: Politics, Society and Culture in the Adenauer Era,* ed. Robert G. Moeller (Ann Arbor: University of Michigan Press, 1997), 439.

45. Klaus Landsberg, "Neues Wohnen im Berliner Hansaviertel," *Die Innenarchitektur* 5, no. 3 (1957/58): 174.

46. "Die Küche in der 'Stadt von Morgen,'" *Bauwelt* 48, no. 44 (1957): 1177.

47. Barbara Miller Lane, "The Berlin Congress Hall, 1955–1957," *Perspectives in American History* 1 (1984): 151.

48. Charlotta Heythum, "Wohn-Zukunftsträume auf der Interbau Berlin," *Die Innenarchitektur* 5, no. 8 (1957/8): 447.

49. Sonja Günther, *Die fünfziger Jahre. Innenarchitektur und Wohndesign* (Stuttgart: Deutsche Verlags-Anstalt, 1994): 49; Hans Gugelot, "Das komplexe Ausbausystem M 125," *Die Innenarchitektur* 3, no. 8 (1956): 477–78. For a brief survey of the variety of modular storage units appearing in the West German marketplace at the time, see Bernhard Siepen, "Typus und Freiheit innerhalb der Kasten- und Kleinmöbel, *Die Innenarchitektur* 3, no. 10 (1956): 601–7.

50. Elisabeth Noelle and Erich Peter Neumann, eds., *Jahrbuch der öffentlichen Meinung* (Allensbach am Bodensee: Verlag für Demoskopie, 1957), 108–9.

51. Tennant, "Design for European Trade," 23.

52. Michael Wildt, "Changes in Consumption as Social Practice in West Germany during the 1950s," in *Getting and Spending: European and American Consumer Societies in the Twentieth Century,* ed. Susan Strasser, Charles McGovern, and Mattias Judt (Cambridge: Cambridge University Press, 1998), 311.

53. Deborah Howell-Ardila, "Berlin's Search for a 'Democratic' Architecture," *German Politics and Society* 48, 3 (1998): 72.

54. "Berlins größte Mietskaserne auf der Interbau," *Berliner Zeitung,* 22 September 1957.

55. Kurt Liebknecht, *Die nationalen Aufgaben der deutschen Architektur* (Berlin: Deutsche Bauakademie, 1954), 74.

56. "Ost Architekten im Hansaviertel," *Der Tagesspiegel,* 2 September 1956.

57. "Analyse der Interbau," Secretariat des Beirates für Bauwesen beim Ministerrat der DDR, 15 March 1958, Bundesarchiv SAPMO, DH2 DBA/4/48.

58. Ibid., 38–42.

59. Ibid., 15.

60. 'Klytaemnestra,' "Wie haben Ihnen die Wohnungen der Interbau gefallen?" *Der Tagesspiegel,* 29 September 1957; reprinted in *Neuer Wohnbau,* ed. Hermann Wandersleb (Ravensburg: Otto Maier Verlag, 1958), 2:110.

61. "Analyse der Interbau," 43.

62. *Rezolucija Internatcionalne konferencije ekonomiskih propagandista,* cited and translated in Patrick Hyder Patterson, "Truth Half Told: Finding the Perfect Pitch for Advertising and Marketing in Socialist Yugoslavia, 1950–1991," *Enterprise and Society* 4 (June 2003): 219.

63. On the Khrushchev-era ideology of managed socialist consumption, see Susan Reid, "Cold War in the Kitchen: Gender and the De-Stalinization of Consumer Taste in the Soviet Union under Khrushchev," *Slavic Review* 61, no. 2 (2002): 211–23.

64. Patterson, "Truth Half Told," 217–18, 193. On the production of the Soviet consumer, see Susan E. Reid, "Khrushchev Modern: Agency and Modernization in the Soviet Home," *Cahiers du Monde Russe* 47, no. 1–2 (January-June 2006): 244–55.

65. This was especially true of abstract art. As Susan Reid notes, "The filtering of contemporary western intellectual and artistic currents into the Soviet Union through the 'soft' border of Eastern Europe was instrumental in the emergence of nonconformist art [in the USSR]." Susan Reid, "Toward a New (Socialist) Realism: The Re-engagement with Western Modernism in the Khrushchev Thaw," in *Russian Art and the West: A Century of Dialogue in Painting, Architecture, and the Decorative Arts,* ed. Rosalind P. Blakesley and Susan E. Reid (DeKalb: Northern Illinois University Press, 2007), 223.

66. Anne Kaminsky, "'True Advertising Means Promoting a Good Thing through Good Form': Advertising in the German Democratic Republic," in *Selling Modernity: Advertising in Twentieth-Century Germany,* ed. Pamela E. Swett, S. Jonathan Wiesen, and Jonathan R. Zaitlin (Durham, N.C.: Duke University Press, 2007), 265.

67. Ibid., 267; Landsman, *Dictatorship and Demand,* 175.

68. Alfred Schneider, "Wir erbauen unsere Zukunft selbst," *Kultur im Heim* 3, no. 4 (1958): 3.

69. Joachim Palutzki, *Architektur in der DDR* (Berlin: Reimer, 2000), 144–45.

70. Duanfang Lu, *Remaking Chinese Urban Form: Modernity, Scarcity, and Space, 1949–2005* (London: Routledge, 2006), 6.

71. Landsman, *Dictatorship and Demand,* 174–75, 205–7.

72. On the development of East German self-service retailing, see Silke Rothkirch, "Moderne Menschen kaufen modern," and Ina Merkel, "Die aufhaltsame Aufbruch in die Konsumgesellschaft," in *Wunderwirtschaft. DDR-Konsumkultur in den 60er Jahren,* ed. Ina Merkel and Felix Mühlberg (Cologne: Böhlau Verlag, 1996), 112–18; 9–20.

73. Landsman, *Dictatorship and Demand,* 187–88.

74. Ranier Gries, "'Help Yourself!' The History and Theory of Self Service in West and East Germany," in *Selling Modernity,* ed. Swett, Wiesen, and Zatlin, 311.

75. This assessment is supported by recent investigations of socialist retailing, including Julie M. Hessler, *A Social History of Soviet Trade* (Princeton, Md.: Princeton University Press, 2004); Mark Evan Landsman, *Dictatorship and Demand: The Politics of Consumerism in East Germany* (Cambridge, Mass.: Harvard University Press, 2005); Katherine Pence, "'You as a Woman Will Understand': Consumption, Gender and the Relationship between State and Citizenry in the GDR's Crisis of 17 June 1953, *German History* 19, no. 2 (2001): 218–52; and André Steiner, "Dissolution of the 'Dictatorship over Needs'? Consumer Behavior and Economic Reform in East Germany in the 1960s," in *Getting and Spending,* ed. Strasser, McGovern, and Judt, 167–85.

76. Steven E. Harris, "Moving to the Separate Apartment: Building, Distributing, Furnishing, and Living in Urban Housing in Soviet Russia, 1950s–1960s" (Ph.D. diss., University of Chicago, 2003), 465.

77. Ibid., 143–44.

78. Palutzki, *Architektur in der DDR,* 139, 187.

79. E., "Neue Form in Finnland," *Bildende Kunst* 3, no. 5 (1958): 190.

80. Horst Michel, "Industrieformen auf der IV. Deutschen Kunstaustellung," *Bildende Kunst* 4, no. 1 (1959): 45–46; and Horst Michel, "Aufgaben des Industrieformgestalters in der Deutschen Demokratischen Republik," *Bildende Kunst* 7, no. 2 (1962): 96.

81. Reid, "Khrushchev Modern," 241.

82. Steiner, "Dissolution of the 'Dictatorship over Needs'?" 170.

83. Ina Merkel, *Utopie und Bedürfnis. Die Geschichte der Konsumkultur in der DDR* (Cologne: Böhlau, 1991), 228.

84. Palutzki, *Architektur in der DDR,* 139, 194.

85. "Kurzanalyse zu Republikfluchten 1959–60," Abteilung Bauwesen (SED Central Committee), 6.12.1960; cited in Palutzki, *Architektur in der DDR,* 192.

86. For an account of Ulbricht's manipulation of the Kremlin policies regarding divided Berlin, see Hope M. Harrison, *Driving the Soviets Up the Wall: Soviet-East German Relations, 1953–1961* (Princeton, N.J.: Princeton University Press, 2003); and John Gearson and Dori Schake, eds., *The Berlin Wall Crisis: Perspectives on Cold War Alliances* (New York: Palgrave Macmillan, 2002).

87. Alexandra Richie, *Faust's Metropolis: A History of Berlin* (New York: Carroll and Graff, 1998), 715–24.

88. *Chronik Bauwesen DDR,* cited in Palutzki, *Architektur in der DDR,* 193. For a more recent history of this vanished monument, see Frederick Taylor, *The Berlin Wall: A World Divided, 1961–1989* (New York: HarperCollins, 2007).

89. Petra Gruner et al., "P2 macht das Rennen. Wohnungsbau als sozio-kulturelles Programm," in *Alltagskultur der DDR: Begleitbuch zur Ausstellung "Tempolinsen und P2,"* ed. Stadt Eisenhüttenstadt, Dokumentationszentrum (Berlin: Be.Bra Verlag, 1996), 92.

90. Horst Michel, "Moderne Wohngestaltung," *Bildende Kunst* 7, no. 11 (1962): 595.

91. Gruner, "P2 macht das Rennen," 92–93.

92. Ernst Könitzer and Jacob Jordan, "Die Ausstellung 'neues leben–neues wohnen' im Muster- und Experimentalbau P2 in Berlin," *Deutsche Architektur* 11, no. 9 (1962): 523; Michel, "Moderne Wohngestaltung," 598.

93. Jörg Peters, "Wohnraum—Möbel—Rundfunk—Fernsehen," *Bildende Kunst* 8, no. 1 (1963): 36.

94. Könitzer and Jordan, "Die Ausstellung 'neues leben–neues wohnen,'" 523.

95. Michel, "Moderne Wohngestaltung," 598.

96. "Meinungen, Kritik und Hinweise zum Versuchsbau P2," *Deutsche Architektur* 11, no. 9 (1962): 543–46.

97. Ibid., 546.

98. East Germany's practice of exporting high-quality furniture rather than sell-ing it domestically became even more prevalent with the expansion of foreign debt under Honecker. Jonathan R. Zaitlin, "The Vehicle of Desire: The Tra-bant, the Wartburg, and the End of the GDR," *German History* 15, no. 3: 366–67.

99. Friedrich Engemann, "Architektur und Wohnkultur," *Deutsche Architektur* 11, no. 9 (1962): 541.

100. "Fachtagung der Möbelbauer und Innenarchitekten," *Deutsche Architektur* 11, no. 9 (1962): 555.

101. Ibid.

102. "Fragen der deutschen Innenarchitekten und des Möbelbaues," Bundesarchiv SAPMO, DH2 DBA A 141.

103. Engemann, "Architektur und Wohnkultur," 542; Peter Bergner, "Möbel," *Deutsche Architektur* 11, no. 9 (1962): 532.

104. Michel, "Aufgaben des Industrieformgestalters in der Deutschen Demokrati-schen Republik," 92.

105. Autorenkollektiv, *wie richte ich meine wohnung ein?* (Leipzig: VEB Fach-bucherverlag, 1961).

106. "Antwort auf Fragen. Diskussionsrede des Genossen Walter Ulbricht auf der Bezirksdelegiertenkonferenz in Leipzig am 9.12.1962," *Leipziger Volkszeitung* 15 December 1962; quoted in Heinz Köster, "Schmerzliche Ankunft in der Moderne," in *Wunder-wirtschaft: DDR-Konsumkultur in den 60er Jahren,* ed. NGBK (Cologne: Böhlau, 1996), 98–99.

107. Karl-Heinz Hagen, "Hinter dem Leben zuruck. Bermerkungen zur 'Indus-trielle Formgestaltung' auf der V. Deutschen Kunstaustellung," *Neues Deutschland,* 4 October 1962; quoted in Köster, "Schmerzliche Ankunft in der Moderne," 97.

108. "Einschätzung der V. Deutschen Kunstaustellung," 27 October 1962, quoted in Köster, "Schmerzliche Ankunft in der Moderne," 98.

109. The *Frankfurt Abendpost* ran a satirical photomontage of Ulbricht with flying cups and saucers captioned "Black cups—black souls?" Köster, "Schmerzliche Ankunft in der Moderne," 99.

110. Kaminsky, "'True Advertising Means Promoting a Good Thing through Good Form,'" 269–70. East Berlin's Council of Ministers decreed that "advertising and fashion shows contradict socialist society" just weeks after the construc-tion of the wall, as noted by Swett, Wiesen, and Zaitlin, eds., in the introduc-tion to *Selling Modernity,* 16. East Berlin's biannual Fashion Week, a popular garment industry and media event, disappeared without warning or explana-tion in 1961, as did the comic operetta *Messeschlager Giesela* about a factory worker's triumphant breakthrough as a socialist fashion designer; on these reversals of fortune, see Judd Stitziel, "On the Seam between Socialism and Capitalism: East German Fashion Shows," in *Consuming Germany in the Cold War,* ed. David F. Crew (Oxford: Berg, 2003), 73; and Landsman, *Dictatorship and Demand,* 209–10.

111. The classic text on the emergence of this managerial cadre is Thomas A. Baylis, *The Technical Intelligentsia and the East German Elite: Legitimacy and Social Change in Mature Communism* (Berkeley: University of California Press, 1974).

112. Martin Kelm, "Die Bedeutung der Gestaltung industrieller Zeugnisse im entwickelten gesellschaftlichen System des Sozialismus," quoted and translated in Eli Rubin, "The Form of Socialism without Ornament: Consumption, Ideology, and the Fall and Rise of Modernist Design in the German Democratic Republic," *Journal of Design History* 19, no. 2 (2006): 161.

113. Martin Kelm, "Es Geht um die Sinnvolle Form," *Bildende Kunst* 8, no. 2 (1963): 92.

114. On the shift of power within the SED, see Monika Kaiser, *Machtwechsel von Ulbricht zu Honecker: Funktionsmechanismen der SED-Diktatur in Konfliktsituationen 1962 bis 1972* (Berlin: Akademie Verlag, 1997).

115. Rubin, "The Form of Socialism without Ornament," 161, 162.

116. Köster, "Schmerzliche Ankunft in der Moderne," 100.

117. Steiner, "Dissolution of the 'Dictatorship over Needs'?" 185.

118. Thomas Topfstedt, "Wohnen und Städtebau in der DDR," in *Geschichte des Wohnens*, ed. Ingeborg Flagge (Stuttgart: Deutsche Verlags-Anstalt, 1999), 5:523.

119. Fred Taylor, *The Berlin Wall: A World Divided, 1961–1989* (New York: HarperCollins, 2006), 348.

120. The term "planned miracle" is from Joachim Nawrocki, *Das geplante Wunder: Leben und Wirtschaften im anderen Deutschland* (Hamburg: Christian Wegner Verlag, 1967).

121. Zaitlin, "The Vehicle of Desire," 358.

122. Taylor, *The Berlin Wall*, 415.

123. Gerhard Schürer quoted in Jeffrey Kopstein, *The Politics of Economic Decline in East Germany, 1945–1989* (Chapel Hill: University of North Carolina Press, 1997), 192.

124. On the use of socialist consumption as a culture of resistance, see C. Humphrey, "Creating a Culture of Disillusionment: Consumption in Moscow, A Chronicle of Changing Times," in *Worlds Apart: Modernity through the Prism of the Local*, ed. Daniel Miller (London: Routledge, 1995). On the role played by consumer dissatisfaction in the collapse of the East German state, see Kopstein, *The Politics of Economic Decline in East Germany*, 192, 195–97; and Charles S. Maier, *Dissolution: The Crisis of Communism and the End of East Germany* (Princeton, N.J.: Princeton University Press, 1999), 89–97.

EPILOGUE

1. Arkadi and Boris Strugatski, *Monday Begins on Saturday*, trans. Leonid Renen (New York: Daw Books, 1977), 129.

GREG CASTILLO is associate professor at the College of Environmental Design at the University of California, Berkeley, and is a research associate at the United States Studies Centre at the University of Sydney, Australia.